MW01091744

Food and Drink in Medieval Poland

Food and Drink in Medieval Poland

Rediscovering a Cuisine of the Past

Maria Dembińska

Translated by Magdalena Thomas

Revised and Adapted by William Woys Weaver

PENN

University of Pennsylvania Press

Philadelphia

Konsumpcja Żywnościowa w Polsce Średniowiecznej *(Food Consumption in Medieval Poland), from which this book is adapted, was originally published in 1963 by the Institute of the History of Material Culture, Polish Academy of Sciences, Warsaw.*

Printed in the United States of America on acid-free paper

10 9 8 7 6 5 4 3 2 1

Published by
University of Pennsylvania Press
Philadelphia, Pennsylvania 19104-4011

Library of Congress Cataloging-in-Publication Data
Dembińska, Maria.
{Konsumpcja żivnościowa w Polsce sredniowiecznej. English}
Food and drink in medieval Poland : rediscovering a cuisine of the past / Maria Dembińska ; translated by Magdalena Thomas ; revised and adapted by William Woys Weaver.
p. cm.
Includes bibliographical references (p.) and index.
ISBN 0-8122-3224-0 (alk. paper)
1. Cookery, Polish—History—to 1500. 2. Food habits—Poland—History—To 1500. 3. Cookery, Medieval. I. Weaver, William Woys, 1947– . II. Title.
TX723.5.P6D4613 1999
641.59438—dc21 *99-12275*
CIP

In Memory of Henryk Dembiński

(1911–1987)

Contents

Editor's Preface

Three Latin words scribbled in the margin of the parchment ledger book of Polish royal treasurer Henryk of Rogów—*ad regalem scutellum*, for the royal pot—not only extended a proprietary reach over the markets and gardens of medieval Poland; they also conjured up a court cuisine unique to Central Europe. Strangely Oriental, yet peasantlike in its robust simplicity, it was a cookery that captured all the complexities of Poland in that far-off age, a nation of great power slowly twisting toward upheaval, of farmlands and towns thronging with emigrants from cultures unable to meld with the Polish countryside around them. And yet for a time, it was also a rare period of peace. Maria Dembińska went back to the royal account books—indeed, to all the medieval records she could find—in order to reconstruct this chapter of Poland's history. Her work is now a scholarly classic.

Maria Dembińska's research was originally prepared in 1963 as a doctoral dissertation at Warsaw University and the Institute of Material Culture of the Polish Academy of Science. Published under the title *Konsumpcja Żywnościowa w Polsce Średniowiecznej* (Food Consumption in Medieval Poland), it was immediately recognized as a groundbreaking study of food in an area of medieval scholarship that is not well known to the rest of Europe. Even today, although her work is often cited by Slavic writers, it does not appear in any of the general works dealing with French, English, or Italian medieval food studies. The inaccessibility of Polish language sources, and perhaps the unduly complex nature of medieval society in the far reaches of Central Europe, provide natural barriers against the sort of cross-cultural exploration that has characterized similar research in England and France.

Maria Dembińska was aware of this difficulty, and she published an English synopsis of the book in the proceedings of the Second International Symposium for Ethnological Food Research held at Helsinki in 1973. It was her hope that this would spur interest in a complete revised edition of her work, perhaps in France, where there was a large émigré Polish community. A son in Paris and a daughter in Los Angeles provided Maria with family contacts outside Communist Poland that served her well in circulating her research at international symposia, a luxury not available to many Polish scholars at the time. This was especially so for someone like Maria, who was not a member of the Communist Party and who was by no means proletarian, having been born Countess Gołuchowska and having married Count Henryk Dembiński. Nor was her study cast in a Marxist framework. In fact, during the period of martial law in the 1980s, she taught underground courses on Polish history that would surely have landed her in jail if she had been discovered. How she managed all of this is material for a novel; to say the least, Maria Dembińska was not easily intimidated.

The focus of Maria Dembińska's study was not a culinary history of the Polish Middle Ages but rather an analysis of the diet as a key to what she termed "the Polish reality of that time." She was well acquainted with the historical refinements of haute cuisine, both Polish and French. Indeed, her grandmother, Countess Anne Gołuchowska (née Murat), was not only French, but a direct descendant of Napoleon's Marshal Murat. Maria Dembińska could have chosen any number of ways to view the Middle Ages; however, her main interest lay in defining social structure in terms of food consumption, a theme she pursued throughout her professional career.

Her approach was completely novel given the Marxist definitions of history imposed on Polish universities before the collapse of Communism in 1989. Yet we must remember that Maria Dembińska began her serious work during the intellectual thaw that followed the death of Stalin. Her approach was innovative for other reasons as well, for she was one of the first Polish scholars to reassess what was meant by "Polish cuisine," and she effectively challenged a number of old but persistent myths. Only a person with a name like Dembińska, a name instantly recognized in Poland as one of the great noble families, could dare assume such an oracular position.

Yet her name alone was no guarantee; it was her extraordinary integrity and determination that carried her through her career. Maria Dembińska's situation was a curious melange of elements that were possible only in Communist Poland: she was by virtue of her birth a symbol of Old Poland, and yet it was this same Polishness that served as a psychological means of resistance. Maria could have left Poland after she and her husband lost their eight-thousand-acre estate at Przysucha, but they chose to stay because they were loyal to the idea of Poland and deeply convinced that someday the country would again be free. Everything she wrote about Poland must be read in this context. While the Communists took away the material world that once defined who Maria Dembińska was, in the end, she gave back to Poland something of even greater value.

For the historian trying to flesh out the history of an age long gone, the task is difficult enough as an intellectual challenge. Adding the restrictions of a police state and a political atmosphere deeply antagonistic to certain types of research, it is a wonder that Maria Dembińska was able to achieve anything at all. Yet she had the party functionaries on her side for one fundamental reason: nationalism. What she wrote about Poland helped to supply missing pieces to the Polish story, indeed to one of the most brilliant chapters of Polish history: the reign of the Jagiellon dynasty. Bits of her research even surfaced in the hugely popular *W staropolskiej kuchni i przy polskim stole* (Old Polish Traditions in the Kitchen and at the Table) by Maria Lemnis, issued by Interpress in 1979.[1]

Dr. Don Yoder of the University of Pennsylvania was one of the first in the United States to recognize that an English edition of Maria's book was overdue. In a seminal article entitled "Folk Cookery" in *Folklore and Folklife: An Introduction*, edited by Richard M. Dorson in 1972, Yoder singled out Maria's book for its combination of historical research with ethnographic sources. In 1977 Yoder introduced me to Maria at an international conference in Wales. Yoder and I had just come from Poland and an extraordinary visit to my maternal grandfather's birthplace. It was in Wales, over a fresh supply of Polish vodka, that Maria and I initiated our friendship and our discussions about an English-language edition of her book. This unfolded into a voluminous transatlantic correspondence addressed to "Dear Willy"; I became a collaborator, a faraway light during very dark times for Poland.

During the next five years, Maria and I outlined the project and discussed the many ways we could render the book in English. I had interested the University of Pennsylvania Press in publishing it, but a great deal of legal work had to be done with contracts, and worst of all, the Polish mails could not be trusted due to petty thefts and overly zealous secret police. So Maria and I devised a means for getting mail in and out of Poland intact. We also agreed to meet in Hungary in 1983 during an ethnographic conference and that I would take from her what was necessary to have the book published in the United States. This included a complete copy of her book, which by then had become extremely difficult to find.

When we finally met at Matrafüred, Hungary, Polish Solidarity agitation was evident everywhere. So were the Hungarian police. It is difficult to describe the oppressive atmosphere that hung over that conference, the food shortages, even the "off schedule" visits to private homes where once we sat drinking wine with the lights out so that the police would not suspect foreigners were on the premises. Maria smuggled out of Poland her own copy of the book, all of the original artwork (stuffed under Solidarity propaganda), and other materials connected with it. The propaganda was discovered at the Polish border, and she would have been detained then and there had she not given the guard one of two antique silver collar pins of the royal arms of Poland she had with her (she gave the other one to me). Our conspiracy was thus a success, and a friend of mine with a diplomatic passport spirited me into Austria with the manuscript files intact. Nonetheless, for me that trip from Budapest seemed a day of pure terror. But coupled with sheer emotional exhaustion was the happy knowledge that the English version of the book was truly launched.

The next problem was finding a translator. Although Maria Dembińska's second language was flawless French and she could move easily into Latin, Greek, Russian, German, and medieval Polish, she nevertheless found English more difficult than her own complex mother tongue and realized that she could not translate the book herself. My own ability to read Polish is not that of a translator. It was necessary to find a specialist who could deal with all the nuances of Maria's style — no simple task. Thanks to a generous grant from the International Association of Culinary Professionals toward this translation effort, Magdalena Thomas, a Polish-born scholar well acquainted with linguistics, spent the summer of 1993 rendering the book into English. This was a monumental task considering the many charts and graphs and the long citations from medieval sources.

However, it was evident after translation was completed that the book would not work in its original form for American readers. Part of the issue was content: what sufficed for a scholarly audience was not necessarily appropriate for more general readers. There was also a problem with redundancy — some of the same material was explained in several ways — and parts of the text veered away from the food theme into an economic study of market patterns in the 1380s. Furthermore, since Maria Dembińska used a non-Marxist approach to her subject, she was obliged at every step to substantiate her arguments with massive amounts of annotation, much of which would have been unnecessary in the West. Thus, it became evident that the book needed streamlining in some places but expansion in others.

Maria recognized this fact, and we often discussed possible solutions. Finally, as Maria's illness began to deprive her of her ability to work, the ultimate task of recreating her book in English fell to me. Using Magdalena Thomas's translation, I forged a new text. It is not the book that Maria Dembińska wrote, but it captures the essential parts of the food story as she assembled it. I have also added material from Maria's later writings (such as her 1973 book on medieval flour mills) and expanded both the historical background as well as some of the details about specific foods. Of special interest to culinary historians is the material I have included about our ruminations over early cookery manuscripts and sources of ideas for the Polish court. It is possible that we shall never know some of the answers, considering that the burning of the Polish National Archives in 1944 destroyed about 75 percent of that priceless collection. On the other hand, there are many untapped archival materials in other countries, and it is my hope that someone more adept in medieval studies than I am will pick up on some of these threads and settle the issues one way or the other. There are good reasons for pressing forward into these unexplored territories.

The Polish royal court was not operating in a culinary vacuum. Indeed the Angevins (Louis d'Anjou—king of Hungary and Poland—and especially his daughter Jadwiga, who became queen of Poland) evidently had access to some of the most important culinary texts of the 1300s, notably a text (or texts) similar to those that evolved into the cookbook attributed to Guillaume Tirel. Maria Dembińska had wanted to pursue this because she had studied a copy of Tirel's *Le Viandier* that had once belonged to the Duke de Berry and determined that it was considerably older than the other surviving manuscripts, thus throwing into doubt Tirel's authorship (a point recently raised by Terence Scully and fielded in further detail by Bruno Laurioux). Maria had reason to believe that an Angevin owned that manuscript before the duke bought it in 1404. Is there a Polish connection here?

The Duke de Berry's copy has been missing since 1945. Maria Dembińska was obliged to use the 1892 Pinchon and Vicaire edition of *Le Viandier* for her book (the only complete text that she could locate in Poland in the 1960s). She could not say in 1963 that she suspected Queen Jadwiga had access to all or part of the de Berry manuscript (or an earlier one on which it was based), but she cited material from *Le Viandier* because she knew of this anterior significance and hoped that the de Berry copy would resurface so that she could revisit some of these long-lingering questions. In any case, the *Le Viandier* strengthened her hand in the analysis of the royal purchase orders for various meals enjoyed by the Jagiellon court.

It was this search for a connecting manuscript that led Maria Dembińska to the Danish cookery books in the Royal Library at Copenhagen. She recognized that this material was incorrectly dated (much later than assumed), but she also realized that the recipes were copied from something older, indeed, some of the recipes could be quite old and probably predated Tirel. The Danish cookery books provided Maria Dembińska with recipes suggestive of an earlier medieval time frame, and this was especially useful, for example, when it came to looking at the ways the Polish nobility may have wanted its fish pickled in the 1300s.[2]

Likewise, I have introduced the Cypriot connection as we sometimes called it: a problem concerning the origin of table forks and certain types of medieval recipes. Polish historians have tended to downplay the "cosmopolitan" character of their monarchs and to restrict the effects of their reigns to inner tickings of the Polish political clock. Yet men like Casimir the Great were indeed personalities on a much grander stage, and whether cause or conduit, Casimir may have been responsible for more than a rapprochement of squabbling European powers. The appearance of King Peter de Lusignan of Cyprus at Casimir's convention of nobles in 1364 had far more ramifications to it than merely a Latin king of a Greek-speaking country (Peter was also King of Jerusalem) politicking for funds for another crusade — his ostensible reason for being there.

At Casimir's convention, however, King Peter was indeed a

"Greek" bearing gifts, surrounded by a mixed court of Hellenized Franks, gasmuls, Maronites, in short, perhaps the most truly exotic medley of all the nobles assembled. They were also fabulously rich, and the court brought with it customs and eating habits that stood in stark contrast not just to the Poles, but also to the Austrians and Germans and others present who perhaps knew Cyprus simply as one of the Crusader states that in collusion with the Venetians was growing wealthy on sugar. Is it an odd coincidence that Cypriot recipes begin to appear in western European cookery books after this event? Or that table forks suddenly surface shortly after it as well? Poland seems to offer a connecting thread.

Another issue that is deserving of comment is the time frame for this book. Based on what is known today about medieval Poland from research carried out since 1963, a fuller account of the Jagiellon dynasty and its foods is entirely possible, certainly down to the 1490s, which is generally accepted as the end of the Middle Ages. However, the documentation for this later period is so rich that it deserves a book of its own. The same could be said for individual food histories of Silesia and the old Prussian states (Pomerania and East and West Prussia). These regions developed politically and culturally separate from Poland, although the exchanges between them were many. Maria Dembińska's use of the records of the Teutonic Knights for comparative purposes should serve as a notice that the archival riches in these parts of present-day Poland offer ample opportunities for further exploration and analysis.

Copies of Maria Dembińska's original work are available in several North American libraries for those who want to consult it. This new edition is intended to move the general reader beyond dissertational particulars now more than thirty years old, and to focus on a somewhat broader culinary landscape than the one covered in 1963—not so much in terms of time as in terms of dimension. I was obliged to include a brief history of Poland so that readers unfamiliar with Poland's past may see Maria's work in its wider European context. Of course, her original audience was keenly familiar with Polish medieval history, but the American reader must be reminded constantly that this is a history with many convolutions and that Polish society then was starkly different from what we know today. Furthermore, I have condensed charts and moved annotations into the main text. In short, the book is a new work reassembled from the old one.

Finally, the section of recipe reconstructions is new to this edition; although much of it is based on Maria's research, the voice in that section is wholly mine. The very closed nature of things in Communist Poland stalled our planned foray into the kitchen, only to have it prevented in the end by Maria's illness. It would have been an extraordinary experiment to have worked with her in person on all of the recipes, along with a crew of hungry Polish medievalists sharing in and critiquing the results. This did not happen, and I was left to proceed on my own to evolve many of the untested recipes out of twenty years of our very loose but productive notes. However, during my 1985 visit to Poland, we were able to "field test" a major part of the basic recipes that follow with the help of the staff of the open air museum at Nowy Sącz, only a few miles from my maternal grandfather's birthplace on the manor of Krasne Potockie. Thus, for me the recipes evoke a personal note, a looking back at roots on a side of my family I know little about. But intellectually, they were developed for this book as Maria would have wanted them, and designed to give material shape to some of the dishes she mentioned in her text.

Maria Dembińska's findings on medieval Poland are now part

of standard Polish scholarship. Her approach was creative, and it is my hope that this edition of her work will provide a glimpse into a rich and intriguing culinary heritage that is now assuming a more visible position in general European culture. Maria Dembińska died on November 1, 1996, without seeing the fruits of these labors. I hope that this book will serve as a testimony to her scholarly contribution and to the deep love that she fostered for Polish culture.

Illustrations

77 *Wine jug from Čataj, Slovakia, eleventh century. Drawn by Signe Sundberg-Hall after the original in the Museum of Viticulture, Bratislava, Slovakia.*

83 *Copper cauldron and pot hook for adjusting it over the fire. Woodcut from Paprocki's* Koło rycerskie *(Cracow, 1575). From a photograph ex collection Maria Dembińska.*

83 *Cheese made using an antique mold, in 1985 at the open air museum at Nowy Sącz, Poland. Drawn by Signe Sundberg-Hall.*

85 *Sixteenth-century woodcut of an aurochs. From an original woodcut ex collection Maria Dembińska.*

87 *Meat claw for removing clods of meat from a cauldron, circa 1350–1400. Polish, private collection. Drawn by Signe Sundberg-Hall.*

91 *Hearth utensils. Broadside of Hanns Paur, Nuremberg, 1475.*

103 *Ceramic mush pot for use on a raised hearth. From Michael Hero's* Schachtaffeln der Gesundheit *(Strasbourg, 1533).*

104 *Woodcut of a miller hauling grain to be ground. Redrawn by Signe Sundberg-Hall from Heinrich Jacob's* Sechstausend Jahre Brot *(Hamburg, 1954). The source of the original woodcut is not identified.*

110 *Clasher for working millet as it cooks. Polish, eighteenth century. Wood. Private collection. Drawn by Signe Sundberg-Hall.*

113 *Harvest tools. Broadside of Hanns Paur, Nuremberg, 1475.*

116 *Obarzanek. Drawn by Signe Sundberg-Hall from original examples purchased in the Old Market, Cracow, 1977.*

117 *Signet ring with inscription, National Museum (Czartoryski Museum Narodowe), Cracow, fifteenth century. Drawn by Signe Sundberg-Hall. The shape of the signet is the same shape used for gingerbread images during this period.*

118 *St. Florian, from a woodcut in* Introductorium Astrologie *(Cracow, 1515).*

121 *Alexanders. Drawn from life by Signe Sundberg-Hall.*

126 *Skirrets. Drawn from life by Signe Sundberg-Hall.*

127 *Küttiger Rüebli, a medieval variety of carrot from Küttigen, Canton Aargau, Switzerland. Drawn from life by Signe Sundberg-Hall.*

128 *Barszcz, woodcut from the 1613 herbal of Szymon Syrennius.*

128 *Buckler-leafed sorrel. Drawn from life by Signe Sundberg-Hall.*

130 *Cracow lettuce,* Lactuca sativa, var. cracoviensis. *A medieval lettuce type resembling the Celtuce of China. Drawn from life by Signe Sundberg-Hall.*

Toward a Definition of Polish National Cookery

This book is about the Middle Ages, but it is also an exploration of culinary identity. Food, like language, is a transmitter of culture, a set of signals that define a people in terms of time and place. Until now, the Polish experience has not been well understood outside Slavic-speaking countries, and nothing prior to this book has been available for English-speakers who wanted to seek out an understanding of Poland's rich culinary past. This volume is intended, therefore, to explore what is meant by "Polish cuisine" and to connect this understanding to the fascinating period of the late 1300s when Poland burst forth on the international scene as a world power. Yet, much like the United States in its formative years many centuries later, the Polish nation had only a pubescent awareness of what it was. This awareness developed rapidly after Poland achieved a sense of purpose as a nation-state. The foods and foodways of the country moved in tandem with this continuing cultural adjustment.

These broader issues are not necessarily medieval problems, yet in terms of Poland and what it has become today, they are vitally important. The pages that follow will create a culinary framework for looking at medieval Poland by gradually focusing the kaleidoscopic materials and complex issues that come to bear on the meaning of Polish identity at table. This includes a thumbnail history of Polish cuisine down to the present. However, the avenues of research are bumpy due to the very nature of Polish records, especially those surviving from the Middle Ages.

During the wars with Sweden in the 1650s, which devastated Poland in a manner not repeated until World War II, much of what remained of medieval Poland sank into ash and ruin. Documentation of the Polish Middle Ages, then, is spotty. Written evidence from before 1300 was never very extensive to begin with, and consisted mostly of documents relating to cloisters or chronicles of events in the lives of certain brave or saintly individuals. However, because it has been spared from many of the vicissitudes of war, southern Poland is especially rich in written materials after this time, with Cracow and its university evolving as a focal point for the preservation and study of medieval records as Polish nationalism grew in strength during the nineteenth century. This scholarly research continues apace, and new editions of early manuscript material as well as new interpretations of their significance now appear in print with great frequency.

Early medieval Poland, however, is quite another matter. This period, dating roughly from 963 to 1194, has been characterized by Polish historian Tadeusz Manteuffel as the period of ducal rule because there was no powerful monarchy to hold the Polish people together as a unified nation. What we know about this period, especially in terms of daily life and food consumption, is derived almost entirely from archaeological finds. The study of Poland's culinary past is therefore predicated on two distinct avenues of inquiry: the interpretation of archaeological remains from the early period and the analysis of manuscript materials dating mostly after 1300.

Polish medieval archaeology received its greatest boost in the years following 1945. Government-sponsored postwar archaeological digs at Gdansk (Danzig), Szczecin (Stettin), Opole (Oppeln), Wrocław (Breslau), and many other places were designed to give political credence to the Polishness of recent German territories. Furthermore, the destruction of many downtown neighborhoods in Polish cities during the war — Warsaw's Old Town being one — permitted archaeologists to explore sites that had previously been covered by buildings. Many spectacular artifacts came to the surface (including the set of kitchen utensils shown on page 63), but the archaeological methods of this period were also quite crude and many culinary materials were misinterpreted.

One classic example occurred at Wolin and Szczecin in Pomerania (northwest Poland), where a small quantity of deer bones was discovered.[1] Some Polish food historians attempted to read this material as culinary refuse when in fact the bones were later shown to have been artisanal waste. They were by-products of a craft industry centered on antlers (horn spoons, utensil handles, the manufacture of hartshorn salts for baking, etc.). Thus, the caveat with all archaeological materials is vigilance, especially with materials relating to food consumption. Fortunately, since 1963 Polish archaeologists have greatly improved their scientific analysis so that today there is far more certainty in identification and in dating. This has been taken into account in the choice of archaeological evidence included in this volume.

However, when archaeology fails to yield evidence, and written sources fall silent, ethnographic sources from more recent times can yield a mine of culinary information. These include a range of materials, from diaries and travel accounts, to interviews with older people still living in the Polish countryside in the 1950s and 1960s.[2] In some cases, due to the overlapping nature of generations, oral traditions can be traced to the end of the seventeenth century. This kind of data proves useful in ascertaining more specific meanings for medieval words like *pultes* (porridge), which may not always be clearly defined in an old text. How did nineteenth- and twentieth-century peasants make dishes of similar consistency? How did these foods fit into the daily diet? Sometimes the answers reveal striking insights that further confirm conclusions based on very old sources. Polish medieval documents are consistent, for example, in placing mead only at lavish feasts. Ethnographic sources made the same point, thus supporting the hypothesis that mead remained expensive until quite recent times.[3]

Aside from oral and written traditions, ethnographic evidence also includes daily objects—culinary tools, for example. This is material culture in its purest sense: the study of things and their social context. Wear on wooden tools shows how they were held in the hand, charring on pottery reveals something about hearth uses, and ornamental patterns on gingerbread prints or cheese molds can tell us a great deal about artistic metaphors that were current when these objects were made. The animal-shaped *redykalki* cheeses from the hill country of Podolia, for example, with their physical reference to folk tales, are the sort of culinary material culture that unites custom with the imagination. Such traditional types of objects, even those of recent manufacture (*redykalki* molds are still being carved), may retain external forms or techniques of construction that link them to medieval predecessors. Such evidence can be as rich a source of information as an archaeological site.

Polish cheese mold with Gothic patterns, seventeenth century. Private collection.

Indeed, many artifacts contain their own narratives. Such commonplace objects as crocks of honey and grain found in many Polish peasant larders even today would hardly seem noteworthy to the casual observer. Yet twelfth-century pots with traces of honey in them, along with small crocks of carbonized millet, have come to light from a medieval house excavated at Gniezno.[4] Thus, objects of the everyday provide a link to continuities from the past, as well as to changes over time. The ethnography of medieval culture is the art of weaving such threads of continuity and change into a cultural texture that can be experienced firsthand, like the creation of the recipes for Polish medieval dishes in the final section of this book.

Another challenging dimension to the exploration of food identity is that of class and standard of living. The two are not equivalent. One of the most intriguing dimensions of medieval food consumption in Poland, from a nonculinary viewpoint, is the extent to which the standard of living of a particular feudal class was reflected in what it served at table. This is a research problem that is neither simple — owing in part to subjective interpretation of the material — nor easily quantified, as some historians have assumed in the past. The most common approach to food history has been to accept a rather arbitrary division of medieval society into four distinct groups arranged in a vertically descending order — nobility, clergy, townspeople, and peasants — allowing that in Poland the lines of demarcation between all of these groups were often hazy. In reality, this schematic division of society is not workable if we want to understand the real differences in eating habits between particular Polish social classes of the Middle Ages. By extension, this same rule of measure could be applied to any society in history. Looking at foods and consumption in terms of standard of living gives us a fuller picture of the society.

In medieval Poland the standard of living serves as a better qualifying principle. Based on this form of measure, we must also include, on par with the nobility, state and court officials who were not always of noble origin, as well as persons closely associated with royal or princely courts, or with the regional courts of the starostas, voivodes, and other high nobility who were the real power brokers during much of Poland's history. The clergy was equally diverse, encompassing a broad range of individuals: landed prelates (such as archbishops, bishops, and abbots of powerful monasteries) who lived like feudal lords, a panoply of rich and poor priests, monks and friars, and the lowest monastery monks of peasant origin. Medieval townspeople were not homogeneous, either. There were at least three subdivisions within this group: urban patricians, middle-class merchants and craftsmen, and of course, the urban poor. Likewise, the peasantry living in the countryside was divided into many groupings, ranging from well-to-do village administrators and rich farmers to middle-class peasants with modest land holdings and rural craftsmen to herdsmen with no fixed address, tenants, rural poor, beggars, and tramps.

The variations in living standards within each social group were so profound that it is not possible to adhere to these four convenient divisions. In real terms, secular and church magnates, royalty, wealthy nobles, high court or princely officials, and rich patricians all shared similar consumption patterns. All of these individuals were surrounded by entourages of servants, minor officials, state clerks, and other lesser folk whose eating habits closely resembled that of their masters. The only exception in this case were luxury foods of high cost (such as almond milk or sugar), which were enjoyed only by a privileged few.

Next in the consumption hierarchy were the landowners of small estates, knights with or without property, middle-class merchants and craftsmen, rich village administrators and wealthy farmers, and the clergy with middle income. The very bottom of the nutritional pecking order was composed of the urban and rural poor, destitute friars, low-level servants, camp followers, and similar individuals with little personal property. These people were numerous in medieval Poland, just as they were in other parts of Europe, but owing to the nature of record-keeping during this period, they are at times invisible in the written and physical records.

The archival materials relating to nutrition in medieval Poland mostly date from the period 1350 to 1492, roughly to the end of the reign of King Casimir Jagiellończyk. Some historians end the Polish Middle Ages at 1506, with the death of King Alexander Jagiellończyk, but no matter what cutoff date is used, two important points must be kept in mind. First, the overwhelming amount of information now available deals with the highest levels of society, and by virtue of this fact, this book is clearly focused on the royal court and the people surrounding it. Second, most of these records were written in Latin, which was the language of the educated classes in Poland even for literary purposes. Not much record-keeping was done in demotic Polish. Although culinary recipes may have been composed in that language, none are known to have survived. The earliest writings in vernacular Polish are sermons and religious hymns.

The Latin records, however, are not exclusive in their coverage of the activities of the rich and powerful. They can also be mined for information about the middle classes, particularly merchant families, small landowners, and other individuals who might have dealings with the high nobility. But we learn very little about the poor unless they were criminals or became entangled in a legal case. Since the original publication of this book in Polish in 1963, a vast amount of new information has come to light on the daily lives of common Poles largely as the result of archaeological research. In time, this material may come to interest food historians enough to explore medieval Poland as lived by the urban and rural poor at greater length.

For the present, although much of the material in this volume dates from the 1960s and earlier, it is still useful as a point of contrast to what can be said about the Polish court. Furthermore, all of the per capita consumption data that Polish historians were relying on for their conclusions about medieval eating patterns, including those of the poor, seemed questionable. These doubts have since been confirmed by other scholars, but an example is in order. In Andrzej Wyczański's study of food consumption in sixteenth-century Poland, a work that was also used to help understand the diet of Poland's late Middle Ages, the food eaten by peasants, urban laborers, and hired help both in towns and on rural manors was calculated in rather positive terms. Wyczański concluded that the average laborer on a Polish manor consumed about 300g (a bit more than half a pound) of fatty meat daily.[5] This was interpreted as not altogether bad.

Several problems with this reasoning are obvious. First, well-being is not necessarily determined by the amount of meat one eats, although in medieval terms, meat was indeed a measure of "good food." Second, and perhaps more important, meat was not eaten alone but in combination with grains, cabbage, and other vegetables, a fact that improves the nutritional picture radically. Furthermore, the meat in question was most likely streaky bacon of some sort, with very high fat content. Boiled, this might even be considered healthful by modern standards given the caloric requirements of heavy labor. But this half-pound of meat was probably distributed to the head of a household and further subdivided among several individuals. If this was the sole source of protein, the picture shifts from not altogether bad to near starvation. If the bacon is merely a garnish to a vegetable-based diet, then perhaps we can see Polish peasant cookery in a light similar to the steady advice of modern nutritionists to cut back on red meat intake. The fact remains that the data are not clear cut, so one cannot say with certainty that the diet was healthful or even adequate by medieval or modern standards. All of the consumption figures provided throughout this book must be read in this light.

With the records written in Latin, traces of everyday life buried in medieval kitchen refuse, and no extant cookery books from the period written in Polish or even claiming to be Polish, how do we arrive at the Polish table with a firm sense of cultural identity? Surely medieval Poles understood who they were and readily recognized certain foods as peculiarly their own. But perhaps this identity was also an evolving one, just as the Polish language itself was evolving at the time. During the thirteenth and fourteenth centuries, Polish was heavily influenced by Czech, from which it borrowed many words and concepts. Was food likewise influenced by this same flow of ideas? The appearance in Polish of Czech terms like *koláče* (from Latin *collatio*) would suggest this.

Yet if an idea is Czech, when does it become Polish? The concept of a national identity in cookery is a tricky one because it intermingles political aspirations with religious, ethnic, and even racial definitions based on food preparation. The Polish experience cannot be readily understood by simply looking at the Middle Ages, or even one narrow slice of it, because the Middle Ages is part of a larger continuum. Viewing Polish cookery from a broader perspective will lead us directly into the tangled matter of national identity in food. If there is a common theme to Poland's culinary identity, it is the synthesis of peasant and the noble into one idea. Buckwheat is raised from peasant fare to haute cuisine by the tap of a queen's fork. Bigos frees itself from the gilded stag draped across the lid of a royal tureen to find company with rye bread in a peasant's open kettle. Queen Jadwiga may be emblematic of this unique combination.

Jadwiga was married off to a Lithuanian prince specifically because she represented political legitimacy. Historians have often characterized her as a mere pawn, useful in so far as she possessed proper papers. But child-bride or not, it is also apparent that she was cognizant of the fact that she was part Piast, an embodiment of old Poland. Therefore, she was also a living artifact, indeed the last in her line. Did the food on her royal table (she had her own chef and retinue) also symbolize this sense of ancient Polish identity? There were probably two sides to Jadwiga: the Jadwiga d'Anjou, daughter of a Hungarian king of French ancestry, who dined at court on the most innovative dishes her chef could conjure; and the Jadwiga who appealed to the popular image of St. Jadwiga (her namesake) when she dined in peasant simplicity among country noblewomen. The evolution of Polish cookery is evident in the synthesis of these two distinct dichotomies: the court setting and peasant food.

The Three Phases of Polish Culinary History

The evolution of this cuisine into something recognizably Polish, at least as we know it today, may be divided rather roughly into three phases. The first ranges from the period of ducal rule (963–1194) to about the middle of the fifteenth century. Polish tribes lived in the region of modern Poland long before 963, but in terms of national identity, the period of ducal rule has provided Poland with much of the written lore surrounding its early foods and foodways. This book is primarily concerned with the second half of this phase, the period from the thirteenth century onward, which witnessed the introduction and development of a rent-based economy. Archaeology forms the basis of our understanding of the earliest period, while the second is better understood thanks to a variety of Polish as well as foreign works, such as the *Ménagier de Paris* of Guy de Montigny and *Le Viandier* attributed to Guillaume Tirel, called Taillevent. These foreign texts represent international influences during the 1300s and, on a technical level, help place the Polish material in context.[6] As a result, we have a fairly accurate understanding of the makeup, ingredients, and preparation techniques peculiar to the food of this era.

In general terms, throughout this phase of medieval history in Poland, there is considerable overlap in the sorts of foods consumed by all classes of society, excluding the obvious contrast between the menus of the royal court and those of the poor. Most of the dishes prepared prior to the mid-thirteenth century in Poland were based on plant and animal products gathered or raised directly by those who consumed them, with only a small percentage sold on the open market. For example, such wild grain plants as goosefoot (*Chenopodium album*) and black bindweed (*Polygonum convolvulus*) appear frequently in archaeological sites of this period. Szymon Syrennius even provided a recipe that used black bindweed in his 1613 *Herbarium*, evidence that such old traditional foods remained popular over a long period of time. In any case, as the rent-based economy evolved from the thirteenth century onward, such foraged foods and the dependence on home-grown produce became more marginalized because better market networks allowed farmers to specialize in cash crops, market gardening, poultry raising, and other income-producing activities. It is within this economic framework that the Jagiellon court operated.

The second phase encompasses the period from end of the fifteenth century to the middle of the eighteenth century. During this time, the quantity of food increased and the quality of food preparation radically improved. Greater emphasis was placed on the aesthetics of serving food, as described by Polish Protestant nobleman Mikołaj Rej in his 1568 poem "Zywot człowieka pozciwego" (Life of an Honest Man). This theme was later taken up by Jędrzej Kitowicz in his *Opis obyczajów i zwyczajów za panowania Augusta III* (Customs During the Reign of August III) published in 1777.[7] Similar books on the culture of fine dining appeared in Italy and France and doubtless served as models for the Polish works. Indeed, it is known that Rej was inspired in part by the Italian author Palingenius.

Other changes included the introduction of foreign vegetables and culinary dishes, especially after the marriage in 1518 of King Sigismund I (reigned 1506–1548) to Princess Bona Sforza of Milan (queen of Poland 1518–1557). Polish historians have assigned Queen Bona a position in Polish history comparable to that of Catherine de Medici of France: both queens are said to have introduced the art of cookery and Renaissance dining into their respective countries. The truth is not as sweeping as hitherto claimed; in fact, the de Medici myth has been debunked by recent scholarship.

Like many other Polish queens, Bona Sforza maintained her own kitchen and chef. She also brought with her a complete retinue of Italian gardeners who introduced to the Polish royal kitchen a number of Mediterranean vegetables — or at least Mediterranean varieties of vegetables that were already known — such as asparagus, broccoli, and certain types of lettuce. But Casimir the Great also had Italian gardens at Lobzów in the 1300s, so Polish histories of some of these vegetables may be complicated.

Furthermore, Queen Bona is said to have introduced to Poland the tomato, pumpkins, and other New World foods. Considering that German botanist Leonhard Fuchs did not illustrate a New World bean until the publication of his herbal in 1542 (he is considered one of the first Europeans to depict a bean plant), Queen Bona's introductions would have occurred late in her life. It is well documented that the Polish ambassador to Istanbul sent Turkish tobacco seeds to Warsaw in 1650, so similar and much earlier Turkish connections to New World plants cannot be ignored, especially in the case of tomatoes, beans, peppers, and maize.

Yet Queen Bona's cooks are known to have introduced the Polish court to a new profusion of condiments and spices, as well as to increased ornamentation of food with gold and various artificial colorings. These included an expanded number of dishes made with marzipan and almonds, all used to showcase the wealth of the high nobility rather than to enhance the flavor of food. Rej jested that such newfangled cookery was soporific because "after eating it, one snores, having gobbled everything up like a hog in a pig-sty . . . all those gilded dishes: golden chickens, eagles, and glittering hares are pretty on the outside but in reality, they are not worth the Devil."[8]

Polish aristocratic cookery has always bowed to the influence of various foreign cooking styles, including French (or what passed for French), German, and Oriental (Byzantine during the early Middle Ages, Near Eastern later on). The Byzantine influence is an important one given Poland's geographical position, but there were also direct political connections as early as Mieszko I (reigned c. 960–992), who maintained close contact with the court of the Dowager Empress Theophano of Byzantium. The rich culinary culture of Byzantium may have reached Poland in several ways. During the early Middle Ages, there may have been direct exchanges through trade. Later, during the 1300s for example, we find Byzantine cookery transmogrified into the body of international recipes that passed for Arabic or French and widely circulated among European cooks. (Tirel's *Le Viandier* represents the tail-end of this process.) Byzantine cookery also reached Poland through Italian middlemen, especially through the Venetians who traded with Byzantium on a tax-exempt basis after 1082. The Genoese competed on the same footing after 1155.

The Italian influence cannot be ignored in Poland owing to Poland's special relationship to the Papal See. High church officials were familiar with the culture of Italy and often traveled there. Italian artisans were commonly brought to Poland to work on medieval buildings. Casimir the Great was especially keen on things Italian, and Louis d'Anjou and his daughter Jadwiga came from a family whose old seat of power was in southern Italy. The d'Anjou family has been called French, but like the Lusignans (originally from Poitou) who possessed kingdoms in Cyprus, Syria, and even Armenia, they were really a type of Mediterranean Creole. Superimpose this on Poland of the late 1300s, and it is much easier to understand the royal larder with its huge array of exotic foodstuffs, even the casks of Sicilian vino cotto.

Italian humanism came to Poland via Hungary during the late fifteenth century. High church officials, the magnates who controlled much of Poland, the urban elites, all of these groups turned to Italy and to Florence in particular for inspiration. For this reason, some of the earliest examples of Italian Renaissance architecture outside of Italy may be found in Poland. And for this same reason, the cuisine of the Tuscan aristocracy was studied and imitated by the Polish nobility. Aristocratic Poles of the eighteenth century often wrote about this supposed golden age as though it epitomized old Poland, but again one could ask the question: when did a Tuscan or Milanese dish become Polish?

During the Swedish Vasa dynasty in the seventeenth century, the center of influence shifted to the Baltic and especially to northern Germany. In coastal cities like Gdansk, a Dutch presence, even in the architecture, became a dominant feature of the culture. By the eighteenth century, the Saxon kings who ruled Poland employed mainly French-trained cooks at the royal court, and thus French culinary ideas eventually prevailed in spite of the earlier German culinary and political inroads. These trends in cookery emanating from the Polish court have been treated in some detail by Polish historian Zbigniew Kuchowicz, who detected an evolution of complex culinary distinctions based on class during that period. (His conclusions are limited by the fact that he did not use standard of living as his yardstick.) Nonetheless, all of these external forces worked together in shaping what we now call Polish cookery, but no matter how diversified, they were still a dimension of the court setting and thus only half of the synthesis, to go back to the duality of Queen Jadwiga's table. But nothing Polish is ever precisely that simple, for there are always strange internal forces at work.

We cannot move toward our understanding of Polish identity as expressed in food unless we also take into account some of these strange pulses. One of them is an escapist mentality called Sarmatism that developed in the late sixteenth and early seventeenth centuries among Poland's ruling elites. Some historians have described it as an inward escape from the political failures of the nation. Others have characterized it as a search for an ancient Polish identity in the serenity of the country estate as opposed to urban life, as symbolized by the hunt (and by extension of this the further apotheosis of dishes like *bigos*). Sarmatism entailed a synthesis of exotic ideas about mythological Polish origins in regions bordering on far-off Persia, imaginary Scythian roots, and a preoccupation with Turkish themes.

One might describe this as the return of the Byzantine, recast in Turkish terms. Clothing, decorative arts, even cookery found their way into the country houses of Poland and further isolated the nobility from the world around it. When Poland was called upon to provide an army to defend Vienna from the Turks in 1683, Sarmatism faded into the ranks of the enemy and France ultimately triumphed as the ideal "other" to Polish self-consciousness.

The middle of the eighteenth century to the end of the nineteenth century has been called the third phase of development in the history of Polish culinary identity. During this time, the food culture of France became fully integrated into the national culture of Poland. Flavorful dishes prepared in the French manner, but based on peasant models, became the center of interest of the rich and middle-class devotees of food. It was during this time that the two old dichotomies, the court setting and the peasant dishes, finally came together as one. Yet the fusion was fleeting, if we allow that Polish cookery, as a culinary art, declined rapidly after that under the onslaught of two highly destructive world wars and almost fifty years of Communism. Even during the short period of its final flowering, this cookery was centered in the cities, and before the reunification of Poland in 1918, this meant only three main cultural centers: Austrian Lvov and Cracow, and Russian Warsaw. There are also several subthemes: the evolution of Polish-Jewish cookery in tandem with the mainstream developments just outlined, the forced Germanization of those parts of Poland under Prussian control, and a steady flow of culinary ideas from the East, primarily from Russia.

The East has always been a source of culinary influences on Poland and Poland has always synthesized these Asiatic ideas into something European. During the Middle Ages, influences came from Byzantium, from the Tartars, and of course from neighboring Lithuanians. But as Poland moved eastward by conquest during the 1300s, Polish culture penetrated regions with highly diverse ethnic identities and in many cases Polish settlers lived side-by-side with peoples who followed the Eastern Church — one more thread leading back to Byzantium. The full effect of Russia on Polish foods and foodways, however, did not occur until after the final partition of Poland in the eighteenth century.

The Russian culinary ideas that came to Poland also did not emanate from a court setting like the earlier foreign influences from the West, but from the peasantry. In this respect, they were radically different in substance and their acceptance by Poles was highly regionalized. Russian influence was most evident in the diet of the rural populations — both the gentry and the peasants — in the eastern areas of Poland that bordered on Russia. The eviction of Poles from these areas in 1945 and their resettlement in western Poland removed this cookery from the land where it was practiced and effectively scattered it throughout the country. In any event, Russian dishes also can be found in many nineteenth-century works printed in the Russian sector of Poland, such as Łukasz Gołębiowski's *Domy i Dwory* (The Town House and the Country House; 1830). Polish food terms of Russian origin, such as *tołokno* (parched barley flour), *salamacha* (wheat gruel with goosefat), *prazucha* (noodles made of parched buckwheat or rye flour), and *knysz* (buckwheat strudel) all attest to this westerly food migration.

Poland's courtly cuisine was kept alive until the outbreak of World War II on the great estates like Baranów, Łańcut, Nieświeź, and Sucha and in private homes. The subsequent reorganization of Polish society under Communism changed the old balance of dichotomies. The breakup of the estates brought an end to the aristocratic structure. The reordering of peasant life in the villages and the urbanization of Polish society changed that dimension of the equation forever. Peasant cookery, rather than serving as a mine for the creative synthesis of the cuisine, has now retreated into the log houses of open-air museums and into ethnographic archives.

The Communist government was committed to improving the Polish diet, yet this endeavor brought it up against deeply entrenched traditional values. A general lack of funds and widespread impoverishment brought extraordinary resistance from a populace that was forced to subsist on hoarding and black-market goods. As a result Polish cuisine as an artistic expression of the country suffered greatly. But the picture is not altogether negative.

Polish scholars are presently studying what is left in an attempt to understand better what has happened. Perhaps in this new search for identity another type of culinary synthesis will surface. In *Przy wspólnym stole* (At the Common Table; 1988), ethnographer Zofia Szromba-Rysowa of Cracow explores the eating habits and festive meals of the mountain villages of southern Poland. In looking at these somewhat isolated cultures, she was able to link their foods and foodways to much older traditions and even detected lost symbolic meanings tracing to the Middle Ages.

It is this bridge from the present reaching back to the Middle

Ages that constitutes the main thrust of this chapter. We have already seen that Polish cuisine was subject to dynamic forces that shaped it in stages. Yet, in order to understand why this cookery evolved in the distinctive ways that it did, it is necessary to understand the shifting meaning of "Polish" and how this concept relates back to the medieval situation. Traditional logic has assumed that there has been a Polish national cuisine as long as there has been a Poland, and this presumption has colored historical research down to the present time.

At the turn of the twentieth century, Zygmunt Gloger attempted to define *kuchnia polska* in his much-cited *Encyklopedia staropolska* (Old Polish Encyclopedia).[9] He detected certain "national" dishes that he determined essentialized Polishness (bigos being one of them). But what is meant by "national"? Whose Poland? *Which* Poland? How old must a dish be for it to qualify as Polish? Are we talking about a body of dishes codified as Polish by such contemporaries of Gloger as Madame Ochorowicz-Monatowa, whose 1910 cookbook *Uniwersalna Książka Kucharska* (The Universal Cookbook) is still considered a classic? Or are we asking what Gloger meant by "old" and "authentic"? The suggestion above that Polish cuisine is a synthesis of dichotomies would imply that the recipe cannot stand alone, for it is only a component of a much broader culinary entity.

The concept of a national or "ethnic" cookery based on certain key dishes is both highly subjective and relative, a product of the prejudice of the times rather than an objective assessment. Some foods characteristic of Polish cooking emerged owing to the natural suitability of the soil and climate to certain grains and plants. Millet and millet kasha, for example, have been consumed in Poland since the very earliest period of Slavic settlement. Written documentation and archaeological evidence for millet crops in other parts of northern

Europe are minimal. Because of its low tolerance to cool night temperatures and its short growing season, millet cannot be grown in most parts of northern Europe. Yet, because of its adaptability to the slash-and-burn agriculture of medieval Poland (it thrives on newly cleared ground), millet formed a key element of everyday diet prior to the introduction of the potato in the seventeenth century.

While it is tempting then to assign millet to the "national" cuisine of Poland during the Middle Ages, archaeological remains of millet can be found all over southeastern Europe, in parts of Russia and the Czech Republic, and even in Rumania. Farther south in the Balkans it is very common. It is easy to prove from archaeological evidence that Poles consumed millet for at least a thousand years, and this by itself should qualify it among the old and authentic relics that Gloger considered worthy of Polishness. But millet is not there.

In its stead we find *bigos* (see recipe on page 169), a cabbage-and-meat dish of more recent adoption. Outside Poland, it is treated as one of the most ubiquitous symbols of Polish culture. A winter dish requiring several days' preparation, bigos has been described as a type of Polish cassoulet. It has also been characterized as a type of hunter's stew, with multitudes of recipe interpretations. It is probably all of these things and more, since it is still a part of the living food culture of the country. But bigos did not originate in Poland, nor is the name of Polish origin. In concept, it appears similar to an Italian dish known in sixteenth-century Poland as *miszkułancja* (from the Italian *mescolanza*, meaning "mixture"). Some Polish historians have accepted this as evidence of Queen Bona Sforza's inventive influence, but her Italian cooks simply may have given an older dish a new and more fashionable label.

Mikołaj Rej did not mention bigos specifically in any of his writings during the sixteenth century, so the dish must have assumed its more familiar name and form within the past three hundred years. Bigos was initially composed of mixed game, which by definition was food reserved for the nobility. It has evolved over time into a more egalitarian preparation, since many Poles make it today, although rarely with game. It is even available in most Polish pubs and bistros.

Some Polish etymological material has suggested that the word *bigos* is polonized from the German *Bleiguss*.[10] This is not a food, but something associated with a custom: pouring molten lead into cold water on New Year's Day. The resulting strangely shaped flakes of metal are then studied to predict the future. This etymology is doubtless erroneous, although bigos was probably a modification of a medieval German dish. The archaic German verb *becken* (to cut up or chop and equivalent to the old English verb *bray*) would offer a more promising possibility. So would *Beifuss*, which appears in old German as *bîbôz*, *bîvuoz*, and other variations. *Beifuss* is a term for mugwort (*Artemesia vulgaris*), a popular medieval condiment for meats.

In any case, we do know what bigos is in medieval terms, since it is made with leftovers and was originally structured in layers. It is similar to the cabbage-and-meat mixture known as *choucroute alsacienne*, although the ingredients in that preparation are not chopped up into small pieces, which may be one of the keys to the origin of bigos. Perhaps it is rather more like another Alsatian dish, *potée boulangère* (*Baeckoffe*), which descends from the medieval *compositum* (meaning a mixture). This braised layered dish made with cabbage, leftover meats, and fruit is known as *Gumbistöpel* in parts of Bas-Rhin and Switzerland.[11] It was traditionally made in many parts of southern Germany and Austria, where it still survives under numerous dialect designations. It is also indigenous to the old Saxon cookery of

Transylvania and has thus evolved into many variant forms in Hungarian cookery. It would be tempting to point toward a Hungarian avenue for the introduction of bigos into Poland, given the flow of other culinary ideas from that part of Europe. But it is also true that Hedwig of Andechs-Meran (d. 1243), later known in Poland as Saint Hedwig of Silesia, would have been perfectly at home with this dish during her thirteenth-century youth in the Bavarian monastery at Kitzingen.

The medieval origins of bigos are oddly alluded to in a most un-medieval source: the *Paradok molodym khozjajkam* (A Gift to Young Housewives), a nineteenth-century Russian cookbook.[12] The author, Elena Molokhovets, never explained where she found her recipe for Polish bigos, but her procedure for making it involved the older, more medieval technique of layering the ingredients in line with the structure of a compositum. The significant part is at the beginning of her recipe, where she layers the bacon and cabbage. This step was technically unnecessary because she could have chopped them just as easily. She was evidently remaining faithful to an older recipe format, yet she was also obliged to stew the dish because she was preparing it on a cookstove.

Cooking pot excavated from the Old Market, Warsaw, fourteenth century.

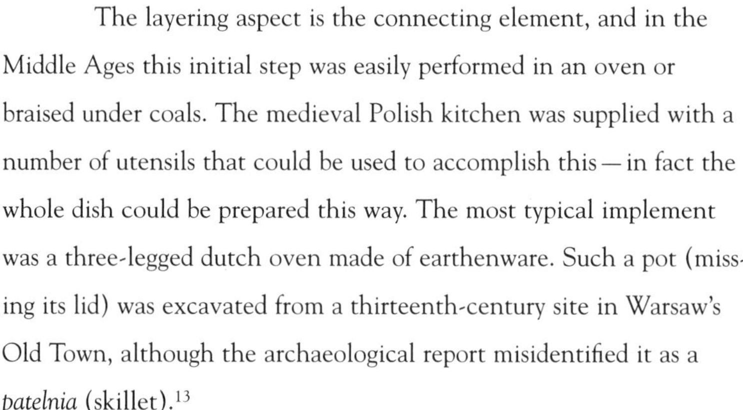

The layering aspect is the connecting element, and in the Middle Ages this initial step was easily performed in an oven or braised under coals. The medieval Polish kitchen was supplied with a number of utensils that could be used to accomplish this — in fact the whole dish could be prepared this way. The most typical implement was a three-legged dutch oven made of earthenware. Such a pot (missing its lid) was excavated from a thirteenth-century site in Warsaw's Old Town, although the archaeological report misidentified it as a *patelnia* (skillet).[13]

If the rest of Molokhovets's ingredients had also been added in layers, the result would still be bigos. In fact, if the recipe for cabbage compositum with mushrooms (see page 150) is combined with the chicken baked with prunes (see page 154), the mixture would remind most Poles of bigos. What separates the modern Polish dish from its medieval roots is the subtle alteration in structure and procedure that took place as the recipe shifted from hearth to stove cookery. While bigos is stewed today, it is not sloppy with liquid because the stewing is intended to cook it down. In any case, the preparation should be thick like Sicilian caponata, which is why Poles today serve it as an hors d'oeuvre on toast or bread before a formal meal.

It should be evident from the examples of millet (a Polish food now largely forgotten) and bigos, a dish that has come down to the present with considerable cultural baggage, that the dichotomies of Polish cuisine are not strictly limited to the court setting and the peasant dishes. These two worlds have indeed fused in the creation of a Polish consciousness at table, but other dimensions also come into play. The Polish fascination with the writings of Sir Walter Scott during the nineteenth century encouraged an Ivanhoe mentality about the Polish Middle Ages. In order to cut through these many layers of romanticized history, in order to see Poland in its raw medieval terms, we must confront the very definition of Polishness. The main players of the Polish Middle Ages have not left us with evidence of their thoughts on food or how they saw themselves when they dined among foreigners. Thus, the presumption here has been that Polish cuisine is the living food culture of the times. It is the reality of the here and now, as well as the particular reality of a past place and time. In the pages that follow, we will tackle the Polish Middle Ages and dissect a particular slice of it with that caveat in mind.

Poland in the Middle Ages

The traditional schema for studying medieval society based on class alone does not work in the area of food consumption and cookery. Standard of living is the only measure that comes closest to the reality of the times. There are also problems in identifying the various social groups who made up medieval Poland based on the nature of medieval record-keeping. But most important, we have attempted to answer the question: what is Polish identity, at least as it applies to food?

Now we shall turn to the question: who is Polish? How do we create a logical boundary for dealing with the people of medieval Poland and their diet? The old borders of medieval Poland were artificial because they were political. They did not always relate to the actual distribution of ethnic Poles in Europe. A national concept of Polishness was likewise diffuse and ill defined. It is more likely that Poles defined themselves in terms of the dukedom where they lived, or perhaps by a particular region during the early Middle Ages. Certainly during the very earliest period of Slavic settlement, Poles defined who they were according to their tribe. The following pages provide a summary of Poland's medieval history up to the early Jagiellon state, which was established in 1386.[1] There we shall pick up the story of Polish food and drink in greater detail.

Historical descriptions of Poland prior to the Jagiellon monarchy, however, have supplied us with some of the material dealing with the foods of the Polish Middle Ages. Of particular interest is the *Cronicae et gesta ducum sive principum Polonorum* of the Benedictine monk Gallus Anonymus, who compiled his work between 1116 and 1119.[2] He composed it along the lines of the chansons de geste then common in Western Europe, thus heroic elements are interwoven with fact and no small amount of political agenda. The anonymous *Chronicon comitis Petri* was less sweeping in its coverage, for it focused primarily on the exploits of Peter Włostowicz of Silesia, a powerful noble who challenged ducal authority.

Silesia (the westernmost part of present-day Poland bordering Germany) has always been fertile ground for various forms of literary and philosophical expression. Perhaps the most exquisite of these that still survives (from a manuscript dating from 1353) is the *Vita sanctae Hedwigis*.[3] This is a richly illuminated account of the life of Hedwig of Andechs-Meran (d. 1243), wife of the Piast Duke Henry I of Silesia. The manuscript is full of pictures relating to the daily life of her period and is especially useful in its visual documentation of drinking cups, hand mills, and other objects.

Born in Tyrol and reared in the monastery of Kitzingen in Bavaria, Hedwig (Jadwiga in Polish) could easily have introduced a number of new culinary ideas to Poland long before the onslaught of things Italian in the 1500s. More important, after the death of her husband, Hedwig retired to the convent of Trzebnica and devoted the remainder of her life to the poor. In 1267, she was canonized as a saint. Indeed, she became the patron saint of all Silesia, the reason for the great popularity of her name in Poland.[4] Because she was connected by marriage to the Piast dynasty that created Poland, Hedwig was also a political symbol. Queen Jadwiga, whose court we shall explore in Chapter 3, owed her name to this much-loved saint, which was doubtless useful in giving further authenticity to her own Piast ancestry.

The first attempt at an organized Polish history, rather than heroic deeds, was the *Cronica de gestis principum ac regnum Poloniae* by Vincent Kadłubek, bishop of Cracow (d. 1223). This was followed by the *Cronica Poloniae Maioris* by Godisław Baszko of Poznan (d. before 1297/1298). All of these early documents refer to food, and all were published in nineteenth-century collections of medieval sources edited by various Polish scholars.[5] Yet, except for Gallus Anonymus, no Polish chronicles survive from the period of ducal rule. What we know about the earliest period of Polish history has been extrapolated from later sources, from foreign references to Poland, and especially from archaeological findings.

Origins of the Polish People

The oldest city in Poland is Kalisz, which was originally built on an island in the Prosna River. It is the ancient Calisia mentioned by Ptolemy in A.D. 142–147, a major trading center on the old Amber Route between the Baltic and Mediterranean Seas. Whether the Calisians were Poles or even Slavs is a matter of debate because the people who are generally referred to by medieval historians as "proto-Polish" do not appear on Polish soil until the sixth century. They were largely engaged in animal husbandry and farming.

Several Byzantine sources describe the proto-Poles and their tribal society. Archaeological evidence has revealed widespread trade contacts with Carolingian Europe, Kievan Rus (modern Ukraine),

Great Moravia (centered on the present Czech Republic), and various Baltic peoples. Furs, amber, and salt appear to have been the leading export products.

Polish society at this time was organized under military leaders called *knędz* (later spelled *książe*). These leaders built fortified settlements and eventually organized the Poles into numerous territorial entities. Eventually, the Polanie tribe (called Polanes in Latin records), situated around Gniezno in the north, and the Wiślanie tribe (called Vislanes in Latin), centered around Cracow in the south, emerged as the most powerful. The Polanie tribal territory was later known as Great Poland, while the Wiślanie territory was later known as Little Poland. Archaeologists have carried out extensive excavations at the old Wiślanie capital of Wiślica. As a result much is now known about the early stronghold and how it was built, in addition to massive amounts of material relating to the foods and foodways of this period.

The military chiefs who headed the various tribal territories fought against one another and against foreign encroachments. After the Polanie leader asserted control over the rest of the tribal territories, all of the tribes were referred to collectively in Latin texts as Polonia. The name Polanes derives from the Polish word *pole*, which means a field. Thus Polonia is literally a nation of field dwellers, that is, people who do not live in villages but in scattered single-family farms. These agriculturalists were pagans who worshipped the sun. Their chief god was Swarożyc.

Medieval texts mention a Prince Mieszko (d. 992), who by 960 appears to have consolidated the various tribal territories of Polonia into one political entity and opened trade with Byzantium. Mieszko was a Piast, and all the various dukes, princes, and other magnates who ruled Poland up to 1370 claimed descent from this ancient family line. The synthesis of court and peasant mentioned in connection with food is epitomized in the legends surrounding Piast origins, for the Piasts are said to have descended from a wheelwright. In short, they claimed to be peasants who became rulers. Thus, when the nobility of postmedieval Poland chose to evoke authenticity and ancient Polishness, it could turn to these legendary peasant origins as a symbol of identity and as a link to the land. Food in this context assumes a dimension of political propaganda, which is quite evident in many of the chronicles of medieval Poland that extol the virtues of certain rulers or high nobles. Yet the Piast legend is nothing more than that. The family name is derived from the Polish word *piastować*, which means "to take care of," or in a political sense "to hold office," but since office holders take care of people, the two meanings are not really separate. Polish linguistic scholars have suggested that the name was originally some type of title, but that interpretation is not firmly settled.

Prince Mieszko and his Piast territories are important because he is mentioned in the 966 account of Jewish merchant ibn-Ya'qub of Tortosa in Spain, who was visiting Prague that year. In 964 or 965 (the exact date is not known) Mieszko married Dobrova, daughter of a powerful Bohemian duke. She came to Poland with Christian priests and in 966 Mieszko and his court were converted to Christianity. The rest of Poland, however, did not convert so quickly; indeed, it took almost two centuries for the Church to eradicate pagan practices.

However, the coming of Christianity to Poland altered the course of Polish history. Mieszko later placed Poland directly under the Apostolic See, dedicating Gniezno (then the capital) and its environs to Saint Peter. This placed Poland under the protection of the Pope and allied it permanently with the Latin West. It also laid the foundations for the enormous political power that would eventually flow into the hands of the Polish Church. For the most part, the high church officials were also Piast princes or close relatives, so the web of dynastic power during this period was tightly woven.

Mieszko's eldest son, Bołeslaw Chrobry (reigned 992–1025), expanded Poland into Kievan Rus to the East and took lands in the West from the Czechs. In 1025, the Pope granted him the title of king and he was crowned on Easter Sunday that year. The choice of that date for his coronation is significant, as it not only equated the event with the widespread feasting following Lent, but in a political sense it also elevated the new king to a type of national savior. Bołeslaw was Poland's first true king, but if the intermingling of political and religious imagery was meant to bolster the success of the state, the gamble failed. He died shortly after his coronation, and Poland was plunged into political upheaval and a full-scale reversion to the old pagan religion.

Bołeslaw the Bold (reigned 1058–1079) pulled the country back together, regaining Silesia, a region that throughout Polish history has slipped back and forth between various rulers. With the assistance of Pope Gregory VIII, the Polish king resurrected the Church. He also established Cracow as the capital. The Piast magnates grew suspicious of his attempts to consolidate power, and in 1079 they drove him into exile. From this time on, the real power behind the Polish throne lay in the hands of a small group of families who controlled vast estates and personal revenues.

In 1226, one of these magnates, Duke Conrad of Mazovia (a Piast), invited the Knights of the Teutonic Order (originally Crusaders in the Holy Land) to help defeat the pagan Lithuanians, Prussians (at

Schedel's view of Cracow printed at Nuremberg, 1493.

that time a distinct ethnic group), and other tribes living on his eastern borders. Because the knights also had papal approval and the support of the Holy Roman Emperor, their appearance on Polish territory became a threat to Polish autonomy. By 1230, the knights had conquered much of Prussia. In 1309, the Grand Master of the Teutonic Order moved the brotherhood from Venice and constructed a vast brick castle at Malbork (Marienburg) near Gdansk that still stands. The duke's fateful invitation set into motion a bitter conflict with Poland that lasted for centuries and did not play itself out until 1945, when Poland absorbed the remnants of medieval Prussia and expelled the German-speaking population from those territories.

The Peasantry

During the very earliest part of the Middle Ages, the Polish peasants may have existed as free farmers holding land as part of the local tribal unit. The actual ownership of the land may have been communal insofar as it belonged to the group rather than to one person. Once the military leaders, like the early Piasts and their warriors, forged control over the tribal communities, they demanded tribute. Some tribute was paid in agricultural products, others were paid in specialized services, such as beekeeping, hunting, sheep herding, or through general agricultural labor.

By the twelfth century, some of these peasant farmers — later called "half-acre gentry" (from *zagradowa,* "fenced in" or "enclosed") — remained free. But most of them experienced some type of restraint on their existence, whether freedom of movement, use of resources, or limitations on the types of activities they could engage in. Some had become outright serfs to their princely rulers; nearly all were required to pay heavy duties. Their rulers endowed churches and rewarded loyal followers with grants of land and the income paid by the people living on them. In this way, the high nobility, the bishops, and the monasteries accumulated landed estates covering large areas with many hundreds, even thousands, of dependents. In some regions of Poland, these landed estates were devoted to cereal crops under the close supervision of the overlord. In others, temporary fields were carved out of woodlands by slash-and-burn techniques and these farmers lived more or less undisturbed by their masters.

The Polish situation was further complicated as the ruling princes and landowners turned their attention to vast tracts of unsettled land in order to increase their incomes. At first, this was undertaken using Polish concepts of land tenure. By 1200, Western European concepts of special privileges in the form of fixed rents, hereditary tenure, and village self-government were brought into play. Lured by these benefits, settlers from abroad (mostly Germans) and from within Poland took up land in the Polish wilderness and carved out new farms and villages.

By about 1300, the success of this settlement plan was obvious to the overlords in all parts of Poland, and special privileges were gradually extended in piecemeal fashion to the older settlement areas. The economic benefit to the landowners lay in the fact that agricultural risk was shifted to the peasant while guaranteeing a steady annual flow of rents in cash. The peasants acquired cash by selling their produce in the market towns which were developing during this same period. Not all Polish peasants achieved legal freedom or economic independence, but from the late thirteenth century through the fifteenth, the rentier economy allowed them to enjoy a relatively decent standard of living. This general well-being was only disrupted if they fell victim to the destruction of invading armies, climatic disasters, or epidemics, especially the plague.

Because economic development of the region now comprising modern Poland relied heavily on immigration during the Middle Ages, Poland became a polyglot society during this phase of its history. Immigration filled large areas of Silesia, Pomerania, and Prussia with German-speaking majorities. From the fourteenth century on, the extension of Polish political control eastward and southeast also brought Lithuanians, Hungarians, and large Ukrainian minorities into the Polish kingdom. Ethnic and cultural tensions between Poles and non-Poles never fully disappeared. When speaking of peasant foods and foodways in medieval terms, we must always keep in mind this great diversity.

The Lesser Nobility

While much of the Polish peasantry during the thirteenth century merged into a class of free rent-paying tenants on land owned by someone else, the half-acre gentry retained a military role and a status equivalent to ownership rights over their property. This class of peasant, divided into those who performed mounted military service in full armor and the so-called *wlodarz* (pages, stewards, and soldiers of lesser rank), began to claim exemption from taxes due to their military service, a privilege already enjoyed by the entourages of the powerful overlords. By degrees, this upper level of peasantry coalesced into a group known as the lesser nobility (in Polish, *szlachta*).[6] Their privileges became more sharply defined after King Louis d'Anjou of Hungary and Poland granted them legal status in 1374. In spite of this, their economic resources were not much better than that of a well-off peasant, and without military rewards or the steady employment of an overlord, the szlachta was always at risk of slipping into a lower rank.

The szlachta was already a recognizable part of medieval Polish society by the Jagiellon dynasty. Since it further evolved as a class during that period, it would be useful to look at an example of one family to see exactly how complex the existence of the szlachta could be, not just in terms of social status but in the constantly shifting nature of their standard of living. Not all members of the Polish szlachta could claim genealogies as old as that of the Woyszkys, but since the fortunes of this family were tied to those of the early Piasts, they serve as a convenient bridge between the early and late Middle Ages. Furthermore, they represent the sort of soldiering class that formed part of the entourage of individuals called *familiares* (retainers) at the Polish court.

Chapter 2

Poland in the Middle Ages

The first appearance of the Woyszky family in medieval records was in an 1183 document confirming property transfers in Bohemia and Moravia by Frederick, duke of Bohemia. Two brothers, Otto and Rediwoi Woizke, acted as witnesses on behalf of the Order of Saint John of Jerusalem (Hospitallers).[7] This may also support the supposition that they are of Czech rather than Polish origin. They are generally described in later lists of nobility (from the 1500s onward) as Silesian or Upper Silesian and eventually became Germanized after most of Silesia came under Austrian rule in the 1500s.

The family reappears in a 1290 document issued by Przemysl II, duke of Great Poland and Cracow (king of Poland 1295–1296), when Bernhard ("eius qui dicitur Woyszky"—he who is called Woyszky) is referred to as castellan of Cracow.[8] The distinction was mentioned because the *wojski* was the title of the official who stood in for the castellan when he was away on a military campaign. Thus the family name derives from a title of office. From this we can gather that the family is indeed a military one, and in the case of castellan, his primary job was to defend the walls of the royal capital. Furthermore, as loyal followers of the Piast princes, the Woyszkys acquired small feudal holdings, which elevated them economically above the peasants, although in real terms the differences may have been small. Casimir the Great mentioned a Petrus Woyszky in 1354, and the family surfaces in many later histories of Poland and Silesia.

Another complicating factor was that of clan (*ród*), which represented a type of political consciousness based on real or imagined genetic relationships with a common ancestor. Knightly clans evolved in Poland during the thirteenth to fifteenth centuries, with groupings called *gniazda* ("nests") forming protective settlements around many towns. Polish families that managed to rise above the peasantry attached themselves through marriage or military service to various clans according to a fixed number of insignia. This recognition of clan gained ground as part of the efforts of the szlachta to further define itself as a distinct class with specific rights and privileges. All members of the same clan shared one insignia and *proclamatio* (battle cry).

The Woyszky clan insignia was the Wieniawa, a head of an aurochs with a ring through its nose, a species of wild cattle symbolic of ancient Poland. It is not known when the Woyszkys were first permitted to use it, but by the 1500s they were considered old members of this clan. That the clans were powerful social forces is not in doubt, for Casimir the Great attempted to create new power elites in the mid-1300s specifically to break the grip of the old clans on the Polish throne—and in that fallout exit the Woyszkys. Later, throughout much of the Jagiellon dynasty, the lords of Brzesie (the Lanckorónski family of the Zadora clan) dominated the court politics via their clan networks. It was through their good offices that many nobles, as well as members of the szlachta, found employment at court.

Wieniawa, a clan insignia.

We find, for example, Piotr Szafraniec of Łuczyce (Starykón clan) employed as assistant master of the royal pantry (1376–1398), a political crony to say the least, but for a person of noble origin, this job was hardly one of influence or prestige. Such positions were more commonly filled by the lesser nobility, who were quite willing to work as military officers at court, as royal huntsmen, royal falconers, and even, as we shall see, as master chefs. In fact, a whole range of duties were viewed as stations above the peasantry offering honorable employment and opportunities for social advancement. There was also the added perk of sharing in the culinary largesse of the master's table. This pattern not only applied to the royal court at Cracow; it was repeated in all the princely courts throughout Poland.

Such courts would have included those of the powerful voivodes of Cracow, Sandomierz, Poznan, Kalisz, and Sieradz, as well as the church elites headed by the archbishop of Gniezno and the bishops of Cracow, Kujawy, and Poznan. But there were others as well, even beyond the immediate borders of the kingdom. One such court would have been that of Wenzel, duke of Legnica, a Piast who was sometimes an honored guest at Wawel Castle. He was doubly powerful in political terms because he was also the bishop of Wrocław (from 1382 to 1417) and is known to have received a barrel of corned aurochs from the Polish king. This was a gift food of high status and would not have been served to members of the szlachta at court, unless in the form of leftovers. Leftovers, as we shall see, form a large part of what was served to the various individuals living at Wawel Castle, and the pecking order involves an understanding of the varying degrees of status accorded to all of these people. A list of some of these individuals and a brief discussion of their professions appear in Chapter 3.

This brings us to the period of Polish reunification coupled with the extinction of the Piast dynasty. Other branches of the Piast family continued to rule in Mazovia and Silesia, and many prominent members married into European royal houses. In Poland, however, the royal line soon died out. True political unity did not come to the kingdom until the reign of the Kujavian Piast, Władysław I Łokietek, called "the Short," who ruled from 1306 until 1333. In 1320, he arranged the marriage of his daughter Elizabeth to the Sicilian Angevin King Charles Robert of Hungary. This political move was one of the reasons for a strong Hungarian presence at the Jagiellon court later in the century.

Upon the death of Łokietek in 1333, his son Casimir III

ascended the throne. Casimir's reign (1333–1370) is one of the periods of Polish history that might justifiably be described as golden. He made Poland into a major European power, but his international successes were mixed. In 1335 and 1339 he signed treaties with Luxembourg recognizing its claims over Silesia. In 1343, he recognized the claims of the Teutonic Knights to Pomerania. As an interesting footnote to those soldiering Woyszkys, a branch of the family soon appeared on estates at Krokau in Pomerania, acquired through service to the Order. Clan loyalties were not shaped by nationalism.

Hemmed in by political setbacks in the west, Casimir turned eastward and in 1340 invaded Podolia, Halicz, and Ruthenia, thus capturing Lvov and doubling the size of the Polish state. In the 1360s, he arbitrated a serious conflict among the Luxembourg, Hapsburg, and Angevin dynasties, and in doing so, perhaps averted a major war that would have broken up the Holy Roman Empire. In terms of Polish culinary history, Casimir's reign marked an important shift in focus. An aficionado of fine cooking with a keen eye for pomp and spectacle, he helped to foster an international interest in Polish cookery.

If Polish hospitality had been a mystery to the world leaders of the mid-1300s, Casimir changed that in 1364 when he hosted an international convention of nobles in Cracow. Period accounts gathered by fifteenth-century Polish historian Jan Długosz have cast this event as one of the most spectacular of the fourteenth century. Other accounts by actual participants are now beginning to surface and suggest that the full story has not yet been told. Roman Grodecki's history of the congress has detailed the complex political ramifications, but not much has been written about the unusual culinary dimensions that set this gathering apart from all others in the late Middle Ages.

Casimir set out to accomplish several things at once. His first order of business was to marry off a granddaughter, Elizabeth of Pomerania, to the Holy Roman Emperor, widower King Charles IV of Bohemia. Charles had been married to another Polish Piast, Anna of Swidnica-Jaworów, who died in 1362. This settled the dust on some irritating dynastic claims and brought the major European powers at that time into better harmony. The second order of the day was to curry support for King Peter de Lusignan of Cyprus (reigned 1359–1369) and his plans to launch a crusade against Egypt. Among the foreign royalty present at this convention were King Charles, King Peter, King Charles Robert of Hungary, and King Waldemar IV of Denmark, not to mention their courts and a vast following of princes, dukes, bishops, and their entourages, including their private cooks.

As host, Casimir was called upon to supply the guests with food and lodging, and his open generosity was everywhere noted. But his most distinguished guests also brought gifts and reciprocated with dinner parties according to their own taste, so that the cumulative effect was one grand culinary bazaar. Casimir took this opportunity to showcase Polish cookery, but his household accounts do not survive, so we can only guess at what this meant, at least in terms of the royal court.

Casimir maintained Italian pleasure gardens at great expense considering the severity of Poland's winters. It is likely that this Italian emphasis was also carried over into his kitchen when he engaged in public entertainments, the sort of pre-Platina recipes of the late 1300s that have come to light in a large Italian manuscript recently discovered in South Tyrol (as yet unpublished). But like most recipe collections from the Middle Ages, regardless of the language in which they are written, such material would represent an accretion of information spanning perhaps as much as three centuries and reaching down into a number of sources. Some of this material may have percolated through several cultures, with adjustments often made when a recipe is copied, translated, or rewritten. Analysis of later cookery manuscript collections—from the seventeenth and eighteenth centuries for example—has shown that this characteristic is inherent in the very nature of manuscript cookery books. This is a demotic literary form based on eclectic derivation.

In any event, we may safely presume that the courtly dimension of Casimir's table was derived from models found in written sources. To complete its Polishness, his cook would have unified this with dishes of peasant origin. For political reasons, he may also have chosen certain foods that reinforced imagery relating to his king's Piast ancestry: wafers stamped with the Piast insignia or shaped like wagon wheels (alluding to wheelwright origins), mead, and dishes featuring turnips, since they figure in the legend about the founding of the Piast dynasty. He would also have served dishes based on the cuisines of the king's most distinguished guests, both to flatter to them, and to show that the king was indeed an international man.

The most exotic food at this convention was doubtless that of the Cypriot delegation. Traditional histories have assumed that the dynastic families of French origin who established themselves in various Mediterranean kingdoms imposed their culture on their dependents. This may indeed have been true of the political structure and the social customs directly connected with it, but in terms of food consumption, all of these societies had very highly developed cuisines in place before the French arrived. Many possessed a long tradition of culinary literature going back to early Byzantium. Time and the destruction of wars have erased much of the original material, but some of it passed into the body of Western European culinary literature.

On closer analysis, it would appear that these new rulers were quickly creolized both through intermarriage and by acculturation. We may cite as evidence the wedding feast of Richard I of England (an Angevin), which took place on Cyprus in 1192. The menu discussed by George Jeffery in his *Cyprus Under an English King* (1973) was anything but English, and it was certainly not French. Even taro was served. It would be tempting to suggest that the "Vyaund de cyprys bastarde" and its Cypriot roommates in the Harleian MS. 279 (supposedly dating from the 1470s), represent material handed down from this much earlier period.[9] But it could also stem from a (now lost) body of recipes that evolved out of Casimir's grand convention in 1364. The recipe for hashmeat (see page 171) is offered as a sampling of the way in which something Cypriot may have been seen through the eyes of a Polish court cook. All that can be said about most of the surviving medieval recipes in Western Europe claiming to be Cypriot is that they have been rewritten to accommodate foods not found in Cyprus.

What would we have expected among the food gifts brought by King Peter to the Polish king? Items that were easy to transport without spoiling, such as olive oil, various wines, rum, and the beverage *soumada* (a form of almond milk taken as a health drink, with which rum was often mixed), or *glygo amygdalou*, a marzipan confection made in Cypriot convents.

This list also would include large quantities of sugar and a number of costly spices. If anything could be called "Cypriot" to the Polish mind of the middle and late 1300s, it was the importation of sugar, two sorts of galingale ("lesser," *Alpina officinarum*, and "greater,"

Alpina galanga), grains of Paradise (*Aframomum melegueta*) used to flavor hippocras, and other spices purchased by Italian merchants in Acre or Alexandria and shipped to Poland via Cyprus. This also included labdanum, an aromatic resin exuded by the Cypriot rock rose (*Cistus monspeliensis* and *Cistus villosus creticus*) which was carried in the pocket as a prevention against the bubonic plague. To this we might further add Cypriot "monk's pepper," the seed of *agnia* or chaste tree (*Vitex agnus castus*). The pepper was added to monastic dishes to suppress venery or sexual desire.

Yet no Cypriot product stood out more than sugar. Sugar cane was introduced to Cyprus from Egypt sometime during the period of Byzantine rule (330–1184), perhaps in the seventh century. It was under later Lusignan (1192–1489) and Venetian rules that it became a major cash crop. After stripping the island of its lumber for shipbuilding, the Venetians in particular created vast sugar plantations along the warm southern coast of Cyprus and traded it out of Les Salines (Larnaca), a city also famous for its salt used in glassmaking. The Genoese, who were important to Poland through Black Sea trade, also entered the picture, especially after they captured the Cypriot port of Famagusta in 1376 and thus gained a foothold on the island.

Byzantine fork, sixth century, wrought bronze. Private collection.

The Cypriot delegation also brought with it the custom of eating food with forks, called *peronas* in Byzantine Greek. This technique for eating food developed in Byzantium and was widespread by the tenth century. It was adopted by Western Europeans who came in contact with Byzantine food culture in the eastern Mediterranean. Byzantine forks are known to date from at least the sixth century and were commonly used for eating sticky foods and cheese. Their evolution from serving forks into personal implements carried by each individual was in part due to the Byzantine style of court cookery, in which the food came to table cut up in small pieces and served in a multitude of little dishes. Byzantine forks (or their copies) have also been found in archaeological sites in Sassanian Persia, which suggests that the Greek custom developed in response to Oriental influences emanating from areas well outside the Byzantine world.

It is quite likely that forks made of precious metal were presented as gifts by the Cypriot king to the other monarchs attending the Cracow convention of 1364, although no documentation has thus far come to light to prove it. These curiosities may have been passed on as gifts to others. Louis d'Anjou, a guest at this feast, listed a fork in his 1368 inventory. Fifteen years later, a fork appeared in the 1379 inventory of King Charles V of France. It took more than a century for European cookery to adapt to the use of forks, and forks do not appear in royal inventories in Poland until 1502. They did not become commonplace on Polish tables until the seventeenth century.

The archaeological prospects for documenting such an exchange remain dim, as it is not likely that a royal fork with a gold handle or encrusted with jewels and Byzantine cloisonné would ever end up on a rubbish heap. But an example of lesser quality was found in a late fifteenth-century site at Stare Miasto "Na valach" in the Czech Republic. That fork was probably old and worn when discarded, implying that it had been in use for some time. Its place of manufacture is unknown, but it was definitely owned by someone of high rank. The find is significant because it places the fork in Central Europe considerably ahead of its appearance in written sources. Other serendipitous discoveries may eventually close the gaps in what is now known about the early distribution of the fork. In the meantime, the

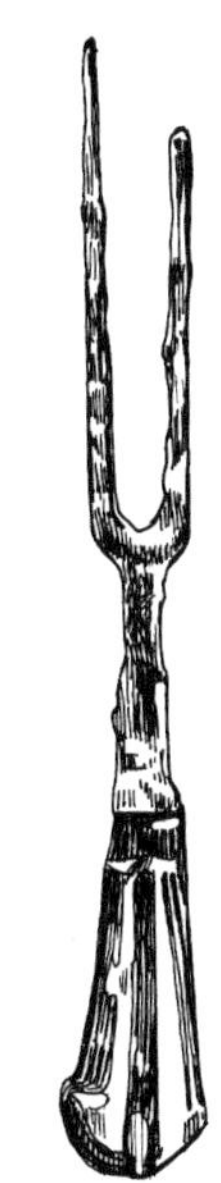

Medieval fork from Stare Miasto.

Cracow congress of 1364 presents itself as one possible point of introduction.

The culinary diversity of that event symbolized in many respects the new Poland that Casimir III had assembled prior to his death in 1370. He recognized the value of a vibrant urban economy and pragmatically invited the Jews to settle in Poland. His royal protection threw open the country to a mass migration of Jews from Western Europe, especially from the German Rhineland.[10] Yet mixed in with the Jews were also Waldensians from Italy and considerable numbers of Armenians fleeing west in the tumultuous years leading up to the Mamluk conquest of Armenia in 1375. Like the Jews, the Italians and Armenians congregated in larger towns and cities and added variety to Poland's urban culinary and intellectual life.

Casimir III died without a legal heir. His nephew, Louis d'Anjou (king of Hungary), assumed the Polish throne and ruled in absentia until his death in 1382. In 1384, after a brief interregnum, Casimir's grandniece Jadwiga d'Anjou became the Polish queen. A child-heiress and symbol of political legitimacy, she was the second daughter of Louis and sister of Maria d'Anjou (who reigned from 1382 to 1395 as queen of Hungary). Jadwiga's assumption to the Polish crown was predicated on an arranged marriage negotiated by the Polish magnates with Jogalia, the extremely powerful grandduke of pagan Lithuania. In return for this union, which brought together Lithuania and Poland, Duke Jogalia and his people converted to Christianity. He then polonized his name to Jagiełło and took the Christian name Władysław. Poland was thus transformed from the rich polyglot state created by Casimir III to an even larger and more powerful kingdom. This political and cultural setting defined the court life of the early Jagiellon state and its royal table.

Poland in the Middle Ages

Jadwiga died childless in 1399, but left a lasting impression on her husband. At her request, her jewels were converted into a trust fund to establish a permanent income for the famous Jagiellonian University in Cracow. Even to the very end of her life, Jadwiga was keenly aware of her saintly namesake, and the meaning of such patronage in Polish terms. She may have been politically powerless, her chancellor Zaklika (Topor clan) and vice chancelor Moskorzewski (Pilawa clan) hemmed in by the Lanckorońskis, but her cultural and culinary effects on the royal court were pervasive. Following her death, Jagiełło remarried several times and went on to establish a new family dynasty that ruled Poland and Lithuania until 1572.

What we know about the foods served at the Jagiellon court have been preserved in the household ledgers. Many of these records are purchase orders for specific meals, and thus serve as a supplementary outline in lieu of a menu. Since quantities are given in minute detail, it is possible to view many of the purchase orders in the same light as recipes. With all or most of the ingredients in place, it simply remains to decipher how they were combined. Yet these records cannot be used alone, but rather viewed in context with similar records from the same period. This helps to better define both the court cuisine itself and food preparation of a more provincial nature within Poland, not to mention a better grasp of subtle differences in food consumption as dictated by standard of living.

To this end, a wide range of regional documents, including the accounts and registers of royal officials and magnates in Niepołomice, and in the cities of Korcyn, Prozów, Żarnow, Ujście Solne, Wojnicz, Cracow, and Nowy Sącz, have been consulted. The income and expense books for the city of Lvov between 1407 and 1417 have provided a glimpse into the far southeastern corner of the kingdom.

The private accounts of the governor of Cracow and state treasurer Henryk of Rogów have yielded rich insights into the lifestyle of powerful state officials. So too did the *Ämterbuch* (central account book) of the Teutonic Knights, with its emphasis on Baltic foodways and the eating habits of a military order. At the other end of the spectrum, records like the account books of the Bochnia salt mines (from 1394 to 1421) provided useful insights into working-class foodways.[11]

From outside Poland, a variety of foreign culinary materials shed light on the similarities and differences between Poland and areas known to have supplied the royal court with ideas about cookery, table customs, and perhaps even written recipes. Poland after Casimir III became a very different place, and the sophistication of the Jagiellon court evolved rapidly. The Angevin connections of Queen Jadwiga to possible foreign sources are extremely important, for it is evident that she possessed a culinary text (perhaps a cookery book) that contained a variety of elaborate recipes. Jadwiga's personal preference for prevailing international styles of cookery is evident everywhere in the type of ingredients mentioned in her financial accounts. Let us turn then to the main figures of this culinary drama as it was played out in Wawel Castle, where Poland's rulers resided at that time.

The Dramatis Personae of the Old Polish Table

Preceding his appointment as viceroy to the king of Bohemia in 1394, an important foreign prince paid his respects to the Polish court. The precise date of this encounter is not clear from surviving records, but it occurred during a trip through his wife's hereditary lands on their return to Germany. Of interest to us is the manner in which this visit played itself out at the royal table. For this was Justus, margrave of Moravia and Lausitz, elector of Brandenburg and prince of Luxembourg. He had spent some time in Italy during 1383, and since 1387 his brother had been the Patriarch of Aquileia, thus adding an important churchly dimension to his family ties. His wife was Princess Agnes of Opole, a Piast and therefore a distant relative of Queen Jadwiga through her great-uncle Casimir III.

Such distinguished visitors would have sat with the monarchs at dinner while the court learned the latest about the cultural events then unfolding in Italy, Prague, and elsewhere. In this situation the Polish court would have dusted off its best linens and presented itself in its international role as a leading European power. The food served would also evoke this high standard of the sort preserved in period cookery manuscripts. The dish of baked fruit (see page 191) is just such a recipe, which reflects the ingredients found in royal purchase orders during the 1390s and their heavy emphasis on such

Hand-washing after the meal, fifteenth-century woodcut.

expensive imports as almonds, lemons, French wines, olive oil, and Cypriot sugar.

One can easily imagine that royal conversation included a discussion of food and the long culinary shadow cast by Casimir the Great some thirty years earlier. The father of Prince Justus, Johann Heinrich, from whom he inherited the title of margrave of Moravia, married Princess Elizabeth of Racibórz and Těšín in January 1364. She was the daughter of Mieszko, Piast duke of Racibórz, Těšín, and Oświęcim. Her mother was another Pole, Princess Euphrosine of Plozk and Mazovia. Both parents and grandparents had been guests at the convention of nobles in 1364. Thus, the medieval protocol for dining with such dignitaries took into account these elaborate dynastic connections. The dinner conversation about the events of 1364 probably served as a jovial common bond echoed in the songs of the minnesingers who entertained that day. But the legends surrounding Casimir's hospitality made it imperative for the Polish court that followed him to live up to his very high reputation, a task that seems to have fallen to Queen Jadwiga.

Generally on ceremonial or state occasions such as this the king and queen dined together. They sometimes dined together privately, but on a day-to-day basis they ate separately at the head of their respective retinues. The male retinue dined with the king, the female retinue with the queen. Gossip often centered on the arrangement or rearrangement of the seating, based on who had fallen out of favor and who had lately joined the table.

Food was delivered according to this pecking order. What the queen passed over went down to the next in line, and so the food traveled down the head table, through the other tables in the room and into neighboring rooms where even larger numbers of lesser nobles and household staff waited to be served. The court records allow us to calculate consumption figures based on the first "flight," that is, divided among the headcount of the retinues who had first choice after the monarch. This provides us with a rough sketch of how much was served, but it does not represent how much was consumed, because hidden behind these figures are all those other members of the royal household who subsisted on the leftovers. Furthermore, most of the people during the Middle Ages were quite short by present-day standards. What served as an adult portion for them was probably more like a child's restaurant portion today. In any case, the style of cooking was heavy and it filled the belly quickly.

This organization of the table, with food traveling downward to individuals of lesser rank, was repeated throughout Poland in the princely and ducal courts, and in the country manors of the lesser nobility. Indeed, even in the peasant households, food was divided up accordingly. The husband and male members of the family ate together first; the wife and other females ate together after the men finished. Guests were accorded special treatment and were normally served first, often with the best food. This rule did not apply to paying guests, who might lodge in a private home for the night. They usually got whatever was on hand or leftover from the day's meal. Such paying guests were a common feature in the Middle Ages due to the lack of inns in rural areas.

Whether at the royal court or in a peasant kitchen, food was eaten with the fingers, except for porridges and soups. No one used personal forks, although some of the royalty in Europe probably knew about forks by 1364, even though they may not have used them. Individuals ate with a knife held in the left hand, or a spoon in the right. At the royal court and in other situations where "good manners" applied, carving was necessary because meats came to the table in large pieces.

All nobles were required to understand the art of carving, which was as essential to a gentleman's training as swordsmanship, equestrian prowess, and falconry. Any member of the royal retinue might be called upon by the king to carve his majesty's portions. This task was generally managed in the French fashion, the carver kneeling directly in front of the monarch. This meant that the food was situated on a table roughly at eye level or somewhat above, and had to be carved in such a way that it could be eaten without a fork—clearly a certain test of a courtier's mettle. We do not have a Polish treatise on such training from the Middle Ages, but Łukasz Górnicki's *Dworzanin polski* (The Polish Courtier) of 1566 describes Polish custom as it evolved during the Renaissance. Górnicki's references to old customs provide a backward glance into the Middle Ages.

Chapter 3

The Dramatis Personae

Burgrave to the bishop of Lvov, vice chamberlain to the crown, grand crown treasurer, castellan of Sącz, hetman to the duke of Masovia — the list of offices held by Polish members of the royal and ducal courts is long and exotic. None of those just mentioned was hereditary, although by the Renaissance many of these offices were assumed only by the nobility. During the Middle Ages, they were administrative positions of power, offices that could be filled even by commoners who were clever enough to work their way up the political ladder. Most of these high officials ate very well because they were seated toward the upper end of the pecking order when royal meals were served. Privately, their incomes often allowed them to live in the same style as a duke or prince. Some of them even acquired choice estates by holding mortgages for princes hard up for cash.

We have compiled a list of the various individuals who are actually mentioned in the records to better understand the Polish royal household and how it worked during the period from about 1390 to 1420. It is fascinating for the light it throws on the way food came into Wawel Castle, who processed it, and who took it up to the king's table. The list has been roughly organized to follow the route of foodstuffs from the forest or garden through the kitchen to the banquet. There were two royal kitchens at this time, one for the king and one for the queen, so some positions existed in duplicate.

In addition, the persons working at court, and most or all of their families, including children, normally resided near or within the fortified area, thus the headcount of the staff personnel becomes huge. Even if all these people did not actually reside on Wawel Hill, they often took their meals there. The wife of the royal potter may have worked as a laundress, and some of the potter's children may have worked with the valets assigned to cleaning rooms. In this sense, the extensive staff was earning its keep. Following each position name below is the Latin designation given in the original documents, then a description of the duties required and some additional information that may help clarify them. Names in italics are medieval Polish equivalents or Polish terms that do not have an exact English counterpart.

Persons Associated with Food Consumption at the Polish Royal Court

Purveyors and Staff Outside the Castle Animal flayer (Listiciarius), *oprawcza*. He worked in conjunction with the butcher. As his duty was to skin the carcasses, he was primarily concerned with hides and leather, and to some extent the parchment on which the royal court kept records.

Beer brewer (Braxator cervisie). He produced beer, yeast, and vinegar for the royal court.

Butcher (Incisor). He slaughtered the animals and divided the carcass into quarters for the kitchen.

Fishmonger (Piscator). The individual who delivered the fish to the royal kitchens was either a royal factor appointed to bring the fish to court or a person not on the royal payroll who made a living by trading in fish. This person was always at the castle on fast days and Fridays.

Gardener (Hortulanus). Large numbers of these individuals were employed to maintain the royal gardens—both the kitchen gardens and the ornamental gardens on the castle grounds. There were also gardeners who worked on the royal estates but who ate at the castle when they brought produce in from the country. The royal estates, or allodia, were the personal property of the king. For political reasons, the royal court never purchased its provisions directly from farms belonging to other nobles. Since the royal allodia never produced enough food (or income) to support the court, the king was forced to rely on the many vendors mentioned in this list.

Herdsman (Pastor). Guarded the royal cattle and hogs.

Miller (Molendinator). He operated the royal mills or the mills under royal contract, produced beer, yeast, and bread, and sometimes fattened hogs for the royal butcher.

Potter (Argillator or Argillarius seu *glynarz*). He made earthenware and cookpots for the royal kitchen. His pottery was usually on or near the castle premises.

Stall-keeper, market vendor (Institor). These traders sold products, mostly in exotic spices, at court. Although they may have been rich, they did not sit with the nobility. They sometimes ate with the household servants.

Vendors (Mangones). These persons would appear at the castle with products to sell. An example is the *mangones musci*, vendors who sold moss (used as toilet paper in medieval times). They were largely transient but they often dined with the servants. Vendors also purchased things from the court as well, such as dog manure from the royal kennels (used by dyers) and rags.

Vessel and barrel trader (Vasator). He sold these products to the court on a regular basis.

Vice procurator, *podrzeczy*. This individual was in charge of managing a particular royal garrison. He reported to the procurator.

In-House Purveyors and Processors Baker (Pistor). The royal baker made all the bread for the court. His ovens were on the premises but he may have had a bakery elsewhere as well. He also ground grains in a quern (hand mill) to make special flour mixes for court use.

Beer barrels.

Cooper (Doliator). His shop was on the premises. He made and repaired wooden vessels and also sold them in the market.

Coppersmith (Faber ereus). He made copperware for the royal kitchen, as well as copper utensils for general household use.

Cutler (Cultellifex). He made and sharpened knives in his shop on the castle premises. He also sharpened weapons for the knights and soldiers stationed in the castle and made kitchen implements for the court.

Oil presser (Oleator). This specialized craft was carried out at court to press poppy seeds, flax seeds, or hemp seeds for oil. The oil presser was always paid in cash. The actual pressing was often done by peasant girls under his employment. He did not necessarily live on the castle premises.

Pharmacist, royal druggist (Apothecarius). He prepared medicines and confections, such as comfits and pastilles, which were consumed at the beginning and end of meals.

Provisioner and warehouseman (Dispensator). He acted as clerk and cashier in dispensing provisions from the royal stores.

Sopny vel Szepny. This Polish term of somewhat vague meaning is the title of the individual at court whose duty it was to supplement the bread supplied by the royal baker with bread bought in the market. He often dealt in trencher bread, which always seemed to be in short supply.

Kitchen and Related Staff Chef de cuisine (Magister coquinae). He supervised the nutrition of the court, discussed food products with the monarch he served, and oversaw the proper functioning of the royal kitchen. He also invented new dishes for state functions and sometimes compiled collections of handwritten recipes. He may have been the only person in the kitchen who could read and write, although this was not a fixed requirement. Sometimes the royal chef was also a member of the lower nobility.

Cook (Coquus dictus), *cuchta*. Staff cooks in the royal kitchen performed all of the duties relating to food preparation. These were mostly young women or girls.

Dishwasher (Abluticius). Washed the dishes in the royal kitchen. Some purchase orders mention horse tails (*Equisetum hyemale*), the common marsh plant, which were used to scour pans and cooking equipment.

Laundress (Ablutrix), *mulier*. She was responsible for washing clothes and table linens. Aside from washing, the laundresses processed starch from *Arum italicum* for the best table linens, napkins, and ladies' head pieces. The herb is highly ornamental and probably grew in the pleasure gardens at the castle or in special gardens at one of the royal estates. Large quantities would doubtless have been used because the starch also went into the manufacture of pastilles and other similar sugarwork.

Persons in Upper Chambers Vicethesaurus. He was actually the royal purser. He was personally responsible for all royal household accounts, dispensed goods and produce from the treasury, the cellars, and the larders, and authorized the purchase of all products for use at court. He was immensely powerful and usually became quite rich as a result of his position. The most famous and shrewdest of these was Mikołaj Wierzynek, chancellor under Casimir the Great. A burgher who was elected to the nobility, he built himself a magnificent house on the market square in Cracow where he entertained the kings of

Poland, Cyprus, Denmark, and Hungary and the Holy Roman Emperor in 1364.[1]

Courtiers (Curienses). Nobles on hand to perform various services for the king.

Marshal of the court (Magister curiae). He supervised the workings of the entire court, the majordomo who was both chief facilitator and head of protocol.

Procurator. His title in Cracow was *wielkorzadca*, something akin to a quartermaster general. He oversaw all product deliveries to the royal castle and controlled all deliveries to and from the royal garrisons.

Royal custodian (Custos thesauri). Specifically a guardian of the royal treasury. As such, he or his men were armed. There were normally several individuals acting as security, both to watch one another as well as to protect against theft.

Steward or chief butler (Camerarius). This was an older valet who served the table in the royal dining room. He was usually a nobleman, and his staff, consisting of "sewers," brought the food forward after it had been sent up from the kitchen. All food was served in "messes," that is, in quantities for four to six persons, thus there was usually a waiter for each mess. The *camerarius* did not touch the food or carve it unless called upon by the king. His staff laid the food on the table, and where appropriate, served it, except to the monarch, for a noble person served the monarch. Whether valet or noble, no one touched the food with the hands. Dishes and implements were held between long linen napkins that were wrapped around the arms of the server, a feature that often appears in medieval banqueting scenes.

Valet (Cubicularius). His duty was to keep the rooms clean,

basically a janitorial function. He may have had a staff of lower-ranking individuals (even children) who worked in teams.

Wine steward (Subpincerna). Although referred to as "cup bearer," this was customarily a person of noble birth who was in charge of the beverages at court and their distribution. The position was considered a great honor.

These anonymous nobles and craftspeople take on a more individual quality in the art of this period. The painted religious panels of southern Poland show an array of kneeling knights in armor and woeful saints draped in clothing typical of the era.[2] The wonderful altar carvings in the Zips region of neighboring Slovakia (part of the same artistic circle led by Veit Stoss in Poland) evoke the very soul of the period in the gentle features of everyday people captured in richly painted wood. One of the panels on the great triptych in the church of St. Jacob at Levoca shows Salome dancing before a group of diners.[3] The table is set with a large platter in the center, manchet rolls are arranged beside each person, and rye bread trenchers lie before them. All of this is spread on a handsome white linen tablecloth with woven stripes. A cup bearer sets a large glass of beer on the table and behind him a valet brings a covered dish of food.

Such vivid everyday images are nevertheless quite rare in Polish medieval art. The best source by far is the richly illustrated *Codex Picturatus* of Cracow patrician Balthasar Behem, compiled in 1505. It contains scenes of tradespeople engaged in daily life, including potters, bakers, and many others who were part of the royal household. The group of portraits of the Jagiełło family by the atelier of Lucas Cranach the Elder gives us the appearance of some of the royalty mentioned in the course of our discussions, but they are a bejewelled and stern-looking lot and quite aloof from life on the street.

Food Consumption at the Royal Court

Before turning to individual foodstuffs and how they were used in medieval Poland, a few words should be said about the actual quantities of food eaten by Poles during this period. First, there was a general belief among medieval Poles that quantity of food was more useful to the body than type of food, although meat was seen as the ultimate source of protein. Bulk foods were also considered important, so a dinner attended by nobility would include not only a large quantity of meat, but also huge quantities of bread and rolls as well as millet mush prepared in some form. Considerable time has been spent analyzing historical data and then converting this into measurable quantities. In some cases, the material defies analysis (uniform measurements were not instituted throughout Poland until 1764), or is so complex that the reader can easily sink into hopeless confusion over such points of discussion as meat mass in medieval pigs, the quantity of beer in a one mug measure, or the proper interpretation of terms like *dunica,* which could be a flowerpot, a bowl of a very specific volume, or even a grater. Rather than repeat the data in full detail, we here summarize the material to show how the dishes re-created in the recipe section of this book fit into the format of a meal. Fortunately, we have nearly thirty years of consistent data relating to the personal eating habits of King Władysław Jagiełło and Queen Jadwiga during their reign.

We have already mentioned purchase orders for food, which can serve as menu outlines, but which lack a breakdown explaining how the food was used. For example, a purchase order for one of Queen Jadwiga's dinners at Korczyn on August 21, 1394, itemized fish, lamprey, crayfish, green peas, dried peas, walnuts, pears, plums, cucumbers, parsley, 360 loaves of rye bread, four achtels of beer, and sixty loaves of white bread.[4] In many cases the exact amounts are given, and these help to create a sketch of food consumption on a per capita basis, although by no means exact.

By averaging this material against retinue lists, we are able to calculate that a royal dinner or supper for the first serving (excluding those "down table") would include on a daily basis forty to sixty pieces of poultry, 120 manchet rolls (each weighing about 60 grams or 2 ounces), and three to four achtels of beer, assuming there are forty to sixty persons attending each monarch. Each person consumed about two to four manchet rolls and one and a half to two liters of beer. Rye bread was mentioned in huge amounts, and if the Wrocław price list of 1362 is used as a base measure, then each individual consumed about three small loaves of rye bread (weighing about 320 to 350 grams or 11 ounces) at a meal. Considering that the bread was used to make trenchers on which each person ate, this is a fair estimate. Much of this bread became waste in the form of trimmings (see the bread recipe on page 180), which were sent down to the servants' dining room, used to thicken sauces, or sent out to the poor. It is also interesting that the three-loaf count corresponds to the general number of courses in a typical meal at court, if we allow at least two trenchers from each loaf.

One must keep in mind that this food was intended to be eaten mostly with the fingers and that there was an elaborate etiquette involved both in serving the food and in raising it from trencher to mouth. Trencher bread was extremely important. We know, for example, that during a meal in 1390, Queen Jadwiga dined with about forty ladies. Forty trencher breads were served, and the main meal consisted

Queen and her retinue at dinner. Pantler (left) serves the royal trenchers. Nuremberg, 1491.

of thirty boiled hens and ten young roast chickens. We are given the impression that in spite of her love of high-style cookery, the queen was in fact eating a very simple country meal, perhaps to emphasize her Polish roots and symbolic role as patroness of the Polish people. But we should not overlook an important feature of this simple fare: poultry was served only to persons above a certain rank. The old hens that were boiled for this dinner were presented to the ladies of lesser rank; the plump roast chickens went to those of higher status at the far end of the room.

During a dinner in 1563, the forty-nine women attending dowager Queen Katarzyna at her meal consumed ninety-five loaves of bread, ninety-five rolls, and 184 mugs of beer (about three mugs each).[5] The bread consumption dropped during the period since 1390 because custom has changed: the court now ate from silver plate, majolica, or gilded pewter. The bread was still either used as sops or torn apart and eaten with the gravies that were served with the meal. On fast days, however, it was customary for the Polish court to eat from bread trenchers rather than from silver plate or fine majolica.

We get a clearer sense of food consumption from a royal meal given on May 10, 1389, with fifty to fifty-four gentlemen in attendance at the king's table.[6] The meat served included a boiled calf's head, two hams, fifty-four pieces of poultry, one mutton, and four piglets. If we calculate the various weights of the animals, accounting for meat and bone mass and how they were butchered, some of which is evident in the royal account books, the yield is 2 kilograms (4 pounds) of meat and one bird per nobleman. This figure would seem substantial were it not for the fact that the meal was a special one where the gentlemen would have indulged themselves more freely, and that a large part of the food was only picked over, then sent down to the lesser tables. Therefore, the meat was actually feeding a much larger number of individuals than the king and gentlemen. For this reason the menus for the royal servants often said "meats" without further description.

Meat was expensive, and in many accounts the food was portioned very carefully to contain costs. In one late case, for the annual *obiady kiermaszowe* ("dining fest") held in 1555 for professors at the university in Cracow, a quarter of an ox was served.[7] Only forty-eight meat portions and four roasts (each equivalent to several servings) were taken from it, with each serving weighing about one pound. This might seem a normal serving size for something like beefsteak in a modern restaurant, but the true context of this meal is not evident unless we also calculate its real price: the dinner cost each professor the equivalent to 20 grosze, or the market value of twenty chickens.

By contrast to what was eaten at court, Andrzej Wyczański calculated food consumption among the people of lower social standing, especially manorial work hands, during the latter part of the sixteenth century.[8] It turns out that slightly more than half a pound of meat *with fat* was consumed by individuals of this class on a daily basis. We now know that such calculations can be misleading, yet one can approximate the daily consumption of other foods, such as dry peas (500 g or 2 cups cooked) and millet kasha (1 kg or 4 cups cooked). By the late 1500s, the manorial system and its gradual pauperization of the peasants had clearly opened a vast chasm between the diets of the nobles and the farmers.

The great flaw of medieval diet was its reliance on quantity as most important to the development of the body, together with its adherence to cooking methods that destroyed a lot of the food value of what was being consumed. After people realized that thick, heavy foods consumed in large quantities required an increase of stomach acids necessary for their digestion, spices were introduced to spur on the flow of gastric juices. This theme is prevalent in old Polish medical works like Falimirz's 1534 treatise on condiments.[9]

Unfortunately, poor nutrition was the source of many diseases and no amount of exotic flavoring could prevent this result. People were aware of which food products were the most valuable in terms of satisfying hunger, but the medieval Polish diet was extremely deficient in iron and in sugar. There were also few raw foods to supply the missing nutrients. Vegetables were always cooked; even lettuce was prepared with a hot dressing so that it wilted before it was consumed. Only apples and other fruits were eaten raw, but these were mostly dessert foods of the rich.

The recipes included in the last section of this book have been plucked out of this overall dietary context. Standing alone, they do not convey the dietary relationship they may have had to other foods on the table. The elaborate ones were only part of a larger meal scheme when they were made many hundreds of years ago.

The Equipment and Operation of the Medieval Kitchen

The small number of surviving iconographic materials showing period kitchens and equipment makes it difficult to present a detailed picture of the Polish medieval kitchen. Polish domestic scenes do not begin until the middle of the sixteenth century, and these are not always as detailed as historians would like. What we know of medieval kitchens is more easily found in English, French, and German sources. Indeed, most of the woodcuts of culinary equipment included in this volume are taken from a broadside printed at Nuremberg by Hanns Paur about 1475. The objects are similar to many of the artifacts excavated from

Hearth utensils.

Polish archaeological sites, thus the cuts can be used with a certain degree of reliability.

While there are several well-preserved medieval buildings in Poland, among them the episcopal palaces at Kwidzyn (Marienwerder) and Lidzbark Warmiński (Heilsberg), as well as Bytów (Bütow) built between 1390 and 1405 in the Pomeranian lake district, only one medieval kitchen survives intact. It is located at the castle of Malbork near Gdansk. Even this kitchen has been extensively restored, rebuilt, and restored again over the years, as Karol Górski pointed out in his 1973 history of the site. In spite of this, it is well furnished and today presents a fairly accurate picture of kitchen life as defined by the needs of a feudal brotherhood. The royal castle on Wawel Hill, where the Jagiellons resided when in Cracow, was extensively damaged by a fire in 1500, then renovated between 1502 and 1535. Thus it does not reflect its former medieval character. However, by combining the relics preserved at Malbork with Polish archaeological remains and iconographic materials, in conjunction with ethnographic sources, it is possible to assemble an impression of the medieval kitchen in Poland. And contrary to common assumptions, fourteenth-century manuscript sources are indeed quite informative if they are read with caution.

The kitchen was one of the most extensively furnished parts of the basement region in a medieval castle. Kitchens were almost always located down in the bowels of the structure to be close to larders, wine cellars, and other storage areas for food. At Wawel Castle, there were two royal kitchens, one for the king and one for the queen. There also seems to have been a third kitchen of lesser importance where food was prepared for the servants, guards, coachmen, musicians, craftsmen, and other members of the staff. This separation was as much practical in terms of workload as it was necessary from the standpoint of guarding against poisoning, even though assassination was not a threat to most Polish kings due to their figurehead status.

The king's and queen's kitchens served their respective monarchs separately, including the retinue of each. The royal entourage normally consisted of forty to sixty people on a daily basis, the king's being men, and the queen's primarily consisting of women. All of these people sat at their respective tables with their monarch according to a minutely defined court protocol. When the court moved to one of the garrisons or encampments, a kind of portable camp kitchen was set up which served the king and all visiting dignitaries *cum familia castri*—it must have resembled an enormous picnic. One such event, held in Cracow in 1415 for a huge contingent of foreign guests and nobles, mobilized all the available cooks in the city.

The king and queen also had their own personal cooks. These cooks were accorded very high honor, and as *magister coquinae* (master chefs) they often presented opinions on economic and commercial matters relating to the state. The Polish term *kuchmistrz* (chef de cuisine) did not come into fashion until after the publication of the first cookbook in Polish, *Kuchmistrzostwo* (1532). Beneath this chef was a small army of ordinary cooks called *coqui*, referred to by the word *cuchta*, a term that today carries certain negative meanings not originally implied in the Middle Ages. The master chef reported to the royal purser, whose job was to keep the king's and queen's accounts and dispense money for purchases. It was also his task to dispense and keep track of all articles in the royal cellars and to direct provisions to the appropriate tables when they were served. He was also responsible for the production of beer and bread. He maintained a staff of people whose sole purpose was to go out into the marketplace and make purchases of produce and utensils and to record every purchase in his accounts. As controller of the royal purse strings, he was a person of extraordinary power and influence. At his fingertips were lists of everything in the royal kitchen.

The diversity of the kitchen utensils installed in the royal kitchens during this time is surprisingly large. They appear not only in quantity but also in a variety of specialized forms and materials. There was a broad selection of wooden, ceramic, glass, and metal utensils, and archaeological explorations in Poland have uncovered remarkable examples from each category. Manuscripts from this period have provided us with technical names for many of the tools, as well as their function. There was a lot of copper and glass, but in the context of a royal kitchen, this would be expected. Indeed, there was even a Polish glass factory at Cudnów, which may have provided the court with some of its supplies. Yet lesser nobles from the medieval period probably did not have as many copper and glass items.

Judging from the frequency of purchases for large numbers of cooking vessels, the majority of which were ceramic, breakage must have been exceptionally high. In the registers of the court administrator there is a section entered by the royal treasurer that a certain quantity of jugs, pots, saucepans, and so forth must be purchased before June 23 (evidently the date of a large dinner) because of shortages in the royal kitchens. Breakage is even more evident in a bill for kitchen utensils and table vessels purchased in February 1404 for the royal garrison at Korczyn, although it is possible that the king was simply outfitting the site in preparation for the crews who were breaking ground for his new palace. In any case, the quantity is telling: 180 cups, 480 mugs, four strainers, ten pans, six griddles, and six saucepans. In July, another purchase order went through for 660 mugs, 480 cups, fourteen pans, six barrels, eight sieves, six strainers, and six saucepans.[10] Certainly, some of this relates to utensils that had to be replaced.

Sometimes the terms used in the royal accounts are confusing because one word stands for two different objects. The term *dolium*, for example, could mean either a wooden barrel or a ceramic vessel, such as the kind used in Spain to store olive oil. In any case, in Poland, the vessel in question was large and was used to store such food products as cabbage. And because it was sometimes repaired in the royal kitchens by a cooper, we must assume that it was a type of wooden barrel of dolium shape, that is, very small at both ends. There were also *kruzki* (jugs) of ceramic and wood; the wooden ones were used in the royal baths or the royal table.

Below is a somewhat abbreviated version of the large list of utensils mentioned in fourteenth- and fifteenth-century Polish court sources. The explanations are intended to provide a better understanding of the tools that actually produced dishes like those in the recipe section.[11] Quantities of measure are included for completeness, but in fact, we can now only guess at the amounts intended since they varied greatly from one region to the next.

Alevus (*neczky*). A pan or trough that was used in the kitchen and bakery.

Amphora. Jug or a vessel in the shape of an amphora. Generally large capacity for storing liquids.

Amphoriculli parvi. Little jugs with ears or lips, normally clay but also sometimes made of wood.

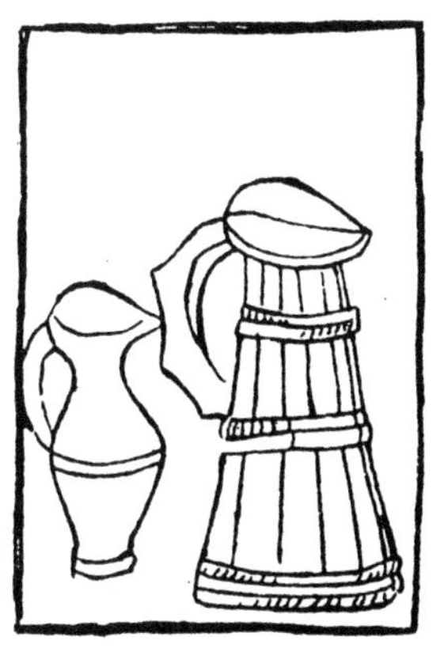

Pitchers.

Amphorule (*krugliki*). Used interchangeably with the above but may indicate a specific measure as well. The amphorule specifically had a narrow neck.

Barila. Large wooden barrels that were used for keeping wine, beer, and other liquids.

Caldarium. Copper cauldron.

Calix deauratus. Silver drinking vessel for the royal table.

Canterum. Beer mug.

Cantharulus. Little jug or mug for beer.

Cantharus. Jug with a lip, also a mug. Appears on the royal table at times.

Cellarium. Cellar. Storing place for provisions.

Ciphus (*hostruhan, dostuchan*). Colander.

Ciste, cistule. Small boxes in which spices and costly foodstuffs such as comfits were stored.

Coclear (*leffil*). Spoon.

Cophinus. Basket. Was made in various sorts and sizes.

Cornuum. Drinking horn, for the royal table. Some were made of silver; others, sheet metal.

Cortina (*kessil*). Small cauldron or kettle, normally copper.

Cribrum (*sitha, pitel, rzessoto, koppersib*). Sifter or strainer. Also, bolters and riddles, utensils used to sift flour and meal.

Cribrum. Unit of measure.

Cubco (*schalen*). Mugs or cups of silver or metal as well as covered goblets. Used for wine and often given as gifts with wine.

Cuffa. A large barrel.

Cultellum. Small knife for use at table or in the kitchen.

Czesze, alias pastina dicte vasa. Wooden kneading trough used in the bakery.

Dolium or dolea. In the Polish context, wooden barrels in a traditional dolium shape: wide in the middle, narrow at both ends.

Flascule (*flashin*). Flask for liquids.

Pottery cooking vessels, fourteenth century, excavated in the Old Market at Warsaw.

Fornax. Stove or furnace to heat a room, or a bake oven.

Futra. Small leather case for personal knives and forks.

Krobe. Bark basket for carrying vegetables.

Linter. Bowl or trough.

Manutergia. Towels for serving as well as tablecloths.

Mensalia (*nastilce*). Tablecloth.

Mortablum ereum. Copper mortar.

Multrales, ollae multrales. Mugs or cups.

Octuale or achtel. Any vessel of 16-liter capacity.

Olle, olla. Cooking pots.

Olliculi. Little pots.

Ollule. Wooden vessels for storing dry sweetmeats, often made of thin bark.

Patella. Iron or clay pan.

Patena (*patenicze, patencza*). Serving dishes, sometimes with silver covers.

Pitel. Half an achtel. Unit of liquid measure equal to 8 liters.

Brass water kettle, fourteenth or fifteenth century.

Schafliky. Wooden wash tubs.

Scutelle. Goblets.

Scutellule. Small goblets.

Sporte dicte *barczcze.* Wastebasket.

Statera dicta *wagry.* Scales, used to weigh ingredients.

Succidulus. Wine glass.

Syarownicze. A ceramic bowl that was used for working cheese into flat cakes.

Tallari. Bread trenchers. The Polish term is very similar to the French: *tailloir.* Both terms imply that the trenchers were round, so there may be a class distinction between those who ate from the trimmed (rectangular) trenchers, and those who ate from the round, untrimmed ones. The latter sort was evidently the most common and therefore the "lesser" of the two.

Urceus. Clay or wooden jug.

Urna. Unit of liquid measure.

Vannus. A sieve in the bakery to winnow grain from the husk.

Vitrum, vitra. Various items of glassware, especially drinking glasses, mugs, and cups.

Wydelki. Flesh fork. Used when roasting meats to poke the meat so that juice runs out. Sauces would be made from the drippings.

Food and Drink in Medieval Poland

The Polish system of daily meals during the Middle Ages was similar to that of the rest of Europe. There were two main meals: the *prandium* (eaten between 9 and 10 A.M.) and the *coena* (eaten between 5 and 7 P.M.), as they are referred to in the old Latin codexes. In terms of time these correspond to the modern brunch and evening dinner, but there the similarities cease. At the royal court at least, these meals differed from one another very little; accounts from the period show that the food dispensed from the royal larder (*spiżarnia*) for both was essentially the same. Alterations to the menus were determined only by seasonality of ingredients and the requirements of religious observance.

During the Middle Ages, the Polish Church strictly enforced meatless fast days (Wednesday and Friday) as well as fasting on certain holy days. Lent was also a period when abstinence from meat prevailed, even the use of butter in cooking. Many Polish religious orders ate no meat at all. However, under the pretense of illness or for a variety of other exceptions, it was possible to obtain—for a price—indulgences that more or less allowed one to turn a blind eye to religious restrictions. Dietary patterns are therefore not as easy to predict as one might assume, and medieval church records are filled with complaints and sermons decrying the flagrant shortcomings of this once widespread practice.

Added to this were the feast days, such as Saint Florian's Day (May 4) in Cracow, when consumption was conspicuous and overabundant. Even the poor could count on a generous dole from the royal court, rich burghers, and nobility. But whether fish day or meat day, it appears that nothing was consumed between the basic two meals, both of which were very heavy. In the early morning, about 7 A.M., some the more prosperous individuals ate light foods to hold them over until the later morning meal. However, Polish sources do not mention breakfast as a regular custom.

Although Polish food preparation during this period was marked by a lack of special refinement, it was not simple. Cooking techniques may have been limited by hearth technology and the fact that there were fewer elaborate cooking utensils compared to the sixteenth century; obviously many foreign dishes were adjusted to accord with the availability of ingredients. While detailed recipes have not been preserved in old Polish sources, there are many clues about specific methods of preparation. These are easier to understand when set against contemporary texts from areas outside Poland.

The *Liber de coquina* (written around 1306) and Taillevent's *Le Viandier* (written between 1373 and 1381) are two valuable documents of French origin that have proven quite useful, especially since Louis d'Anjou owned a copy of *Le Viandier*.[1] Likewise, two small cookbooks in the Royal Library at Copenhagen, one with twenty-five recipes and the other with thirty-one, accurately record dishes prepared in Denmark during the thirteenth century.[2] All these recipe books contain instructions specific enough to re-create the dishes with a certain degree of authenticity. There are also German menus from the thirteenth to fourteenth centuries, as well as regulations governing the diet of monks in German and French monasteries, that have thrown some light on the Polish situation.[3]

After comparing the ingredients mentioned in the French and Danish cookbooks with those that appear in Polish registers, we found that the Polish lists were almost identical. The condiments were the same. Meat was often seasoned with pepper, saffron, parsley, and mustard. Mustard was the most common Polish condiment for flavoring meat sauces, although Poles appear to have preferred their mustard seeds whole, a texture similar to some of the coarse-grained or "rustic" mustards made in France and Germany today.

In both Western Europe and Poland, pork lard was the primary cooking fat. Where the French may have used olive oil, Poles used hemp or poppy seed oils instead. Enormous quantities of eggs were consumed in all the royal courts, for they were used not only for pastries and baking but also as ingredients in various meat preparations such as dumplings and mincemeat. For example, the chopped cooked meat of roast suckling pig was bound as a paste with eggs, or eggs figured in the stuffing of a suckling pig. Finely chopped goose meat was similarly bound with eggs, and stuffing for chicken was made in a like manner.[4] During the 1390s, in the course of one year alone, the Polish court consumed 266,450 eggs, an average of 730 eggs per day.[5]

Ceramic skillet.

Also common were recipes for fish, which was served in a variety of ways, especially in styles peculiar to Poland (see recipe for Polish Sauce on page 190). The most numerous fish dishes in both Polish and French sources were those involving fish aspic. There are many dishes that would even pass for modern-day Jewish gefilte fish, which may suggest a time frame for Jewish appropriation of the recipe from upper-class cookery. The abundance of these recipes is probably due to their complexity, the reason it was necessary to write them down. Manuscript recipes generally represent the dishes one is most likely to forget rather than the simple preparations that were learned by rote at hearth side and used frequently.

Comparisons could be multiplied tenfold, but the similarities between French and Polish cuisine of the period are not of as much interest as the differences, especially how ingredients common to France but not to Poland found Polish substitutes that in time changed the spirit of the dish. Examples of this would be the Polish use of sweet flag (*Acorus calamus*) as a flavor substitute for bay leaves, and the use of the young stems of goutweed (*Aegopodium podagraria*) instead of spinach to create green soups and sauces in the spring. Such cultural adaptations determine the specific character of a regional cuisine.

Another example would be the French use of wine or *verjus* (the sour juice of unripe grapes) in meat dishes. In Poland, these are almost always replaced by vinegar (most commonly apple cider vinegar and malt vinegar) or beer, or even the juice of sorrel. Where the French used sugar, the Poles more often used honey. And in the case of condiments, the Poles use fewer than the French, therefore the flavors were doubtless less complex or at least not spiced in the same way. However, black pepper was the most important spice in both cookeries, with surges of popularity for such related peppers as cubeb (*Piper cubeba*), Indian long pepper (*Piper longum*), and West African Guinea pepper or pepper of Benin (*Piper guineense*). These differences must be viewed against the fact that Polish living standards of all segments of society during the reign of Władysław Jagiełło (1386–1434) compared favorably with those of Western Europe, thus the dietary choices were not necessarily based on economics. Indeed, the West

African Guinea pepper is mentioned several times during the 1390s in the registers of royal treasurer Henryk of Rogów, but like nutmeg, mace, and cloves it was used primarily in connection with the flavoring of comfits and pastilles.

Drink

Truly elaborate ways of serving food appeared in Poland only in the sixteenth century, coupled with the appearance of a great variety of alcoholic beverages.[6] The much criticized Polish custom of drinking distilled spirits, called at the time *gorzalka* (vodka), was introduced during this era. This older name for vodka is derived from the verb *gore*, "to burn" or "to be on fire." *Goro* is a Polish word for throat, so taken together, *gorzalka* may be rendered into English as "something that burns in the throat" or euphemistically, "fire water."

Wine The production of domestic wine in Poland during the Middle Ages was extremely limited. It would appear from the records in which wine references are found that viticulture was undertaken on a small scale by monasteries and by some of the prince bishops so that they would have wines for private or sacramental use. Most of Poland's climate zones is not ideally suited for viticulture, so wine in any large quantity had to be imported — as it is even today. Wine was sold in Cracow, Lvov, and Warsaw by wine merchants who catered mostly to the royal court, the upper nobility, and the wealthy patrician class dwelling in larger Polish towns. As the standard of living in Poland increased during the later Middle Ages, wine consumption also went up among the well-to-do.

Wine tester.

This shift in consumption took place over one hundred years. During the reign of King Władysław Jagiełło (1386–1434), wine was considered a luxury, but it was mentioned much more frequently during the reign of his son, King Casimir Jagiellończyk. By the time we reach the reign of King Sigismund I (1506–1548), wine is mentioned in the royal accounts almost every day. In the records of King Władysław Jagiełło, wine was given out only as a kind of honorarium to mark special occasions or to recognize certain persons of talent. For example, he served wine to the new king of Hungary at a meeting held in Sącz in 1395, and sent two barrels of red and white wine as a gift to Italian artists frescoing a religious building in Lisecz.[7] But the workers who build his palace at Korczyn were rewarded only with beer. Earlier, in 1370, to celebrate the wedding of a granddaughter, King Casimir the Great put out barrels of wine in the Cracow market for everyone to drink, but this was an unusual event and done in any case for its political effect. Slovakian wine historian František Kalesný has pointed out that the bulk of that wine was of the cheaper Hungarian variety.

There were attempts to plant wine grapes and apricots in the royal orchards at Proszowice in 1394. Although the experiment with viticulture was less successful, we know that there were small vineyards in Poland at this time, for they show up in several old views of Cracow. The Jagiełło accounts mention on occasion a Polish wine referred to as *vinum proprium* from a vineyard in Zagoszcz, which was considered worthy enough to supply the court.

Actually, the history of Polish viticulture is not as spotty as one might imagine.[8] It is known, for example, that in the twelfth-century Bishop Otto of Bamberg brought with him a tub full of grapevine cuttings to establish wineries in Poland. There are many villages in Poland which have names like Winiary (from the root word *win* as in Polish *wino* for wine) or which contain *win* in some fashion. Most of these are situated near large administrative centers that in the Middle Ages were also important centers of worship. Since these village names date back to the second half of the tenth or to the first half of the eleventh centuries, they must have originated in connection with the production of liturgical wines or with an attempt among the high nobility to establish a viable viticulture within the kingdom.

Wine jug from Čataj, Slovakia, eleventh century.

We know from extant records that the wine imported into Poland came from a wide variety of places. From Hungary came medium-priced red and white wines, as well as very expensive wines (probably Tokay). There were wines from France, Austria, Spain, Rumania, and the eastern Mediterranean. The better quality wines were often labeled by vineyard as well. Malvasia dessert wines were imported from Cyprus, and a wine called *rywula* in Polish is now known to be the *vino cotto* of Sicily. All these wines are mentioned in fourteenth and fifteenth century documents, but Hungarian wines occupied first place in terms of quantity. Absent altogether from the records in southern Poland are references to German Rhine wines. These appear mostly in northern Poland, and the inventories of the Order of Teutonic Knights at Malbork (Marienburg) contain the largest variety of German wines. Even the middling red and white wines from Hungary were only slightly less expensive than mead, which was itself a luxury item; all the better sorts of wine surpassed mead in cost.

On the subject of wine, it is impossible to ignore the amazing contrast between the cellars of the royal courts of Casimir the Great, Władysław Jagiełło, his son and successor Casimir Jagiellończyk, and those of the Teutonic Knights in northern Poland. The annual cellar inventories of the Teutonic Knights surpass those of the Polish kings in fine luxury beers from Gdansk, Elblag, and other Baltic towns, as well as many barrels of mead, wine, wine must, and sour cherry wine.[9] They also had supplies of raspberry and plum juice, which were added to beer and mead to improve their flavor. Did the knights also attempt to make *nalewka*, an infusion of fruit in spirits? The manufacture of such cordials was quite likely, considering their technical similarities to some of the complex beer infusions made at the time, as well as to popular fermented drinks flavored with such aromatic plant ingredients as bay leaves, yew, sage, rue, blackthorn, and absinthe.

Beer During the fourteenth and fifteenth centuries, king and small landowner alike mainly drank beer of varying alcoholic content. But beer did not always mean the same thing it does today. The word *piwo*, the modern Polish term for beer, derives from the verb *pic*, which simply means to drink, and originally any prepared drink other than water was called beer. However, fermented beer reached Poland with the proto-Poles of the sixth or seventh centuries, one of the earliest documented being the so-called *piwo macedonskie* (Macedonian beer) made from toasted millet that was fermented two to three days. Furthermore, early medieval archaeological sites are rich with remains of important beer-making ingredients, including hops (*chmiel*). It is not clear whether the hops was gathered from the wild or cultivated, but it is clear that beer was fermented from a number of grains, sometimes in combination. Millet, barley, wheat, rye, and oats were the most common. A Lithuanian barley beer called *alus* was sometimes mentioned in old texts, but because it resembled Russian *kvas*, a sweet-and-sour beverage of slightly fermented bread, it was not looked upon as something essentially Polish. Wheat beer, on the other hand, appears to have been the preferred drink, for Jan Długosz commented in his *Opera Omnia* of the 1470s that Poland's native drink was prepared from wheat, hops, and water.[10] Poles called this wheat beer *piwo*. Wheat beer was so valued that Konrad, Prince Bishop of Kujawy, declined to take the position of Archbishop of Salzburg in 1303 because he was told he could not obtain wheat beer in Austria.

One other feature of old Polish beer-making that set it apart from other nationalities was the use of *poraj* or "marsh tea" (*Ledum palustre*, called Labrador tea in North America) to heighten the beer's inebriating qualities. The leaves were prepared as a tea which was mixed with hops. This preparation was then strained until clear. Finally, yeast was added and the mixture was combined with barley and wheat. This resulted in a fermented brew called "thick beer," which was also used as a starter for sourdough bread. The inebriating effect was due in part, however, to a poisonous compound in the plant called andromedotoxin, which is quite harmful if consumed in large quantities. In smaller amounts, it may have acted on microbes or viruses in the body and thereby offered perceived therapeutic benefits.

Beer was even made into soup, according to the register of the royal garrison at Korczyn under the year 1394: "to beer for *caseata*"—an old Polish soup made with beer, egg yolks, and cheese (see recipe on page 159).[11] In Korczyn, it was served to King Władysław Jagiełło. Hence it is not surprising that one of the better breweries in Poland was located at Nowe Miasto near Korczyn, where the king later built a palace. Some beer was homemade, such as *oskola*, a drink fermented from the sap of birch trees favored for its high alcoholic content.

Medieval records are quite clear in singling out certain breweries for their beer, and there was even a royal brewery, although its exact location is not specified. For the most part, the leading breweries during the Jagiellon reigns were located in Proszów, Wislica, Bochnia (also known for its salt), Busko, and Cracow, which made a famous "double" beer (*potus marcialis*) recommended for invalids. There were also well-known breweries at Niepołomice and Wieliczka, and Żator produced a famous black beer (perhaps a type of stout). The best Silesian beer, made at Swidnica (Schweidnitz), was also sold in Cracow. Warka beer was by far the best beer produced in Mazovia, although breweries at Sierpiec and Gostynin are also mentioned. The list of Polish beer breweries from the medieval period is huge, and these are only a few of the best known ones.

How does all of this beer translate into drinking patterns? One achtel of beer was the typical measure mentioned every day in the registers of the royal household. The average daily consumption of beer in this period seems to have been about 1.5 to 2 liters per person. This accords with remarks by Mikołaj Rej in his "Life of an Honest Man" (1568) that in the "good old days" Poles had very modest eating and drinking habits.[12]

Mead The modern Polish word for mead and honey is the same, *miod,* but medieval records clearly differentiate their uses. The Old Slavic word *med* (equivalent to the Old German word *meth* or *met*) meant the fermented beverage called mead, designated as *medio* in Polish Latin texts. Honey squeezed from the combs and used in that raw state was called *mel* in Polish records.

Mead was consumed at weddings and baptismal parties, but never to the extent of beer. In fact, there is a common misunderstanding that mead was the everyday drink of the ancient Slavs, but this was not at all the case. This idea originated, no doubt, from a fifth-century A.D. Greek reference by Priskos of Panion (in Thrace) that Slavic tribes settled on the Danube drank a beverage called *medos*.

Honey was scarce, and what documentation we do have from the early Middle Ages is consistent in casting mead as a beverage only for the rich. City account books show that mead purchases were always categorized as a luxury product served to the king or highly ranked nobles. The everyday drink of Polish royalty, their guests, their staff and military advisers, as well as the servants in the royal household, was wheat beer. Priskos should have said that mead was the drink of the Slavic chieftains, served at diplomatic meetings when they arranged treaties and other state contracts. Throughout the Middle Ages, mead carried with it this contractual connotation, which is why it was served at weddings and important feasts.

The high intrinsic value of mead may be inferred from the fact that in 1251 the magnate Casimir, Książe (duke) of Leczyca, collected three large *urnae* of mead from the village of Czernin as a gift to the cathedral in Cracow.[13] In that period, one *urna magna* of mead was valued the same as one cow, although the precise amount of liquid that this represented can no longer be calculated accurately. Nonetheless, the duke made a gift of no small importance.

Polish sources do not provide us with a recipe for mead prior to the sixteenth century, but it certainly was little different from the mead described in later works. The simplest way of making mead was to combine honey and water to obtain a mixture called *czemiga* in Polish (see recipe on page 163). Czemiga, mentioned in the sixteenth-century *Pandecta Medicinae* of Matheus Silvaticus, was only slightly fermented.[14] It was similar to the drink called hydromel mentioned in many medieval French texts.

The oldest description of Polish mead preparation may be found in Olaus Magnus's *Historia de gentibus septentrionalibus* (1567). Magnus included a recipe given to him by one Marcin of Gniezno in

1543.[15] Ten pounds of honey are cooked with forty pounds of water, and the ensuing foam skimmed off. One pound of hops is then boiled in water and placed in a sack. The sack is put into the honey and water mixture after it has cooled, along with beer yeast or bread starter. It is then allowed to ferment. In his 1613 herbal, Szymon Syrennius provided a recipe dating from the sixteenth century in which fennel is also added to the fermenting mixture.[16] Other flavorings occasionally added to mead were pepper, cloves, and cinnamon.

The Teutonic Knights kept a large variety of meads in their cellars at Malbork. The meads appear to have been inventoried on a yearly basis according to strength, using such terms as *aldis methes* (aged mead), *gerines alt mete* (old, clarified mead), *donne mete* ("weak" mead), and *coventmethes* (thin and watery mead). The amount of mead stored by the knights seems impressive, but there is no way of knowing whether it was for their own use or for sale. Furthermore, there is no consistent unit of measure that can help us translate the quantities mentioned in the various vats and barrels. However, if one Prussian barrel contains 114 liters, then the transfer to barrels on the order of the Grand Marshall in 1404 was 7,524 liters of mead and 3,762 liters of honey. This would work out to a total daily consumption rate of 20 liters of mead for all 375 knights in residence. This is not very much, considering the various qualities of mead involved, for some of the knights of lower rank would drink the less desirable sorts or none at all.

Overall, mead was far more popular among the nobility in the northern parts of Poland than in the South. In Pomerania, for example, honey was often mixed with beer, as records indicate from as early as the twelfth century. Mazovian sources also mention a mead-like beverage called *trojniak* produced at Zakrocym. It is first mentioned in the accounts of Duke Janusz Mazowiecki dating from 1477 to 1490.[17] The fact that mead was restricted mostly to the upper classes is confirmed in archival material dealing with peasant wills from the end of the fifteenth century. There is no mention of mead in these wills unless for a specific purpose, such as leaving money to a church so that the monks might purchase some mead. In such cases, mead is treated as a charitable gift of the highest kind. Indeed, as a gift, mead was considered equal to imported spices and wine. For this reason the cities of Lvov and Cracow often presented foreign dignitaries with gifts of mead.

Copper cauldron and pot hook. Polish woodcut, 1575.

Meat

It is evident from contemporary sources that meat was considered a basic food to be consumed on a daily basis, and not only by royalty. Its quality and method of preparation, however, varied greatly, and of course, meat was always replaced by fish on fasting days. The most frequently mentioned meats were pork and beef, then poultry, especially guinea fowls and chickens. Lamb was rare, although its consumption increased in the middle of the fifteenth century. By 1568, lamb became part of the royal court's weekly menu, according to the expense accounts of Queen Katarzyna, wife of King Sigismund II.[18] Yet the small quantities of sheep and goat bones from medieval kitchen refuse do not argue against extensive sheep and goat raising, as suggested by some Polish food historians. Rather, the archaeological evidence supports the hypothesis that due to their small meat mass, goats and sheep were valued primarily for their wool and milk. Even today, *oscypyck*, a smoked molded cheese of goat's or sheep's milk, is considered a delicacy by Polish gourmets.

Traditional molded sheep's curd cheese.

Beef A typical royal dinner or supper menu from the Middle Ages usually consisted of several courses involving various kinds of meat: beef, pork, hens, or capons.[19] Beef, however, was king, for it was entwined in the ancient Polish myths of migration and identity. This mythology drew upon a kernel of truth in that cattle traveled with the ancient Polish tribes, but they were not the first peoples to introduce short-horned cattle into Europe. This type of cattle was perfected in Asia Minor and spread (via the Celts and others) into Central Europe as early as 3,000 B.C. The *Bos taurus* was preferred by ancient peoples due to the cow's ability to give good yields of milk. Since the cow or steer was owned by the peasant for draft purposes, it had (in medieval terms) the intrinsic value of a tractor. One only ate beef, generally, when the draft animal died, or when the most important son was married off in a favorable land deal.

The *Bos taurus* evolved genetically from an ancient long-horn type, and both of these animals trace their ancestry to the aurochs (*Bos primigenius*). Also called "wild urus," among other things, the aurochs was indeed the granddaddy of most modern European cattle. The European aurochs roamed wild in Polish forests during the Middle Ages but died out in 1637. There have been recent attempts to back-breed cattle to reproduce this handsome lost ancestor.

The aurochs — standing six feet tall at the shoulder — must have been especially impressive considering how bony and lean cattle were in the Middle Ages. In fact, the animals were often very small due to poor foddering and bad inbreeding practices. Thus, cattle were only about 45 inches (112 cm) tall in the rump and "weedy," resembling donkeys in size. This is no vision of opulence in culinary terms, yet beef was valued monetarily above all else in the hierarchy of cui-

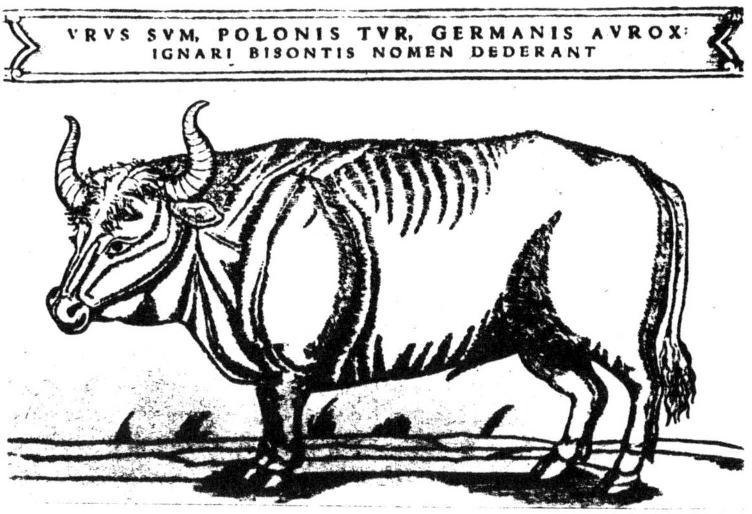

VRVS SVM, POLONIS TVR, GERMANIS AVROX:
IGNARI BISONTIS NOMEN DEDERANT

Aurochs. Sixteenth-century German woodcut.

sine. Beef took second place only to game meats on the table of Polish nobles, specifically the above-mentioned aurochs, the European bison or wisent (*Bison bonasus*, *żubr* in Polish), and European elk (*łoś*). These wild animals were protected in the forests of the high nobility, which also insured their existence against extinction. Banquets using the meat of these animals in various creative ways are commonly noted in Polish records, and even today bison are allowed to range in the old primeval forests of Białowieza.

In 1417, Ulrich von Richental chronicled an interesting gift of aurochs by King Władysław Jagiełło to the Holy Roman Emperor during the Council of Constance.

> On Tuesday after St. Valentine's Day the Holy Roman Emperor received a huge animal caught in Lithuanian territories, which was sent to him by the Polish king. The king had ordered three such animals to be brought from Lithuania alive. However, by the time they arrived at Cracow, due to their

> being wild and bound with shackles, the creatures went mad to such an extent that it was no longer possible to send them on to Constance alive. Thus the king ordered them killed.
>
> The king further ordered that the meat of two of the animals be packed in herring barrels. The third was cut through, left in its skin, "salted" with gunpowder and rubbed down with spices. The barrels filled with the meat were sent to the Polish bishops then attending the conference at Constance, while the salted animal was offered to the king of England by the Emperor. The beast resembled a large ox, only its head was larger and its neck thicker. It had a huge chest and two small, sharp-ended horns. Its forehead between horns was one foot wide. With its short tail, it resembled a buffalo similar to those that live in Italy. Its inner organs were taken out. When the animal arrived it was lying on its back with its legs raised up. As soon as it arrived at Constance, more gunpowder was put on it as well as spice powder. In this condition it was sent on to the English king then on the Rhine. As the animal was being carried out of Constance, the Emperor ordered that a servant go before it playing a trumpet.[20]

The hapless aurochs is now a historical curiosity, yet its eventual extinction was no less tragic than the loss of Polish cattle breeds during World War II. Hunger, combined with the Nazi determination to exterminate all vestiges of Polish culture, not to mention predatory Russian troops, eliminated all old Polish cattle breeds that would have provided a link with the Middle Ages. These include such breeds as Polesian (Polish gray steppe cattle) generally found in the Pripet Marshes, as well as breeds like Polish whiteback, Polish marsh cattle (Żuawka), and several rare Silesian races.[21]

Although the royal registers frequently mention beef on a daily basis, it is usually in reference to deliveries of quarters or sides of beef, rather than about modes of preparation. Polish archaeology has proven that beef bones were consistently cracked open to remove the fatty marrow, a part of the animal that was highly relished during the Middle Ages. Records of the royal court make very little reference to this. We do know from royal purchase orders that beef was often served *assatura*, that is, grilled or spit-roasted (and normally marinated before cooking), or seared then roasted in a pot. This is the only form of preparation specifically mentioned in Polish court sources.[22] In nutritional terms, it is also the healthiest.

There is considerable information on sources of the meat in medieval Poland. For example, in the *Codex Diplomaticus Civitati Cracoviae* under a regulation dated July 23, 1453, the Cracow city council ordered that "anyone driving oxen from Russia for sale here, should drive them through Sandomierz, whereas oxen that Cracow butchers purchase in order to slaughter to sell in their stalls, should be driven along a shorter route through Ropczyce, for which the butchers have royal permission."[23] Obviously, such a regulation had its origins in concern over the quality of the meat, in this case, the short-horned Podolian steppe cattle. Bony and swayback at their very fattest, they needed the shorter route to maintain their weight—and their market edge. This took them through the large cattle trading centers at Busko and Nowe Miasto near Korczyn.

Polish meat claw, circa 1350–1400. Used for lifting clods of meat from a cauldron. Wrought iron. Private collection.

The lowest quality beef, what the old sources called *truncelli* (a term also applied to the intestines and offal), probably came from discarded parts of oxen or old milk cows. Apart from the meat itself (eaten mostly by the poor after boiling), the intestines were converted to sausage casings, and the suet (in Polish, *sadło*) was used as a cooking fat. Oxen suet was also added to food for hunting dogs and mastiffs.

We can infer both from the kitchen utensils uncovered from the period and from recipes discussing other meats that beef was important in the medieval Polish diet, and that it was generally stewed, boiled, or spit-roasted, depending on the cut.

Pork Beef appears less frequently in the records than pork in part because it was not processed in as many different ways. Pig farming had the advantage of easy foddering and rapid reproduction, although pigs had no value as a draft animal, which therefore placed it at a lower economic status.

Like beef, pork was also grilled and roasted, although it was bacon that made the most frequent appearance on the table. Streaky bacon, called *rąbanka* in old Polish documents, was evidently the most valued product of the pig. *Loszijna* (possibly derived from Polish *locha* for "sow") was a type of lard prepared expressly for the king and may have been the medieval equivalent of leaf lard, the most delicate type of lard, taken from the underbelly and loins, and used primarily in pastries.

In medieval Poland, two distinct types of pigs were raised for general consumption and there were doubtless a number of gradations between the two extremes. The first was called the "great swine," a half-wild, half-domesticated razorback often illustrated in medieval manuscripts. The other—small, mean, and not easily domesticated—was known in Polish as "swamp hog" (*Sus scrofa palustris*), which not only captures a sense of its fierce independence, but also hints at its culinary qualities. While they may have resembled wild boars in flavor, swamp hogs were considered livestock as opposed to true wild boar (*dzik*), which was hunted only as game.

The hogs belonging to the king were specially raised on

acorns, beech mast, and forest pasturage on royal lands to yield superior bacon. By contrast, analysis of pig manure excavated in Gdansk confirms the supposition that hogs belonging to commoners foraged for food in public garbage dumps and ate kitchen refuse. Bacon was therefore of greatly varying quality, but its consumption was widespread, and not just limited to the nobility. Indeed, it was the most common form of meat eaten in Poland during the Middle Ages.

This is streaky bacon as we call it today, except that it often came to market with the outer rind and hair attached, like bacon shown in a number of Italian and Spanish paintings.[24] It was also sold as *perna lardi*, that is, with the sidemeat still attached to the ham, a cut similar to the old English bacon known as a Wiltshire side. Most hogs were fully mature when butchered, anywhere from one to two years old, and their average cost in Poland during the 1380s was about 21 grosze, or the market value of twenty-one chickens. As a point of comparison, a fat ox cost about 54 grosze, and a fat cow about 44.

Archaeological evidence confirms the high proportion of pork in the Polish diet at this time. Animal refuse recovered from medieval sites at Wolin broke down into the following percentages: cattle 31.5 percent, hogs 63.4 percent, and sheep (or goats) 5 percent. Reassembled, this represented the remains of 65 cattle, 219 pigs, and 46 sheep or goats (their bones are similar and cannot be differentiated). Similar percentages were determined for animal remains from medieval sites at Boników.

Specific pork products mentioned in period texts include *szoldre* or *soldre* (ham), *salsucia* (sausage), and *farcimina* (blood pudding or blood sausage—called *kiszka* in modern Polish).[25] Blood sausage was introduced to Poland before A.D. 1000 from German-speaking areas. It is known that beer was supplied to the royal kitchens for the purpose of preparing a blood soup called *czernina* or *juszka* in old Polish and referred to as *iusculum* in Latin. Blood from ducks, geese, and pigs was used.

A fourteenth-century text from Weissenfels, Germany, mentions ham served with cucumbers, a combination that was likewise popular in Poland (see recipe on page 179).[26] Ham is also called *perna* in old Polish sources, but this term can be confusing because it is also used for certain types of flitch bacon. In modern Polish the word for sausage is *kielbasa*, but the older medieval term *salsucia* implies that the meat is in some way salted or brined, not necessarily that it is also smoked as many Polish sausages are today.

The *farcimina*, according to Szymon Syrennius's discussion in connection with millet kasha, "are used for stuffing blood sausages of pork and beef, having first been cooked in the fat."[27] *Farcimina* appears in much earlier sources in a similar context, so there is little doubt as to what is meant by it. Similar sausages using various types of grain stuffings are still made in Poland today.

Toward the end of the fifteenth century and the beginning of the sixteenth, small sausages similar to frankfurters appeared in Polish sources for the first time. They were referred to in a royal account of 1502 as *circinellas pro prandio* — sausages for dinner.[28] Pork sausages gained in popularity because they could be introduced into a great number of dishes, thus giving more variety and imagination to the menu.

Regarding methods of preparation, fried pork must have been popular because Polish texts often mention frying pans. This would also be consistent with the many references to eating bacon, which is generally fried. However, frying is normally discussed in connection with fish in medieval Polish texts, not with meat, thus the evidence is more indirect. Nevertheless, frying was certainly known, and it is shown in old manuscript illustrations along with barbecuing, spit-roasting, and grilling.

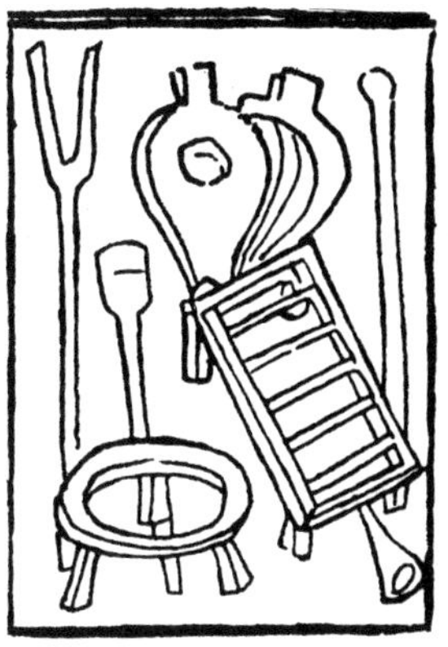

Hearth utensils.

Archaeology has revealed another cooking technique that has been confirmed in manuscript sources: boiling to create an aspic or souse.[29] Large pieces of meat were boiled with finely broken bones in a cauldron so that the bone marrow would cook out and form a thick stock. This stock was then strained and used as a component in other dishes such as stew, gruel, or mush. We can assume that the *pultis* mentioned in numerous royal bills and registers incorporated this type of enriched stock.

Meat cooked and pickled in its own jelly was also an important source of food. Large provisions of meat *ad salsandas* were stored both at the royal court and at royal military stations. Huge amounts of both corned beef and corned pork are mentioned among the provisions of the Teutonic Knights. The *Libellus de coquinaria,* dating from the thirteenth century, contains a detailed recipe for corned meat that may be one of the few surviving from this period.

Polish royal registers occasionally use such expressions as "thirty haunches of pork for preserving in fat" or some variation of this.[30] They appear to refer to the purchases of meat intended for salting, then preserved in lard. Gall's chronicle mentions pork stored in wooden tubs, and this method of preserving meat over the winter is still in use in many rural areas in Poland.

Organ Meats and Veal Lesser meat products also appeared on Polish royal menus, especially organ meats. Tripe (called *trippe* in the early texts) was frequently mentioned, as well as *intestina de porco* and sometimes the more generic term *truncelli.* It is not clear how these were prepared, but in general, this was considered food for the poor, for servants, or for common soldiers. There are two documented cases where organ meat was served to military commanders while visiting encampments, but we do not know whether it was tripe or liver or lungs. However, tripe put up in sauerkraut appears to have been used as an emergency or convenience food during cold weather for all classes of people (see recipe on page 187).

It is worth mentioning that in the charter of 1140 for the Cistercian monastery at Jędrzejów (later known in Poland for its fine gardens), the townspeople were required to give the local prince and his posterity all the hearts of cattle slaughtered in that place.[31] It is not clear whether these beef hearts were considered a special delicacy or whether they were simply food intended for servants connected to the princely household. The context would suggest that the hearts were set aside for the monks, who were of low social standing. Mikołaj Rej referred to beef hearts in his writings as something only fit for monks, servants, and the poor.

Piglets and calves were consumed less frequently than adult animals, but their mention is not rare. Veal, for example, is noted in Polish records as early as the fourteenth century, but such things as *assatura vitulina* (veal sauerbraten) only appear in Cracow during the 1460s.[32] The dish seems to have originated at the Holy Roman Court in Vienna, or at least made fashionable by it, for it is said to be a Hungarian invention which originally relied on *csombor* as a flavoring ingredient. Csombor is an herb with a taste that resembles mugwort (*Artemesia vulgaris*). It may be replicated by grinding together equal parts tarragon, dill seed, and caraway seed.

A little over a century after the appearance of the dish in Poland, Marcus Rumpolt mentioned it in his *Ein new Kochbuch* (Frankfurt, 1581). He called it Kälbern Braten in ein Duba (pot-roast saddle of veal); any large cut of veal could be used. Rumpolt, himself a Hungarian (born in Wallachia), cooked in Poland sometime before the coronation of Queen Barbara Radziwiłł (1550), and noted that the dish was then a great favorite with the Austrian court. In his 1581 recipe, the roast was taken from the loin or saddle, scored, and laid in a marinade of spring water, wine vinegar, garlic, and sweet marjoram (*Origanum majorana*). After marinating overnight, the meat was seared on a spit, then pot-roasted along with the kidneys in a mixture of melted butter and the marinade, all well flavored with herbs and garlic. The meat was served in its sauce with grated pepper. The preparation is simple and invariably results in tender meat. But then as now, veal was expensive.

For farmers, calves and other young animals are "sacrifice" foods in that slaughtering them eliminates their larger economic potential later on. Therefore, it is not surprising to find these meats limited to menus of the royal court and upper nobility. Servants and people of lower station simply did not consume this kind of meat. Lamb and kid were eaten even more rarely, but the references are clear that when lamb was cooked, it was always served with onions (we mention this because the medieval cookery of Poland relied heavily on onions).[33]

Poultry The most commonly consumed meat after beef and pork was poultry, especially chickens, capons, and poussins. Poultry raising must have played a very significant role in the economy of medieval Poland judging by the vast orders that would be quickly filled for the royal and princely courts. Poultry, too, figures significantly in the payment of manorial quitrents. For example, peasants were required to pay annually anywhere from six hens, two cheeses, and two eggs to eight hens, two cheeses, and twelve eggs above and beyond what was owed in grain harvest (these quantities varied from manor to manor). At the royal court, which received payments of this sort from its serfs, tithe poultry was generally spit-roasted or prepared in aspic, depending on its quality.

The royal accounts also mention ducks more often than geese. The ducks were either young or specially fattened. Wild ducks were mentioned only once and pigeons only on occasion. The nature of these references seems to suggest that all of these last-mentioned fowl were consumed on a seasonal basis. The Weissenfels text from the fourteenth century made mention of chicken baked with prunes (see recipe on page 154), goose baked with turnips, and small birds fried in lard, preparations that definitely had their counterparts in Poland.[34]

Archaeological evidence confirms this general schema, although only in Gdansk is the record clear enough to draw conclusions about the relative consumption of chickens, ducks, and geese. Oddly, the archaeological record for poultry during the fourteenth and fifteenth centuries remains puzzling, for remains are scarce. This is particularly strange given the fact that this period was characterized by an increase in specialized poultry raising.

Game Game is perhaps one of the most perplexing of all the food categories of medieval diet in Poland. The archaeological record is quite clear in its scarcity of game remains, and written sources confirm that game was rarely eaten by rich or poor. Yet these same sources also make abundant mention of hunting, indeed the royal court maintained huntsmen almost year round. What happened to the quarry?

The Polish *ius regale* (law of royal privileges) regulated hunting of big game throughout the kingdom. No one could hunt for big game without the express permission of the king. Game killed by the king or at his order was eviscerated on the spot. All parts of the animal with any value, such as the hide, some of the bones, and of course the meat, would be taken back to town. Bear provide a particularly interesting example of the practice, for only the paw bones show up at archaeological sites connected to food consumption. These parts of the animal enjoyed culinary esteem among the nobility, along with bear bacon and smoked bear tongue, which were treated as gourmet fare. Of course, the fur was also highly valued. The rest of the animal was left in the forest.

On occasion, the archaeological record provides surprising evidence about the hunt, although it is difficult to interpret. For example, excavations at a twelfth- and thirteenth-century settlement of artisan-fishermen in Gdansk revealed bones for elks, aurochs, wild boars, and stags. Several Polish historians have rightly pointed out that these animals were not hunted by individuals but by large groups of men. A single hunter could not have carted the dead animal alone, and in the case of the material from Gdansk, it is obvious from the types of bones found that the game was dressed in the village, not in the forest where it was killed.

The explanation for this is that the local prince arranged for collective, organized hunting by men from settlements in the area. The meat and hides were sent to him for his own use, while the bones, horns, and antlers went to local workshops specializing in the manufacture of utensils. This hypothesis was confirmed when archaeologists discovered bones and skulls with traces of saws, axes, and sharp knives.[35] It appears that in return for hunting, the men were paid with animal parts useful to their craft industry.

Royal accounts do not contain any references to big game in

spite of the fact that there are ample references to hunting dogs and royal huntsmen. Only small game, such as beavers, badgers (*borsuk*), hares, partridges, and black grouse, was regularly prepared for royal menus in season. This kind of game was commonly hunted by village officials or privileged peasants who had the legal right to hunt it and sell it to the royal court.

Venison presents an interesting puzzle, for it is not mentioned very frequently in medieval Polish texts. Gallus Anonymus devoted a lengthy passage in his chronicle to "magnanimitati mensae et largitati Boleslai," which described the wealth and hospitality of King Bołeslaw Chrobry (reigned 992–1025).[36] The king expressed his generosity in receptions given to large numbers of people who were closely associated with him. According to the menus described by Gallus Anonymus, the king's feasts abounded in a variety of venison dishes prepared from animals caught by professional hunters. This pattern of professional huntsmen delivering game to the court is confirmed both by written sources and by archaeological evidence. Hunting in medieval Poland played a different role than in other parts of Europe, for it was less a form of food acquisition and more an extension of court diplomacy. Game was more than just meat, it was a political expression of high esteem and appreciation.

Big game was not common in Poland to begin with, and its consumption was reserved exclusively for large royal celebrations, high military officials, or, most important, a luxury gift food to visiting dignitaries.[37] Indeed, a good-sized elk was valued at 90 grosze, almost twice as expensive as an average ox. It is known that King Władysław Jagiełło organized hunts mainly for the purpose of offering venison to distinguished officials. It is also well documented that he gave "salted portions" of venison as gifts to various state visitors. Indeed, salted meat of all sorts appears to have been quite popular, since purchases of fresh meats were as a matter of practice specially designated as *carnes recentes* in the royal registers.[38] This preference is probably why venison was normally salted, rubbed down with condiments, and then partially smoked or treated in some other way, and then stored in barrels. Otherwise, fresh venison was always placed in a vinegar marinade before it was cooked. This practice was done as much for sterilizing the meat as for flavor and tenderizing.

The kings of Poland were well aware of the symbolism attached to venison, and King Casimir Jagiellończyk used his royal privilege in 1448 to accomplish an interesting political point. That year he granted the citizens of Cracow the right to hunt for venison in the royal forests, but only to satisfy their needs. It may be that the deer population was multiplying too rapidly or that the king wanted to curtail hunting on a large scale by asserting his rights over venison. Whatever his ulterior motive, the immediate result was to win over the sympathies of the townspeople, who at least for a short time enjoyed the luxury of a food formerly served only at the royal court or at princely estates.

The maintenance of royal hunters and falconers was a large expense in all the royal accounts for this period. In fact, there are quite a number of purchase orders for specific dinners where the royal falconers entertained foreign guests. One of the royal purchase orders for Korczyn in August 1405 covered the expenses for entertaining Russian falconers as well as the king's own men: two boiled beef heads, sixty chickens, two sheep, and three achtels of beer. The falcons themselves were fed thirty live chickens.[39] At another dinner, which included drummers, hunters, falconers, bakers, vendors, and lute players, much less meat was served, but almost twice as much beer. The beer came from Busko (a very cheap quality), which may suggest how the court managed to contain some of its costs. Since hunting was considered a diversion with no real economic object in mind, it is easy to see how entertainment expenses could quickly eat into royal reserves.

Yet the kings always viewed hunting as one of the perks of office and a certain way to escape the pressures of work. King Władysław Jagiełło's letter to the master of the royal hunt at Pryzów expressed this sentiment when he remarked that hunting existed "for the salutary refreshment of our body following the exertions of labor."[40] There were high costs involved, for the royal huntsmen had to be prepared at all times to accommodate the king, should he decide, on a moment's notice, to spend a day at the hunt. The entire community of Jedlina in the Radom forests enjoyed the privilege of hunting venison in return for being ready at all times to handle every aspect of the hunt, from driving the animals to transporting the trophies back from the woods.[41]

The preparation of game at court might be inferred from the huge inventories of vinegar consumed by the royal kitchens. The Polish love of sour marinades is constantly referred to in medieval texts under the term *salsum dominorum*. One of the marinades discussed in the Danish *Libellus de coquinaria* called for cloves, cinnamon, ginger, and pepper thoroughly mixed (with the cinnamon predominating), white bread dissolved in it to thicken it, and strong vinegar. Such thickened marinades were also cooked with pan drippings to make sauces or gravies for the meat. Another marinade recipe in the same text consisted of honey, vinegar, and mustard seeds, a combination that reminds one of the honey mustards popular today (see recipe for green mustard on page 156). The royal kitchens always listed abundant supplies of honey, so there is no doubt that some of it at least was being used to create sweet-sour combinations.

Fish

Fish, which constituted the second basic food product in Polish medieval cookery after meat, was eaten in large quantities and was prepared in a variety of ingenious ways. Its consumption was directly connected to the religious practices introduced by the Catholic Church, since fish always appeared on the table during Lent, every Wednesday and Friday, and on other fasting days. It never appeared on the menu on regular "meat" days (Sunday, Tuesday, and Thursday). Quite the opposite was true in Germany, where fish and meat might appear at the same meal. Because the Polish Church strictly enforced fasting days and because such days were far more frequent in the Middle Ages than in later periods, there was a steady demand for fish of all sorts. The royal accounts of Władysław Jagiełło and Jadwiga are very precise in their mention of fish as *recentes* (fresh), *sicci* (dried), *salsi* (salted), or *semiassati* (pickled). The archaeological record, however, is not as easy to interpret. What is evident from the remains, however, is that fish consumption was about the same across all levels of society and that fish in the Middle Ages, were larger and of a higher quality than is seen today. Modern pollution and overfishing have contributed to this decline.

The remains include such fish as sturgeon and wyż (a Polish relative of sturgeon); salmon, sea trout, lavaret (a type of whitefish), trout, and grayling; pike perch and perch; pike; wels (European catfish); carp, ide, roach, *boleń* (*Aspius rapax*), barbel, tench, bream, crucian carp, *certa* (*Abramis vimba*), and *krępie;* cod and turbot. These have been grouped by family and some of the fish do not have common English names. This is complicated by the fact that there are fewer remains of fish with small bones because these bones degrade more quickly in the soil. For example, herring bones are rare, yet we know from written sources that herring was very popular in the early 1100s. In fact, ruins of salt-processing sites connected with herring and dating from the eighth to ninth centuries have been discovered at Kołobrzeg in Pomerania.

Manuscript sources from the fourteenth and fifteenth centuries further confirm the archaeological findings for the earlier period, and add a few more species of fish to the overall list. This is particularly useful in the case of eel, fish imported in barrels from Hungary, and crayfish, none of which were identified from archaeological evidence prior to the 1970s. However, it is very difficult to determine the fish most commonly consumed as opposed to those considered rare delicacies. If we simply list the fish according to the number of times they are mentioned in the written sources, then herring is always at the top. Following this would be eel, then salmon. Trailing far behind these were grayling, perch, ide, pike perch, pike, wels, and at the very bottom of the list, sturgeon and sterlet. These last mentioned fish may have become scarce by this time, a fact supported by the very high prices quoted for large fish in general. A whole large salmon cost 20 grosze, but a portion of sturgeon cost 70 grosze per piece, or more than an entire ox.

Records from the fourteenth and fifteenth centuries also mention various forms of preserved fish, particularly herring and *stracfusz* (pike processed like dried cod). There is also a clear inference that salt-dried cod was extremely popular. Three pieces of cod cost 1 Polish kopa or 8 to 11 grosze. Food in late medieval Poland was generally sold by kopa units, with 1 kopa divisible into sixty "bits." In currency terms, these served as pennies. For comparison, one hundred pieces of herring during this period cost roughly 8 grosze.

The only smoked fish mentioned frequently is lamprey, although the remains of smoked eel are now becoming common due to improved archaeological methods. Because sea lamprey was considered the most flavorful, it was generally smoked so that it could be shipped to inland markets. It was sold by the *wózanka* (bundle) at a cost of about one-half grosze per Polish pound. All of these fish, whether fresh, salted, or smoked, do show up in the culinary record, for we find a number of specific dishes mentioned in period manuscripts.

Two common preparation methods at the royal court included fish fried in olive oil and fish made into aspic. Another cooking method was hinted at in a bill in the accounts of Władysław Jagiełło and Jadwiga for the purchase of fish and herring with oil.[42] It is probable that the herring was preserved in oil, as it is often preserved today. Herring was quite popular during the medieval period, and as a commercial product prepared in the Baltic ports, it came to market in oil, salted, smoked, pickled, and on occasion sold stuck on wooden spits, thirty fish to the spit. Salt herring was cheap and was often sold to nunneries and monasteries. For example, in 1214 the Cistercian nuns at Trzebnica in Pomerania were granted the privilege to transport salt herring on their own boat rather than to pay a middleman for delivery.[43] In any case, the better grades of herring were poached in vinegar stock with mustard and onions or commonly served with a green sauce. There are also references to baking them with cinnamon, or with white wine and condiments.

Other fish that appear with some frequency were perch poached in wine with parsley, in soup, or stewed with vegetables; carp with green sauce or in aspic; and various types of galantines using fish blood to color them black. The galantines were made only on special occasions, usually with pike or some other large fish, and several Polish references are quite clear that the fish was served whole or in large nicely carved pieces (one of the defining features of a Polish galantine). Aspics, composed of meat cut into small bits or shaped into dumplings, were evidently prepared from mixed fish of lesser quality; and in Poland, vinegar rather than wine is the most consistent ingredient (see the recipe for an ornamental aspic flavored with lavender vinegar on page 166).

Salted fish is commonly mentioned, but not by species. It was consumed by rich and poor alike, and even pike and eel were sold this way. Eel was the second most frequently mentioned fish in Polish sources following herring. By the 1300s it was sold by the barrel for about 1½ to 2 grosze per barrel and consumed while rather young.

Wels or sheet fish (*Siluris glanis*), known in Polish as *sum*, which can attain a length of four meters, is mentioned in written sources much less frequently than one would assume, judging from numerous archaeological remains dating from the eighth to tenth centuries. Bones and vertebras found at Biskupin during digs in 1956 suggest that large pieces were smoked to supply the table of the local feudal lord.[44] Excavations also uncovered impressive smoking pits. These sheet fish, the largest of the European catfish, probably came from the lake at Biskupin, but similar smoking pits have been discovered throughout the lake districts in the Pałucko region of Poland. There may be an interesting explanation for this.

Fish was often mentioned as a tithe in medieval documents, and several city registers mention fish specifically as honoraria for important officials. Owing to its perishable nature, fish is more easily transported and stored when salted, smoked, or dried, so we may presume that these methods were used when the fish was given to officials en route to other places or sent as a gift to a locality that would have required several days or even weeks of travel. Smoked lamprey and dried pike were often prepared specifically for this purpose, and the accounts of the Teutonic Knights are full of references to such provisions, mainly cod and herring. Herring was usually listed by the cask (containing six hundred to eight hundred fish), whereas cod was listed by the piece.[45] Such barreled herring became common in the 1300s. Earlier it was sold in bundles of a thousand.

We also find references on occasion in the fourteenth and fifteenth centuries to fish sent in barrels from Hungary, which must refer to some type of migratory river fish (perhaps sturgeon) taken from the Danube. The royal accounts under the year 1412 mention Hungarian fish sold by the cask while Queen Anna (second wife of King Władysław Jagiełło) was returning to Poland accompanied by her Hungarian guests. The royal entourage paused at Sącz, where a merchant from Kosice (in present-day Slovakia) sold them the fish. The merchant evidently trailed the court as it moved toward Cracow so that he could turn a good profit by supplying it with daily provisions.[46]

Mush pot.

Grains: *Kasza* (Grits) and Old Polish Porridge

The polish term *kasza* (kasha in English) refers to a texture rather than to a particular type of grain. However, in the context of medieval Polish cookery, millet is almost universally implied, and porridge made with finely ground millet or millet grits was the staff of life for all Poles, princes and commoners alike. Millet was also one of the distinctive features of medieval Polish cookery that differentiated it from cookery in Western Europe. Today, the potato has replaced millet in

Miller hauling grain to be ground.

Polish diet, but this is a change that came to Poland much later, in the late seventeenth century. Until the potato, millet kasha was one of Poland's defining regional foods, and this has been confirmed by archaeological evidence.

Millet, wheat, and rye were equally in demand, yet were utilized in very different ways. The first was primarily for domestic consumption while the latter two grains were generally converted to flour and therefore served as commercial commodities for breweries, mills, and bakeries. In terms of units sown, rye held absolute priority, and millet never appeared as *sep* (medieval tithe payment), whereas rye is mentioned often in this respect. Yet millet has left a far clearer archaeological trail, for unlike wheat and rye it resists decomposition.

One of the most revealing aspects of millet culture from the archaeological record is the huge biodiversity of plant stock that once existed on Polish soil. Archaeologists have discovered not only a wide variety of seed colors (red, brown, orange, yellow), but also evidence that the plants themselves had undergone many local adaptations. This implies that there were many regional varieties specially selected and adapted to particular soil types. The very existence of such remains has caused historians to reassess the prevailing image of agriculture in Poland during the early Middle Ages. Evidence points to a level of sophistication not previously appreciated, and all the more intriguing given the fact that of all the grains grown in Poland, millet is also the most demanding in terms of soil and weather conditions. The only logical explanation for this is that the Polish preference for millet was cultural and that millet must have arrived with the earliest Slavic migrants. The oldest cultivated species from that period was the so-called foxtail millet (*Setaria italica*), but it was soon replaced by

Panicum miliaceum, the species best adapted to Polish climate due to its shorter period of vegetation.

There are no direct references to millet flour or to breads made from millet flour from early medieval Poland, although the ethnographic record is rich in material on millet *placki* (flat breads). Hearth breads and ash cakes made with millet must have played a role in the medieval Polish diet, especially in rural areas. Since it contains very little gluten, it may have been mixed with other flours. But millet was not, per se, a food of the poor. Indeed, grits made from millet were a feature of meals for all levels of society in medieval Poland. Furthermore, millet was eaten during Lent, on "meat" days, on fast days, and on holidays. Quite simply, it was an everyday dish and was prepared in a wide variety of ways. On exceptional occasions, it was substituted with other grains such as rice (an imported luxury) or with *kasza manna*, grits from *Glyceria fluitans*, a type of grass that grows wild in Poland. Both of these were delicacies consumed by the rich. In fact, rice was considered so precious during the Jagiellonian reigns that it was locked up in the royal treasury along with valuable spices.

Polish medieval records make two distinctions regarding the way in which millet was prepared. One of the most common designations was *pultes* (pulse), which refers to the coarse texture in porridge. It was cooked like modern oatmeal until thick, then eaten plain or with milk, or it was cooked with meat or vegetable stock and such ingredients as dried peas, fresh root vegetables, and sometimes cheap cuts of meat. This form of millet porridge made with coarsely broken grain was rarely consumed by the higher social classes. It was strictly village fare and was considered rustic by the prevailing standards of Polish court cookery. The English word *gruel* best conveys its character. The concept survives in Polish cookery today under the name *polewka,* a cheese gruel consisting of hot milk, water, and fresh curds that is eaten like soup.

Its counterpart among the nobility was *zacierki,* commonly referred to as *pulmentum* in Latin texts, a contraction of *pulpamentum.* In this case the millet was ground very fine to yield two distinct textures: a true flour consistency, and a fine, even-textured form of grits resembling modern polenta. The Italian word for polenta is itself derived from the Latin *pulmentum,* and before the introduction of maize, was made with a variety of other grains, primarily barley. In any case, old Polish *zacierki* may be equated with pap mentioned in medieval texts in England and France. It was a thick soup or porridge with a smooth puree-like consistency. Egg yolks, milk, meat stock, and various spices were also normally added to the millet to create a range of distinct recipes (see recipe using capon stock, honey, and saffron on page 160).

A dish called *pulmentum avenaticum* is also mentioned in some of the noble accounts. This appears, from seventeenth-century ethnographic evidence, to be similar to the *tołokno* of Lithuania and Russia, which was made with parched oats ground into flour and used as a provision during long travels. It was cooked as needed with water, pork fat, and salt. Barley flour and millet kasha were sometimes prepared the same way. Evidently, the Polish oatmeal counterpart was considerably more refined, at least as it was served at the royal court. The records of Klemens Watrobka, voivode of Cracow in 1419, offer a contemporary explanation: "to a half measure of oats for soup called *kucza.*"[47] Thus, Polish soup made with fine oatmeal was known as *kucza.*

Oats did not appear in Poland until the eleventh century,

mostly in connection with improvements in animal husbandry and brewing. This grain was not held in high esteem, and coarse grits or meal made from it (referred to as *gruellum de avena* or *avenata*) were sometimes consumed, but usually by servants and laborers. In contrast to this, *avenata* was a dish of some dignity in Western Europe. Chiquart, a fourteenth-century Savoyard cook, included a recipe for *avenast* (his spelling) in his cookery manual.[48] And the Catalan *Liber de Sent Sovi* of the same period featured an *avenat* sweetened with sugar and intended primarily as a porridge for invalids.

In general, aside from kucza, oats were viewed as fodder for horses or as a component of *tłucz* ("mash"), a food made for hunting dogs by mixing cooked oatmeal with beef suet. Otherwise, oats did not play a pervasive role in the medieval Polish diet but they do show up on occasion as payment by peasants in exchange for the so-called *wrąb*, the right to hunt in manor forests. Such payments are recorded during the 1380s in the accounts of the manor of Niepołomice. Quitrents were also sometimes paid in oats, although the nobility always preferred cash.

Likewise, barley is not mentioned with regularity until the fifteenth century. It was used for grits and meal, but this was not common. The importance of barley can be inferred from the fact that it was planted only in small plots on a scale much more restricted than other grains.[49] We do know, however, that barley was used to "stretch" rye flour in bread making.

Barley was also the main component of a yogurt-like dish referred to in Latin texts as *glycerius* and in medieval Polish as *kyssel;* the modern Polish spelling is usually given as *kisiel.* Normally characterized as nobleman's fare, this thick soup was prepared by pouring boiling water over barley flour, then adding a liquid yeast called "thick beer." It would ferment slightly and thicken, then honey, milk, or fruit was added (see recipe on page 164). There are references to this dish in Polish records as early as A.D. 997. It was served for dinner at the royal table, and the king often served it (without milk) to guests during Lent. For example, in 1394 King Władysław Jagiełło served kisiel at a meal attended by Prokop, titular margrave of Moravia; the duke of Raciborz; Janusz, duke of Oswiecim; and others.[50]

Today, this preparation has evolved into the dish known in Polish as *żur,* a loan word from Russian. Żur has further evolved into a number of regionalized forms. Buckwheat rather than oat flour is used in eastern and northeastern Poland, while oat flour is more restricted to the South. Rye flour is used in the rest of the country. Until quite recently, many peasants reserved a ceramic pot especially for making żur. It was not washed, allowing the fermentation from one batch to act as starter for the next. During Lent, the soup was flavored only with salt and garlic, and so symbolic was it of fasting and self-denial that it is often used in Polish literature as a metaphor for sacrifice and asceticism. In fact, at the end of Lent, the żur pot was symbolically "killed" either by smashing it or burying it in the ground. A new pot was bought, and thus began another annual cycle. Archaeology has uncovered many such pots in medieval Polish sites, lending material evidence to the age of this tradition.

Because of the peculiar role of oats and barley in the old Polish diet, we are led to wonder about the nature of the *gruellum compositum* mentioned in some early sources. Was it a mixture of grits made from millet, barley, and oats as some scholars have suggested? Each of the grains has a different cooking time, oats being the shortest, barley the longest. But because the term *gruellum compositum* is singular, we must assume that the grains are being cooked together and that more likely than not, the whole mixture was reduced to a thick mush. What remains unclear is the mix of grains.

Several texts from late antiquity and from Byzantium make reference to similar porridges or gruels made with mixtures of grains. A type of polenta called *chondrogala* by Galen (about A.D. 165) consisted of barley, wheat, millet, and cracked chickpeas cooked until thick in water and goat milk.[51] The mush became so thick that it resembled mashed potatoes and could be molded into the shape of a cheese. Medieval Poles may have had a variety of other grains available to them, but the end result would have been similar in texture. The recipe for gruel of mixed grains, which combines broken wheat groats and millet kasha in a stock of pureed greens, strikes a middle ground (see recipe on page 147). Its makeup is based on ethnographic evidence; similar dishes were made in rural Poland into the late nineteenth century. The fact that it works as intended in the medieval texts — as a side dish for boiled or roasted meat — further strengthens the case for this interpretation.

Perhaps the most pertinent question is, how was millet consumed in medieval Poland? We know that millet was ground to a sandy cornmeal consistency and cooked, yet sources from the fourteenth and fifteenth centuries do not contain much material on actual millet preparation. Only in the 1613 herbal of Szymon Syrennius do we find actual descriptions of dishes. There are references to millet in Taillevent, and at least one "French" recipe of the same period is of possible Polish origin. The foreign recipes are most useful for information about preparation techniques and methodology, which may provide clues as to how similar processes were accomplished in Poland.

One of the preparations described by Szymon Syrennius stated that millet kasha was "cooked in milk with butter and sugar."

Such a recipe would have been exceptional in medieval Poland, although Cypriot sugar was known in the fourteenth century and shipped on a regular basis from Famagusta via Genoese factors. Some of the very rich could have indulged in millet prepared this way, although honey was far more likely as a sweetener. Sugar would have been used mostly in the preparation of *konfekty*—confections and candied fruits for the beginning and end of meals—rather than to sweeten porridge.

More realistically, at least in terms of mainstream diet, Syrennius's reference to another method of preparation comes closer to the point. He noted that servants ate millet kasha "cooked with water, butter, and salt." Or, hulled millet was "cooked until fluffy and loose, then browned in butter and thus served."[52] This last dish would resemble fried rice.

One fourteenth-century French recipe is more elaborate, although it is simple enough to have been used in Poland and the ingredients were available.[53] Grits were soaked and rinsed three times in boiling water, then poured into hot milk and left to cook without stirring until the milk came to a full boil. After they boiled, the grits were removed from the fire and beaten vigorously with the backside of a wooden scoop or "clasher" to make the mixture smooth. They were then placed over the fire again, saffron was added, and the porridge was cooked until thick.

Clasher for working millet. After an eighteenth-century artifact.

The millet clasher may be peculiar to Polish cookery, for nothing quite like it has come to light in other parts of Europe. It was shaped like a dipper, but with the inside of the bowl left unfinished. The backside was used to mash the soft millet against the side of the cookpot.

At truly refined meals, millet was replaced with *manna* (*Glyceria fluitans*). Known in Poland as Mazovian semolina, manna grows in wet meadows or near water and yields a grain similar in size to common grass seed. According to archaeological evidence, manna did not enter the Polish diet in a large way until the end of the thirteenth century, which suggests that the concept of harvesting it may have come from outside Poland. Large quantities of manna remains have been found during excavations of the Rynek Glówny (the main marketplace) in Cracow, clearly suggesting that manna was an important article of commerce and not just a luxury foraged for the nobility.

The Poles also differentiate between several species or subspecies of manna, among them *Glyceria maxima* (large manna, with grains resembling miniaturized wheat) and *Glyceria lithuanica* (Lithuanian manna, with grains no larger than celery seed). In North America, the native manna is more commonly known as floating manna grass under different taxonomy (*Panicularia fluitans*). Polish manna's slightly sweet flavor is far more delicate than millet and it was historically much costlier than any other grain consumed in Poland. It was purchased in large quantities by the royal court and appeared on the royal menu almost exclusively, usually under the name "semolina."[54]

As we have mentioned, on rare occasions, rice was served to important guests of the royal household as a further substitution in the hierarchy of costly ingredients. Rice was often combined with hashmeats (see recipe in the Cypriot style on page 171). To substitute for rice, rural people gathered the seeds of a plant known as manna lichen (*Lecanora esculenta*) that they used in cookery the same way as rice. This seed was widely used in rural Poland until rice became inexpensive in recent times.

Likewise, on the more modest end of the culinary scale, we come to buckwheat, which was primarily consumed in the villages. During the Middle Ages, only two types of buckwheat were known in Poland: Tartarian buckwheat (*Fagopyrum tataricum*), called *paganca* in old Polish texts; and true culinary buckwheat (*Fagopyrum esculentum*). In Mazovia, both species were called buckwheat since both were prepared the same way as kasha, or *kasza gryczana,* as buckwheat grits are properly known in Polish. Tartarian buckwheat came to Poland from central Asia during the thirteenth century, along with sweet flag (*Acorus calamus*) and Tartar bread plant (*Crambe tatarica*), a potherb often cooked in porridges prepared with buckwheat grits. The fleshy, sweet root of this latter herb was grated into vinegar like horseradish or cooked with parsnips, carrots, or skirrets. The leaves were often used by country people to wrap around bread baked downhearth in ashes or in bake ovens, which gave bread a nice, golden crust. The popular dumplings made with buckwheat and known today in Southern Poland as *pierogi ruskie* did not enter Polish cookery until the nineteenth century, when they came to Poland from Russia.

Another medieval grain dish mentioned in Polish records appeared under the name *prazmo*. Judging by remarks made by Szymon Syrennius, this was a pottage consumed mostly by the poor, although on occasion it was also eaten by the upper classes. It was made by oven-drying the unripened grains of rye and using these as the basis for a gruel. When needed, the green grains were soaked in warm water, then cooked with milk and bacon. Upper-class versions of this dish used capon stock and better quality ingredients. Various traylike grain roasters (*praznice*) made from earthenware have been excavated from sites in Poland dating from the sixth or seventh centuries to the thirteenth century, so there is physical evidence that this practice was in place even in the early Middle Ages, and before literary documentation.

The practice of oven-drying green grain continues in southwest Germany, where the process is applied to *Grünkern*, the unripe kernels of spelt, a species of wheat (*Triticum spelta*). It is known from archaeological evidence that spelt was dried in this manner prior to the Roman occupation of the Rhineland in the first century B.C., and in fact was a widespread practice among the Gauls and other Celtic peoples. Today, *Grünkern* is considered a health food. Like spelt, green rye also cooks more quickly and is easier to digest than the ripe grain. More important, this process intercepted the grain at a stage before the onset of ergot, a toxic fungus that resulted in a disease called St. Anthony's fire, prevalent in medieval times. Ergot is commonly associated with rye, but it attacks other grains as well. Oven-drying was doubtless also applied to Polish spelt, since spelt was the primary winter wheat grown in Poland from the tenth to twelfth centuries. Other wheats grown were club wheat (*Triticum compactum*), a starchy wheat most useful for its flour; emmer (*Triticum dicoccum*), the oldest cultivated wheat (called Alexandrian wheat by the Romans); and common bread wheat (*Triticum aestivum*), which has yielded many modern cultivars.

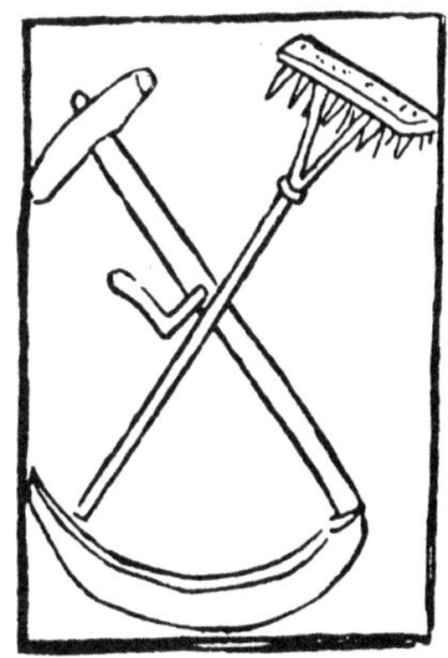

Harvest tools.

Last, hemp seeds appear to have been used as grits for porridge, especially by the rural poor. Evidence for this comes mainly from the Ruthenian (ethnic Ukranian) parts of Poland, and documentation can be traced to the eleventh century. Several Polish historians have suggested that the large quantities of hemp seed supplied to the royal court were also intended for soup. This is a possibility, but we cannot discount the fact that hemp seed oil was used in lamps. Perhaps the crushed seed had a culinary use after the oil was extracted. There is a tradition that such seed mash was used to make soup in monasteries, so soldiers stationed at the royal court may have dined on similar rations. Whether it satisfied hunger remains to be seen; it certainly would have induced a pleasant and incapacitating stupor.

Breads and Baked Goods

Many kinds of bread flours were available in Poland during the Middle Ages. There were two types of rye flour, one coarse (*siliginis*) and one finely ground (*niger*), as well as common and specialty wheat flours. The flour designated as *farina triticea* ("common") in the royal accounts of King Władysław Jagiełło was used for loaf or trencher bread, while the *farina alba* ("white" flour) was used for baking manchet rolls, cakes, and better quality baked goods. The best grade of wheat flour, called *farina alba cribrata* ("finely bolted" white flour) was the most delicate of all and was used for only the highest quality cakes, cookies, and pastries.

Based on medieval baking regulations and the daily listings of bread in the royal registers, we know that there were nine broad categories of bread, not counting the many variant transitional forms, or the unregulated breads baked in homes: common rye bread, black rye bread, common white bread, *binavice*, wheat or manchet rolls, bagels or ring pretzels, *rogale* or crescent rolls, *placki* or flat cakes, and *tortae*.

Common rye bread (*siliginis*) would equate roughly to a modern whole meal rye bread. This type of bread was commonly used for trenchers, as described in the recipe for Wrocław trencher bread (see page 180).

Black rye bread (*niger*) was a fine-grained bread very dark in color. When baked down-hearth in kettles, as was often done in rural farmhouses, this bread resembled a dense pudding like German pumpernickel.

Common white bread (*albus*) was made with *farina triticea, farina alba*, or a blend of the two. Thus there were several subgrades, ranging from bread resembling modern whole wheat to very white sourdough types. The very largest of this sort were made for harvest feasts. After harvest, the peasants would present to the landowner a huge loaf of bread and a crown made of various grains and flowers. The landowner in return was obliged to prepare a feast. This custom was carried over from pagan times and was derived from the belief that this exchange would protect the community from hunger.

Binavice (*biscotum*) is generally rendered into English as rusks, although the Polish term actually means "in a double way." These breads, which are first baked, then sliced, and finally dried at a low temperature in the oven, are not necessarily of fine quality. The earliest references to this sort of breadstuff come from early medieval accounts of requisitions for soldiers' rations. Syrennius even defined it as "soldier's bread" and noted that anise seed was normally added not so much for the flavor as for health reasons.[55]

The benefit of *binavice* was that they could be stored for a long time and reconstituted as needed by dipping in beer or some other beverage. Large quantities were consumed at the royal court, perhaps as part of the servants' mess or as part of the rations for the considerable number of soldiers stationed at court to protect it.

Wheat rolls or manchet breads (*semellae*) were the finest sort of white bread. They are most often depicted in medieval banqueting scenes or in Last Supper scenes using details from medieval life. The rolls came in various shapes, some perfectly round called *bulki*, others elongated with pointed ends. At the royal court and in large cities and towns, rolls were consumed at every noon and evening meal.

Bagels or ring pretzels are called *circuli* in Polish Latin, but *bracellus* or *brachitum* elsewhere in Europe. The Polish plural terms, *obarzanky* and *obwarzanky*, appear often in the royal accounts of King Władysław Jagiełło and Queen Jadwiga. Later they are also referred to as *praczliki*, a term that first appeared in the 1502 accounts of Prince Sigismund I. A common street food in Cracow even today, obarzanki are generally made of two pieces of dough twisted into a ring and then baked with poppy seeds scattered over them. The name does not imply a specific recipe; it is only a reference to the dried-out texture. Thus, obarzanki could be made from any type of dough. In fact, the recipe for trencher bread (page 180) will make both dry obarzanki and fresh raised dough pretzels (*bracellus recens*) of excellent texture and flavor, similar to bagels sold in Wrocław and other Silesian towns in the 1300s.

Obarzanek (ring pretzel).

A round pretzel identical in shape to the bagel was known in classical antiquity and is even illustrated in a Roman codex in the Vatican Library. It is generally assumed that obarzanki came to Poland with the large migration of Jews from Germany during the period of Casimir the Great (reigned 1333–1370). However, these pretzels may have appeared even earlier, perhaps two or three hundred years, since they were already well known to the German bakers who operated in many of the large towns.

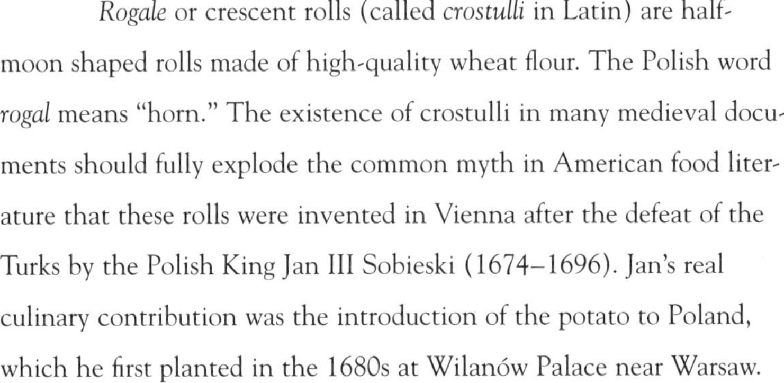

Rogale or crescent rolls (called *crostulli* in Latin) are half-moon shaped rolls made of high-quality wheat flour. The Polish word *rogal* means "horn." The existence of crostulli in many medieval documents should fully explode the common myth in American food literature that these rolls were invented in Vienna after the defeat of the Turks by the Polish King Jan III Sobieski (1674–1696). Jan's real culinary contribution was the introduction of the potato to Poland, which he first planted in the 1680s at Wilanów Palace near Warsaw.

The Polish term for flat cakes, *placki*, derives from the Latin *placenta* (cake) and covers a variety of forms without conveying a fixed meaning other than flat shape. One kind resembled ravioli (stuffed with cheese) and was fried like a Spanish empanada as a dessert served with strawberries or other fruit. It was sometimes called a *krepel* or *kreple* when referred to in Polish. The word is derived from the German *Krapfen* or dialect *Kräpfl*. Placki was likewise applied to *praskury* or *plaskury* (derived from *prosfora*) or wafers. The royal accounts specifically mention saffron wafers, which were probably baked in wafer irons (see recipe on page 173). They were unleavened and generally eaten on fast days. Special recipes were prepared for Good Friday and stamped with appropriate religious symbols. There were also flat cakes baked with apples, evidently something akin to an apple pizza, and related in form to the *koláče* of Moravia. Additionally, there are specific references in the royal accounts to purchases of poppy seeds, cheese and frying oil for Easter pancakes.

In general, honey served as the main sweetener, but when it was added to a flat cake in large amounts, the cake became a *miodownik* or "honey cake." From the 1300s on, this was the accepted term in Poland. Only much later did Polish adopt the term *piernick* from German *Pfefferkuchen* (pepper in Polish is *pieprz*). The term *pierniky* appeared for the first time in the accounts of Prince Sigismund I during the years 1502–1506. Like wafers, these flat cakes were normally stamped with elaborate images. Toruń (Thorn) became a famous center for ornamented honey cakes as early as the fourteenth century.[56]

Polish signet ring, fifteenth century. Similar patterns were used for images on gingerbread.

Tortae were dessert foods made with only the finest grade of bolted flour, since according to the royal accounts only *farina alba cribrata* was used. Eggs and cheese purchases also frequently appear in connection with tortae, and it is fairly clear that in the Polish context something filled or rolled is referred to, perhaps a type of strudel with a rich filling (although strudel is of Byzantine origin).[57] By contrast, the first use of *torte* in German, which dates from 1418, generally referred to small, flat cakes, although the medieval Latin *tortum* was sometimes equated with *gewundenes Gebäck*, a rolled pastry, as in strudel.

Another likely possibility, especially in the case of the royal registers dealing with purchases for Easter cakes (eight hundred eggs, one sack of fine flour, and 180 cheeses for one purchase alone) would be a cake resembling cheesecake.[58] Indeed, because both cheese strudel and cheesecake were known in medieval Poland, it is difficult to second-guess some of these royal shopping lists.

Of the categories just mentioned, trencher bread and white wheat rolls were the most popular, and there was an active trade in selling them in most large towns and cities. One's ability to pay was the only determining factor, not social position. According to the Wrocław bread assize introduced in 1362, one loaf of bread weighed about 300 to 350 grams, which is relatively small. On the other hand, such "standard" loaves must also have served as common trencher breads, and thus would have been consumed on a daily basis. The same Wrocław regulations also introduced a new unit of weight and stipulated that each loaf would cost 1 denar.[59]

St. Florian, patron saint of Cracow. Polish woodcut from 1515.

The fact that class was not necessarily a determining factor in the sort of bread one consumed is made quite clear in the accounts of Queen Jadwiga. Certainly, bread was the most important component of the menu for servants, retainers, and other members of the royal retinue. When the queen left Wawel Castle on one occasion, she ordered that the servants and retainers who accompanied her be given beer and good wheat bread. They were treated to a dinner in the parish church of St. Florian, where they joined the retinue of the king, who was there for the day to inspect the renovations at his expense.

We know from the accounts for the meal that 240 loaves of wheat bread were served. This was one of the major expenses for the servants aside from the beer, so it is possible that the rest of their meal consisted of items left over or sent down from the royal table. In any case, they enjoyed their food with good bread. More important, one must visualize the quantities of food that needed to be transported to the site. Were there bakeries conveniently situated nearby? Sometimes bread was baked right at the gristmill, which may offer a possible explanation, since there were mills in the neighborhood of the church. Fortunately, we know a great deal about the technical side of old Polish bread baking thanks to a large body of archaeological evidence. Ovens excavated from tenth-century sites at Gródek Nadbuzny, Santok, and Budziszyn have yielded a wealth of information about oven construction. The ovens were all essentially the same "beehive" type.[60]

Remains of bread peels, such as a nearly intact one from the eleventh century discovered at Gniezno, have provided vivid details about baking tools often only alluded to in medieval documents. A *praznica* or ceramic tray for roasting grain has come to light from an eleventh-century site at Bojanowo near Koscian, and a wooden grain chest (now much carbonized) from the same period was excavated at Brodno Stare in Warsaw.[61] This accumulation of data has helped Polish food historians to better imagine what the loaves were like based on existing technology, and in some cases to reconstruct old bread recipes.

Breads that resembled types known since the Neolithic era were being made in Poland at the same time. Called *podplomyki* in Polish (a term also applied to middling bread), and equated to breads baked *sub cinarus* (under ash) in medieval Latin texts, these were the

Polish version of the common ashcake. They were baked in hot coals (usually in some type of vessel buried in the coals) or between two hot stones. It is possible that no leavening was used, and if made with millet meal, they would have resembled, in appearance at least, American cornmeal johnnycakes. During periods of famine, the peasantry made ashcakes from knotgrass (*Polygonum aviculare*). The seeds were gathered and ground to flour, while the greens were used in pottages.

On the other hand, the early use of yeast was widespread in Poland, as confirmed linguistically in the old Slavic word *zakwas* (yeast or a yeasty ferment). The modern Polish term for yeast, *drożdże*, can lay similar claim to great age, and probably evolved from "thick" beer made from barley and wheat.[62] Thick beer was used both as a starter for making beer and as an ingredient in bread dough. We know that in the fourteenth and fifteenth centuries thick beer was added to dough by bakers to enhance sponginess. This dual use is why both bread and beer were often produced at grist and flour mills.[63]

Produce from the Kitchen Garden

By combing medieval Polish records for references to vegetables, it has been possible to compile a list of twenty-five species. This does not even touch upon the possibility of cultivar diversity, which we know existed but is difficult to ascertain from vague texts or from the archaeological record. In any case, such a broad representation of species is large enough to fully reject the theory strongly maintained in the literature (popular as well as scholarly) that medieval vegetable cultivation was undeveloped and that vegetable consumption was low. Quite the contrary: by the sixteenth century, which marked the introduction of so many new vegetables from Italy and the New World, there was less a shift to vegetable consumption than a simple expansion of the basic selection. The preference for vegetables did not change, but uses did, and many older vegetable types, like alexanders (in Polish *gker* or *gier*), were often supplanted in court cookery while they remained in the rural diet.[64]

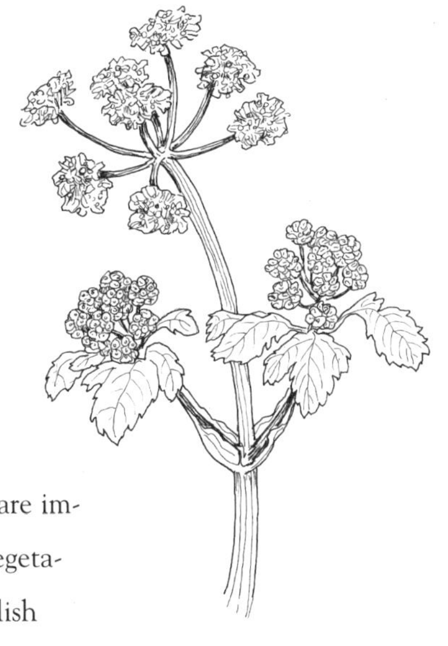

Alexanders.

One of the complicating factors for historians researching vegetable consumption in the Middle Ages is the vague manner in which the texts often refer to vegetables. Terms such as *olus, olera,* and *holera,* which appeared in works like Jan Stanko's 1472 handbook on Polish gardening, referred in general to vegetables for boiling. Similar vegetables are implied in the French *jardin potager,* and in modern Polish such vegetables normally include parsley, leeks, celery, and carrots. The Polish term for these vegetables, *włoszczyzna,* was introduced in the fifteenth century and originally meant "something Italian." In the fifteenth and sixteenth centuries it was the Italian kitchen garden that served as a model for the Polish, not surprisingly, because there was free exchange of ideas and seeds between the officials of the Polish Church and those in Italy. Indeed, Casimir the Great's pleasure gardens at Łobzów, his summer residence in the 1350s, was erected in the manner of an Italian villa suburbana. Before this, however, the main influence outside Poland appears to have been from Germany and Bohemia, or the general movement of ideas and foods up the Danube Basin from Byzantium.

References to medieval menus as well as to household expense accounts show that the daily menu in Poland included at least one vegetable either as a side dish or as an ingredient in a one-pot recipe. Field peas and cabbage are most frequently mentioned, but the most popular potherb was parsley. It was more common in Poland than in Western Europe, and its known curative properties for helping digestion and "cleansing the blood" guaranteed it a prominent position in many dishes of the period. It was also eaten to kill the odor of onions which lingered on medieval Poles after every large meal. From greens during the spring and summer to roots during the fall and winter, there was not a season when parsley was absent from the daily menu. It is interesting, too, that parsley was not viewed simply as an herb, but as a green vegetable to be eaten boiled. It was also used to color green sauces and to enhance or modify their flavors.

Likewise, onions figured largely in Polish diet, and the smell of onions cooking doubtless permeated the midday air of medieval Polish towns and villages. Onions were supplied to the royal kitchen daily and in liberal quantities. In terms of frequency, onions appear in the accounts just about the same number of times as parsley. Like parsley, onions were known to contain strong medicinal qualities, so the two may be seen as complementary in their perceived effects on health.

Other ingredients used for seasoning included dill—popular with crayfish and with mushrooms, garlic, leeks, and mustard—and Poles used both the seeds and the greens. Mustard seeds appear in the royal accounts on a daily basis, while garlic and leeks appear only on occasion. Szymon Syrennius mentioned Florence fennel as well, and even included a recipe for pickling it in vinegar and salt so that the "leaves and bulbs last all year around." He further noted that fennel was used in making mead. We know from linguistic evidence, however, that fennel was a latecomer to the Polish kitchen garden since its name in Polish, *koper włoski,* literally means "Italian dill."

It is not possible to discuss Polish condiments without mentioning poppy seeds, which were a source of cooking oil during fasting days (when animal lard could not be used), as well as an ingredient in cakes. Poppy and hemp seeds were commonly pressed together to make a blended cooking oil. Much of this processing was done at royal oil mills or at mills belonging to the magnates. Poppy seeds also appear frequently in culinary references, but especially during Lent. The seeds offered a way on abstinence days to give complex flavor to food that would otherwise contain meat products. Like the beet, the various uses of poppy seed came to Poland from Byzantium.

Peas and cabbages—consumed by all levels of Polish society during the Middle Ages regardless of affluence—were the most common Polish vegetable between the tenth and fifteenth centuries. The most widely used were the field types grown on low rambling vines that could be harvested with a scythe, threshed when dry, and then stored for winter. When medieval references noted peas, dry peas were intended. They were reconstituted for cooking by soaking in boiling water much the same way that beans are prepared today or ground to flour and used as a thickener in soups and sauces. Indeed, medieval pea varieties were not selected for their qualities as fresh vegetables, although both the pods and young peas were relished in spring cookery among the nobility. This was true in the royal household, for the royal kitchen gardeners are known to have exerted considerable effort in sending young peas (*pisum iuvenum*) as well as early carrots and radishes to the king's table, a fact confirmed by an entry dated June 14, 1394.[65] June vegetables are considered "early" by Polish standards. The royal accounts even differentiated peas by the terms *purrum* (plain), *electum* (choice), *mundum* (elegant), and *simplicior* (common).

Broad beans (fava beans) appear in the archaeological record almost as commonly as peas. They consist mostly of the type known in English as "horse" beans (*Vicia faba, var. equina*) or the *Vicia faba, var. minor.* These were not considered culinary quality, for the seeds are small, somewhat round like gray field peas, and generally dark brown when dry. They were used as animal fodder, but were commonly consumed by the peasants as well. These beans were rarely eaten fresh, but harvested as dry food for the winter and even ground for flour. However, in order to increase pod production, favas must be cropped at the top. These clippings of new leaves and buds were generally cooked as a potherb much like spinach and no doubt provided rural households with a welcome source of greens. The *equina* and *minor* varieties are not well suited to kitchen garden culture because of low productivity per plant, therefore this type of broad bean was generally grown in fields; after harvest the dead plants were often used as barn straw, a fact confirmed by archaeological evidence.[66] For kitchen purposes, the flat-seeded *maior* varieties were preferred. The plants are bushier and pod production is prodigious.

Cabbage was also eaten year round. For winter consumption, it was either stored in root cellars or converted to sauerkraut. Mikołaj Rej described a method for making sauerkraut that includes many elements also found in earlier medieval texts: "Having removed the outside leaves of some nice heads of cabbage, cut them in half and fit them neatly into a vat, spreading beet chards and dill between the layers."[67] (A recipe for a *compositum* using these raw ingredients is on page 150.) It should be noted that sauerkraut was made with the cabbage heads intact rather than shredding them before fermenting, as is the custom today. Pickled vegetables like sauerkraut were so important in medieval diet that the pagan Lithuanians even invoked a god called *Roguszys* to preside over these matters, as King Władysław Jagiełło well knew. But then, the pagan Lithuanians were known during the Middle Ages for their exquisite cookery, so it is not surprising that they should have gods to preside over each aspect of their cuisine.

During early spring, when cabbages began to sprout, the young buds and leaves (collards) were greatly relished for their flavor. The old Polish term for these young greens was *odroszli*, and they were quite often stewed or prepared in layered dishes like the compositum mentioned above. We also know that there were several varieties or types of cabbage: plain white cabbage (*caules albi*), "black" cabbage (*caules nigri*) — actually deep red or purple cabbage — and *caules compositi*, which were probably a type of primitive cauliflower believed to have been developed on Cyprus.

Various types of kale were also grown in medieval Poland, but the old Polish word for it, *brzoskiew*, meant "black cabbage," which naturally has led to considerable confusion concerning the exact meaning of the early texts. Later, once Polish adapted the term *jarmuz* (derived from German) for kale, confusion with red cabbage became less of a problem. In any case, this kale was most likely blue-gray, very dark green, or even slate black (like the black kales of Tuscany). Most kales could be planted, left in the ground all winter, and, if necessary, harvested from under the snow. Thus kale was a useful source of greens for nobles and peasants alike.

Another winter vegetable was the lentil, which was cultivated in the royal estates. It was most commonly consumed by the peasants and other lower classes in medieval Poland, although at times it was eaten by the royal family. The recipe for lentils stewed with skirrets (see page 157) illustrates how lentils would have been used in the context of a rural late winter meal.

Late winter was defined by a shift to Lenten dishes, and

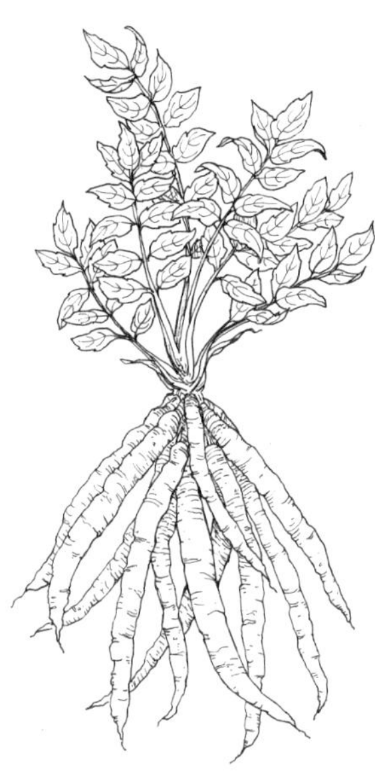

Skirrets.

among these certain vegetables appeared consistently. The most important were parsnips, alexanders (*Smyrnium olustratum*), and skirrets (*Sium sisarum*). The last two are no longer part of the Polish diet, although both still grow wild in many parts of the country. Alexanders (in Polish, *gier*) is a tall-growing relative of angelica, with large, dark leaves. It is resistant to cold and thus can provide greens all winter if covered with straw. Skirret, called *kruczmorka* in Polish, is a root vegetable that prefers damp sandy soil, and therefore can be cultivated on waste land or along drainage ditches around fields. With a flavor similar to parsnips, it was a good forage vegetable that required little care. Szymon Syrennius claimed that skirret was introduced to Poland from Moguncja or Mainz (Moguntiacum), which in itself points to an interesting and convoluted history since the plant actually originated in East Asia.[68] In any event, all three vegetables were eaten with fish.

Carrots are not mentioned very often in Polish sources dating from the fourteenth and fifteenth centuries. Carrots may have been implied under the general term *olera* (vegetables for boiling), but even the archaeological record is slim because the seeds do not preserve well in the ground and cannot be differentiated from wild carrot (Queen Anne's lace). Carrots are only mentioned four times in the accounts of King Władysław Jagiełło and Queen Jadwiga, yet in each case the implication is that these are specially cultivated and brought early to market. We also know from carrot strains surviving from the Middle Ages that the mature carrots were quite large and resembled parsnips, as in the case of the *Küttiger Rüebli* of Switzerland. Since medieval carrots were white or yellow (such as the *carotte jaune longue* or "lemon" carrot of Flanders), the young ones were doubtless the best to eat and would have been cooked in ways similar to parsnips. The old Polish white carrot, designated biała zielongłowa ("green-topped white") by horticulturists, actually resembles a parsnip with green shoulders. Its flavor is sweet and delicate.

Beets are mentioned more frequently than carrots, but usually in combination with other vegetables. The old Polish word *cwikla* (from Latin *cicla*) referred to the entire plant, and may have alluded to chard or spinach beets, a type of beet known since classical antiquity. The Latin word *cicla* traces to Punic (Phoenician), thus providing a long genealogy for a vegetable so basic to the Polish diet. The medieval term for the root part was *cwikielka;* in modern Polish it is known as *burak*. Surprisingly, no material relating to pickling beets has been found in fourteenth- and fifteenth-century sources, although the subject is treated exhaustively by Mikołaj Rej in the sixteenth century.

Küttiger Rüebli.

Beet soup or *barszcz* (commonly Germanized in the United States as borscht) never appeared on the royal table during the reign of the Jagiellonian kings, nor was it consumed by the royal servants. Furthermore, it was not even made with beets in its original form, but from the European cow parsnip (*Heracleum sphondylium*) — also called barszcz in Polish — that grows on damp ground.[69] Its roots were collected in May for stewing with meat, the shoots and young leaves were cooked as greens, and the unopened flower peduncles were eaten as a vegetable or added to soups and pottages. Szymon Syrennius discussed this plant in his herbal and further stated that soups made with it were highly valued in Poland, Lithuania, and Russia. During the Middle Ages it was prepared in soup by itself or it was cooked in chicken stock with such additions as egg yolks, cream, or millet meal. The dry leaves exude a sweet substance that was used to create sweet-sour flavors, especially when used with vinegar. The adaptation of cow parsnips to Polish cookery appears to have come from Lithuania.

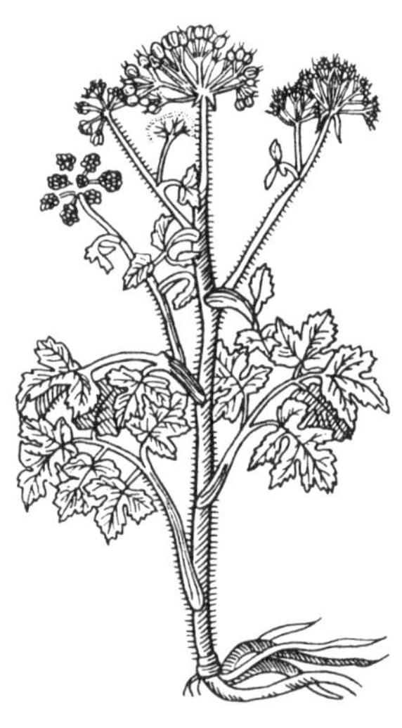

Barszcz from the herbal of Syrennius.

Another wild plant called "water" barszcz or *niedzwiedzia łapa* ("bear's paw") belongs to a related species (*Heracleum mantegazzianum*) and was also used to make a similar soup, although it was considered best when cooked with meat. Collecting and selling these and other wild plants like *dziki szczaw*—in English, buckler-leaved sorrel (*Rumex scutatus*), lamb's quarters (*Chenopodium album*), and *locyga/loczyga* or nipplewort (*Lapsana communis*)—were important features of village economy. But where does this leave the beet soup we know today? Mikołaj Rej mentioned a "broth from pickled beets" in the sixteenth century, but it was not known in all parts of Poland. The evolution of barszcz into a recipe using sour beets is of much later date than most Poles would suspect. In fact, the well-known *barszcz białoruski* (beet soup with meat, cabbage, eggs, and sour cream) did not arrive in Poland from Russia until the nineteenth century.

Rutabagas, turnips, large black radishes (both long and turnip-shaped varieties), and small delicate white radishes appeared quite frequently on Polish medieval menus. Radishes were often cooked like other root vegetables; the tops were also cooked as greens. Yet it is the turnip that served as the "potato" of medieval Polish cookery, the recipe for turnip gruel (see page 200) being an example of how it was prepared to be eaten with sops.

Buckler-leafed sorrel.

In terms of Polish culture, the turnip is also connected with some of the earliest folk myths. For example, the Polish diminutive *rzepka* (from *rzepa*, an old word for turnip) was claimed in the chronicle of Gallus Anonymus to derive from Rzepka, the name of the first mother of the Piast dynasty, the founding rulers of Poland. This false etymology, which created a noble yet peasant origin for the vegetable, has often clouded Polish food history, and stands in open contrast to the fact that turnips were not just peasant fare; they were also consumed at the royal court frequently. The other fact obvious from the royal records is that turnips were mostly purchased, which means that they were not raised in the royal estates. In his 1590 treatise on Silesian agriculture, Martin Grosser discussed turnips in terms of strains and varieties, a point pertinent to this discussion.[70] Furthermore, he observed that turnips were used as payment in feudal lease agreements, which would only confirm the fact that turnips were far more valuable than many sources imply. Just the same, the crop was not easy to measure or to predict, and the confusion in period records certainly accounts for this.

The unpredictability of the turnip crop is quite evident from Grosser's observations. He described three basic types: the best sort, which yielded low crops, and a third, least desirable one that was in his words "watery." This last variety was not desirable because it became moldy and rotted easily in storage. The lack of a reliable high-yielding turnip that stored well may be one key to understanding why turnips are mentioned the way they are in medieval records. Their presence in the Polish diet did not increase until intensive farming became commonplace in the twelfth century as a result of improved networking between monasteries, not to mention the appearance of well-trained horticulturists (mostly German) who settled on Polish territory at that time.

At the Polish court, radishes appear to have been more popular than turnips, especially large long white and black varieties. We know that the king was able to purchase young radishes as early as March, which implies that Polish gardeners were already familiar with the techniques of cold-frame culture. A preference for strong radish tastes in food is also evident in the former popularity of nipplewort, a

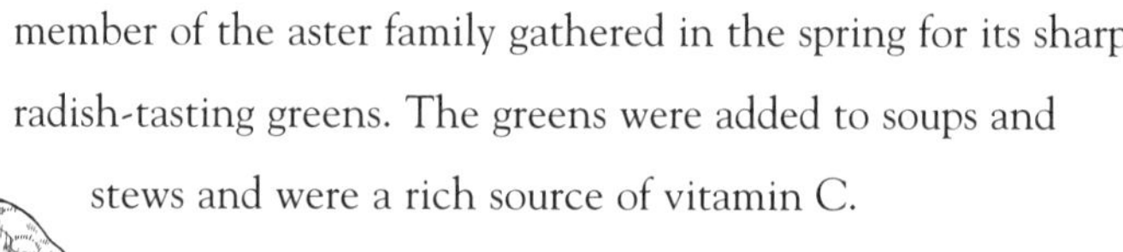

*Cracow lettuce (*Lactuca sativa, *var.* cracoviensis*), an old strain of Polish lettuce.*

member of the aster family gathered in the spring for its sharp radish-tasting greens. The greens were added to soups and stews and were a rich source of vitamin C.

Regarding cold-frame gardening, we also know from a royal account that in February 1415 when King Władysław Jagiełło and his entourage stayed with the military garrison at Nowy Korczyn, they were served lettuce from the garrison gardens. All of this should add more proof to the argument that the level of Polish horticulture was by no means undeveloped, and that Poles were eating many vegetables long before Queen Bona Sforza arrived from Italy.

The most telling proof of this is the early Polish documentation for cucumbers, as seeds have been found in Polish archaeological sites dating to the ninth century A.D. Cucumbers are not the easiest vegetables to cultivate, yet they are one of the most prominent vegetables in the medieval Polish diet. Curiously, in the fourteenth century, they were almost always mentioned in connection with fruit, which seems to imply that they were consumed like apples, fresh during or after the meal. The royal accounts taken at Korczyn in 1389 stated this quite clearly: "to pears and cucumbers for her majesty's dinner and dessert."[71] The cucumbers were evidently served with fresh pears, King Władysław Jagiełło's favorite fruit.

The combination of cucumbers and honey must have been known by this time, too, for at least one reference from the same royal accounts at Korczyn has surfaced in connection with a dish made from cucumbers, pears, and honey (see recipe on page 153). The resulting mixture tastes very much like ripe melons. That cucumbers were treated like melons is evident from the fact that they were served with melons on occasion, as verified in the royal register for the Wislica garrison in 1414.[72]

Oddly, there are no references from the medieval period to pickled cucumbers, which we would expect, given that pickling them is a very old technique. We know that cabbage and even shredded turnips were pickled, so it is hard to imagine this not being common knowledge. In the sixteenth century, Mikołaj Rej discussed salting cucumbers in such a way that would assume his readers well understood the entire process: "pickle cucumbers in salt, add some dill and sour cherry or oak leaves — the leaves make the pickles crisper."[73] There is no mystery that we have here the famous Polish dill pickles, yet pickled cucumbers do not even appear as ingredients in the royal kitchen. The royal family ate sauerkraut, which only makes this absence of pickles all the more puzzling. It is possible that the cucumbers eaten in medieval Poland were distinctly different from the green warty type used later for pickling and illustrated in Leonhard Fuchs' *De historia stirpium* (1542). The seeds found in archaeological sites would not reveal this because the genus and species are most likely the same. However, the physical characteristics could be quite dissimilar.

An explanation may require going back in the history of the cucumber. Cucumbers originated in the Himalayan region and one of the oldest and most archaic sorts still cultivated there is the so-called Sikkim cucumber (*Cucumis sativus, var. sikkimensis*), also known as the Russian netted cucumber. This short season cucumber, or something like it, may have been known to medieval Poles, and it does not pickle well at any stage of development. It was grown in Russia and Western Asia well into the nineteenth century and in form resembles a small muskmelon with brown, netted skin. The fruit has white flesh and a melonlike flavor, but the small, immature fruit, which would otherwise make decent cornichons, is extremely bitter. Perhaps the smooth-skinned types of cucumbers better suited to pickling—and therefore more valuable as a winter food—were not introduced into Poland until the late Middle Ages.

Another puzzle surfaces in the use of the term *boleti,* which was used in the royal accounts to indicate mushrooms. However, *boleti* covered all types, thus the precise species is not clear. This is especially annoying from a research standpoint, considering that there are some thirty-one edible mushrooms known to grow in Polish forests. However, April mushrooms were sometimes designated *smarze,* as in the case of an entry in the garrison records of Korczyn in 1394. A specific variety was intended, perhaps morels. In any event, mushrooms gathered from the wild were consumed from early spring until late fall. They were an integral part of Polish medieval cookery because they could be eaten on fasting days. They were treated as vegetables in side dishes and as components of sauces, and were often cooked with meat.

Fruits and Nuts

The most frequently mentioned fruits in the fourteenth and fifteenth centuries were apples, pears, plums, and cherries (both sweet and sour), and hazelnuts. At court, they were served either raw or cooked almost always after the main meal. Hazelnuts were often pressed for their oil, which was used at court like olive oil, especially in recipes containing nuts. Baked apples or apples candied in honey were commonly eaten on fasting days. Mikołaj Rej also noted that apples were cooked and eaten as a puree and used as stuffing for roast goose; they also could be dried and stored in boxes for consumption all year.

According to the thirteenth-century *Vita ducissae Annae*, Duchess Anna of Silesia gathered various fruits in the autumn specifically for the purpose of making electuaries or fruit butters and she was accomplished in making many sorts of fruit confections. Indeed, fruit in some form appeared on the menus of the nobility all year. Only in the months of April, May, and June are orchard fruits missing.

The menu of King Władysław Jagiełło and Queen Jadwiga rarely included walnuts, yet archaeological remains prove that walnut trees were planted in Poland during this period. Toward the end of the fifteenth century documentation of walnuts appears more regularly. And during the early sixteenth century, walnuts are mentioned quite commonly in the records of Prince Sigismund I (reigned 1506–1548) while he held court at Budziszyn. Also at Budziszyn, we find direct references to consumption of peaches, a fruit totally ignored in other Polish records. Yet the presence of peach pits in many earlier archaeological sites suggests that, like walnuts, they were widely cultivated in Polish orchards.

Regarding exotic fruits, only raisins, almonds, and figs seem to have been known in the fourteenth century. Lemons and oranges are mentioned in royal records only in the following century, and there they are strictly ingredients rather than dessert foods. For example, the account book of the city of Lvov contains an early fifteenth-century reference to purchasing lemons for the king's kitchen. In the accounts of Prince Sigismund I a reference to oranges stated specifically, "oranges for cooking."[74] These oranges were for recipes, not fruit served at the table. What is more, these oranges were expensive because three were valued at the same price as six to eight chickens.

Figs and almonds often show up as gift foods, doubtless due to their cost. In the 1394 register of Henryk of Rogów, the royal treasurer, it was noted that King Władysław Jagiełło ordered him to purchase figs and almonds for Italian painters who were working on a fresco for a church in Cracow at the time. This gesture has the appearance of a special favor.

Almonds were also used as a source of oil in the royal kitchen, although royal accounts do not mention them on a regular basis until the fifteenth century. The accounts of Henryk of Rogów show that from June 20, 1393, until February 13, 1395, he made copious purchases of almonds for the king, evidently to satisfy Queen Jadwiga's passion for French and Hungarian cookery. Her reign was later referred to as a period of great lavishness, for the almonds were used almost exclusively for their oil and milk.[75] Her extravagance has been blamed on Janusz of Boturzyn, the queen's chef, who was accorded unusual dignities. His name appeared in a list of nobles on a 1396 document ordered by Queen Jadwiga and therefore he may have been a member of the *szlachta* (in the 1500s there was a noble family by the name of Boturzyński from the same place with the clan arms *Łzawa*). He is documented as royal chef for the years 1394, 1395, and 1397, although the actual length of his service at court is not known. He may have come with the queen from Hungary as part of her marriage settlement. Whatever his origins, doubtless Janusz was well versed in French and Hungarian court cuisine, among other things, and was quite capable of compiling his own recipe book since he spoke several languages, including Latin.

Jadwiga's culinary enthusiasm appears to have carried over into other projects, as is evident from attempts to plant wine grapes and apricots in the royal orchards at Proszowice in 1394. Extracts from the pits of the yellow apricot (the variety mentioned in the accounts) can give a bitter almond flavor to foods; undoubtedly the queen was acquainted with this fact.

The only wild fruits that consistently appear in the royal accounts are strawberries. We know from market regulations, however, that blueberries were also gathered and sold extensively. The inventories of the Order of Teutonic Knights at Malbork in northern Poland list many more wild fruits: raspberries, sloes, cranberries, and rowans, to name a few. But these fruits were purchased for their juices to make or to flavor various distilled or fermented beverages.

Now that we have surveyed the range of ingredients consumed in medieval Poland, as well as the manner in which many of them were prepared, let us transform this material into actual recipes and dishes. The thirty-five recipes that appear in the next section evolved from a desire to explore the food combinations and seasonings, as well as meal preparation techniques, of medieval Poland.

Medieval Recipes in the Polish Style

William Woys Weaver

183 *Thick Beer or Sourdough Starter (Gęstwina z Drożdzy)*

184 *Turnip Kugel (Kugiel z Rzepki)**

187 *Tripe in Sauerkraut (Flaczki w Kiszonej Kapuście)*

190 *Polish Sauce for Fast Days and Tripe (Polski Sos na Dni Postne i Do Flaków)*

191 *Court Dish of Baked Fruit (Pieczone Owoce po Królewsku)**

192 *Skirrets Stewed with Fish (Kruczmorka Duszona z Ryby)**

194 *Stewed Pig Tails with Buckwheat Gruel (Wieprzowe Ogony Duszone z Kaszą Gryczaną)*

196 *Pomeranian Trójniak (Trójniak Pomorski)**

197 *Hungarian-Style Spit-Roasted Shoulder of Venison (Mostek Jeleni z Rożna po Węgiersku)**

199 *Cubeb Vinegar (Ocet Kubebowy)**

200 *Turnip Gruel (Kleik z Rzepy)**

Recipes marked with * are considered the most likely to appeal to modern palates.

There is something compelling about the unusual and rather exotic flavors that once characterized Poland's old court cookery; there is simply no better way to understand them than to experience the food firsthand. One might say that this truism did not strike home for me until a fortuitous meal at the famed U Wierzynka in Cracow, where I was able to try *zając do zimnej zastawy* (cold stuffed hare), a buffet dish from the waning days of the Austro-Hungarian empire entwined in the story of my great-grandfather's elopement with a governess.

Dealing with medieval recipes is often an exercise in curious abstractions. As Bruno Laurioux has pointed out in his recent voluminous study of Taillevent, manuscript texts may have been created for a discrete patron with material representing everything from the practical to the fantastic. It is probably wise not to accept such collections as broadly representative, but rather to see them only in terms of their narrowest context. Several able food historians have tackled this issue head-on. The efforts of the late Rudolf Grewe with old Spanish texts, Jean-Louis Flandrin's work on French medieval cookery, and Constance Hieatt's excursions into English sources all spring to mind.

Indeed, I shall never forget a medieval Catalan dinner based on the *Libre de Sent Soví* prepared by Rudolf Grewe and served with appropriately selected wines. That feast from the 1380s, so radically different from Polish cookery of the same period, will always stand out as one of the culinary highlights of all my eating experiences. Nor will I ever forget the comment of Dutch medievalist Johanna Maria Van Winter as we were challenged during a banquet in Cardiff Castle to surrender to platters of whole mackerel replete with fixings in the style of the fourteenth century. As we were armed only with knives and trenchers of bread, and not a fork in sight, an appalled silence descended on my table. Johanna Maria smiled cheerfully and said, "I have a medieval stomach." With that, she proceeded to demolish the fish.

It may take a medieval stomach to give proper attendance to the finer points of cookery from this period. Certainly there is a persistent temptation on the part of recipe reconstructionists to cast their fare in a light most favorable to the present age. Constance Hieatt's *An Ordinance of Pottage* (1988), based on an untitled fifteenth-century codex at Yale, is probably the most accessible source to the general reader which also skirts some of these pitfalls. Yet Hieatt is quite aware that all of her interpretations are just that. And so, I cannot claim more for the recipes here.

In any case, my recipes are as "archaeologically correct" as possible. By that I mean that my spelt flour was hand ground from my own harvests of *Triticum spelta, var. bingensium* (the so-called Hildegard of Bingen's spelt), the oldest strain I could find. Oat flour was made from *owies szorstki* (*Avena strigosa*), one of the most primitive of the medieval types still available. Indeed, most of the plant ingredients came directly from my kitchen garden, even to the skirrets, the alexanders, the Good-King-Henry, the peas and broad beans, the old varieties of white carrot, the rare cabbages, and the Carpathian rocombole garlic (of which I grow several varieties). Having the right ingredients at my fingertips, I made no effort to reconfigure the dishes according to modern precepts of fashion or nutrition or healthy diet, for there is a definite scientific and perhaps a culinary need to know what this old food was like in its unadulterated condition.

This also applies to the method for preparing saffron wafers (the success of which owes more to technique than to ingredients), as well as the procedure for spit-roasting meat, one of the key elements of medieval Polish cookery. Medievalists tend to skim past these bald realities in defense of almond milk and other such period extravagances that are easier for the modern mind to grasp, but the truth is, fat pervaded the medieval table, from the finest butter-basted piglets down to the rankest lard. Fat takes precedence over all the ingredients of the kitchen garden that I painstakingly raised by hand because without it, they would not have been relished at all.

Yet, in defense of the fat, keep in mind that medieval bodies burned calories more abundantly given the hard physical nature of everyday work, the penetrating cold of buildings without central heat, and the basic bodily need to digest large amount of coarse bread and grains. Added to this was the prevailing attitude (still common in some nonindustrialized countries) that plumpness equaled good health, especially among men. Only the wretchedly poor and sick were thin.

Simply put, these are teaching recipes that have been tailored to convey the peculiar Polish character of food from the Middle Ages. Although they are total recreations, they are well based in historical fact. Recipe titles have been translated into modern Polish because I did not want the reader to imagine that these titles were lifted from a medieval cookbook. I was obliged to follow this course because no Polish cookery texts have survived from the medieval period, even though we know that such books existed and were probably written in Latin.

Indeed, the oldest known cookbook in Polish, the *Kuchmistrzostwo* (The Art of Cooking and Cellaring) was not published until 1532. It was printed at Cracow and survives today in the form of a collection of loose pages from one lone copy.[1] The *Kuchmistrzostwo* is actually a translation of the bestselling *Küchenmeisterei* first issued at Nuremberg in November 1485 by Peter Wagner.[2] Within a short period of time, the book evolved into a somewhat expanded form now called by bibliographers the "False Platina." It earned this dubious honor because it was claimed (quite fraudulently) by the Strasburg printer who issued it in the 1500s that the author was Bartolomeo Sacchi di Piadena, the venerable Italian humanist who published a famous recipe book in 1474 under the pen name Platina Cremonensis. The Polish edition of 1532 is based on the "False Platina." However, the original Platina, published in Latin, did influence cookery among Poland's nobility, and copies of Platina are known to have existed in many private libraries. In fact, the first original Polish cookbook was also modeled on earlier Latin works. It was written by Stanisław Czerniecki under the Latin title *Compendium Fercolorum* (Cracow, 1682). A member of the Polish szlachta, Czerniecki served as royal secretary to King Jan III Sobieski.

The absence or doubtful nature of material freed my hands from court showpieces of the sort commonly treated in cookbooks dealing with food of the Middle Ages, as well as from a narrow textualist mentality. A myopic focus on obscure words or phrases sometimes misses the larger picture, or indeed the obvious, such as the unfortunate yet widespread presumption that Brussels sprouts (as we know them) existed prior to their genetic mutation in the 1780s. Using historical sources as well as living informants in Poland, I was thus able to explore everyday cookery as well as middle-class and manor foods, not to mention court dishes of a non-banquet character, the sort of thing, for example, that the royal family might eat in its privy chambers when it was not entertaining the full entourage before a standing crowd of onlookers. There are many pitfalls in such free interpretations and they demand an extremely cautious approach. There were many recipes I did not dare undertake. "Where in doubt, leave it out" prevailed, for it is no use creating new myths to replace old ones.

A case in point is Toruń gingerbread, which I had wanted to include in all its gilded sumptuousness. There are numerous extant recipes for making this culinary delight, each so different from the others that it became difficult to extract a sense of what may survive as a medieval original and what may represent later accretions. Due to its festive nature, especially its traditional connection with Christmas, gingerbread tends to remain quite conservative in its composition and general presentation.[3] This old-fashioned and nostalgic quality lies behind the popularity of gingerbread even today. Unfortunately for the food historian, gingerbread recipes belonged to the gingerbread bakers, who were of course organized into guilds. Their recipes were proprietary and taught to apprentices orally. While large numbers of professional recipes for Toruń gingerbread survive from the nineteenth century, when such things were thought worthy of writing down, they cannot be called medieval. Even the few recipes for Toruń gingerbread dating from the 1550s cannot be fully trusted, since they resemble similar preparations from Nuremberg and elsewhere. The ethnographic museum in Toruń owns one of the finest collections of gingerbread molds in Europe, but very few of the molds predate 1500.

The Polish gingerbread story has an interesting twist that is outside the scope of this study but relevant to the ways in which Poles took foreign ideas and reinvented them. Toruń gingerbread was sometimes baked in sheets like giant cookies then laid over a succession of fillings made from spiced plum butter, marzipan, and various mixtures of ground nuts. This was then baked so that it solidified into one soft cake. The cake was iced like *Basler Leckerli* (a type of Swiss gingerbread) and sliced into bite-sized pieces. Polish cooks evidently adapted this idea from related "cakes" (made with cookie dough rather than gingerbread) found in several eighteenth-century German cookbooks.[4] The story of Polish medieval cookery is a similar story of creative adaptation: simple things artfully reshaped to fit a Polish notion of appropriate taste.

Gruel of Mixed Grains (Kasza z Różnych Ziaren)

This genre of dish is often referred to in Polish Latin texts as gruellum compositum, *with no clear indication of grain type or precise texture. However, field interviews now housed in Polish ethnographic archives underscore the persistence of a wide variety of peasant recipes that would conform to this once-popular medieval side dish. The one chosen here is indeed a mixture. The intention was to serve the gruel with meat and of course with wheat beer. The consistency could be thick, as given in the directions below, or the gruel could be thinned with pan drippings or with additional meat stock. It must be thick enough, however, to be sopped up with bread.*

*This recipe represents everyday fare as opposed to a festive or banquet dish. It does not include an array of exotic spices but relies instead on local ingredients for its robust flavors. The most unusual of these ingredients is Good-King-Henry (*Chenopodium bonus-henricus*), which makes an excellent richly flavored sauce. It is often compared with spinach, but the two are not the same. The best parts of Good-King-Henry are the small leaves, which turn a strong green when cooked and lend their distinctive color to the recipe.*

Serves 4 to 6

1 pound (500 g) wheat groats coarsely broken (see note)

2 quarts (2 liters) strained ham or meat stock

6 ounces (175 g) Wrocław trencher bread (page 180) or any dense rye bread that is not flavored with caraway

6 ounces (175 g) Good-King-Henry (small leaves and tender shoots)

1 cup (100 g) chopped smallage leaves (leaves of soup celery)

½ cup (50 g) minced parsley

½ cup (100 g) coarsely chopped onion

1 teaspoon minced rocombole garlic

1½ cups (265 g) millet kasha

2 tablespoons (30 ml) apple cider vinegar

coarsely ground pepper and salt to taste

Put the groats in a deep bowl and cover with boiling water. Soak 2 to 3 hours or until the grains begin to swell. Drain the groats and put them in a deep stewing pan with 2 cups (500 ml) of ham stock and 2 cups (500 ml) of water. Bring to a gentle boil and cook uncovered over medium heat for about 1 hour, or until tender.

While the groats are cooking, put the bread in a bowl and cover with 2 cups (500 ml) of boiling ham stock. Let the bread soak until soft (about 30 minutes).

Put the Good-King-Henry, smallage, parsley, onion, and garlic in a stewing pan with 3 cups (750 ml) of ham stock, cover, and cook for 15 minutes over medium heat. Combine the vegetables and their liquid with the bread and its liquid, and puree to as fine a consistency as possible. Add this to the pot with the cooked groats, then add the millet and any remaining ham stock (about 1 cup/250 ml). Continue cooking for 20 to 25 minutes or until the millet is tender and the gruel is thick. Stir often to keep the mixture from scorching on the bottom. Additional ham stock or water may be added.

When the millet is thoroughly cooked, add the vinegar and pepper. Be generous with the pepper. Season with salt.

Note: For authenticity's sake, Polish wheat (*Triticum polonicum*)—a good boiling groat—or poulard wheat (*Triticum turgidum*) can be used. The latter is very small-grained and resembles rice when cooked. These old wheats were used by both the peasants and the rural nobility mostly as groats or grits or for pasta flour. To create the broken texture, mash the groats in a mortar so that large portions of the berries are broken in half or into small bits. The texture need not be even.

Good-King-Henry.

Courtier's Pottage (Strawa Dworzanina)

This one-pot dinner for rich peasants or petty nobles is made with millet kasha, which must have the consistency of coarse cornmeal so that it cooks down thick. The most historically appropriate dry peas would be those that are small and red-brown or violet-brown in color. The tiny medieval field pea known in Sweden as Jämtlands Gra Forderärt (Jämtland gray fodder pea) or the old English Carling pea are recommended. The Swedish pea would represent a true peasant's pea, while the English variety would represent a better garden sort.

Serves 4 to 6

1 cup (200 g) small, dry field peas

4 cups (700 g) millet kasha

8 ounces (250 g) streaky bacon, diced small

½ cup (100 g) coarsely chopped onion

2 tablespoons (30 ml) vinegar

1 cup (100 g) minced parsley

salt and black pepper to taste

Cover the peas with boiling water and let stand overnight. The next day, drain and cook in salted water until tender (about 25 to 30 minutes). While the peas are cooking, put the millet in a deep stewing pan and pour 5 cups (1.25 liters) of boiling water over it. Cook over medium heat and stir from time to time to keep the millet from sticking to the bottom. Add more water if necessary, and beat vigorously to create a smooth texture. The millet should become very thick (like polenta) after about 40 minutes total cooking time.

After the peas have boiled, drain and add them to the millet. Clean the pan in which the peas were cooked and add the bacon. Brown the bacon lightly for 5 minutes, then add the onion and cover. After the onion is tender (about 3 minutes), add this to the millet, including all the drippings from the bacon. Add the vinegar and parsley, and season to taste. Pour the pottage into a large, shallow serving dish. Guests serve themselves at the table from the common bowl.

Compositum of Cabbage, Chard, Dill, and Mushrooms (Komposjtum z Kapusty, Ćwikły, Kopru i Grzybów) *

This recipe for a middle-class burgher family in a large city like Cracow is both a fasting dish for meatless days and a side dish for fish. A semi-dry white Hungarian or Rumanian wine would have appeared on the table in wealthier households, at least on special occasions.

Surviving foodways practices among peasants in Poland and other parts of Central Europe support the idea that composita *were always baked or braised, usually in large, covered earthenware pots. Recipes that have survived elsewhere in Europe, especially in Switzerland and southern Germany, share one common feature: the ingredients are arranged in layers. The Romans and Byzantine Greeks also made dishes of this type, owing to the recipe's flexibility. This one can be converted into a meat dish by adding slices of sausage instead of mushrooms.*

Serves 4 to 6

---

1 medium onion cut in half lengthwise, then cut into thin slices

8 cups (680 g) white cabbage shredded as for sauerkraut

4 cups (200 g) chard shredded as for sauerkraut

1/4 cup (25g) finely minced lovage

1 cup (100 g) chopped dill

4 ounces (125 g) mixed wild mushrooms, coarsely chopped

1/4 cup (60 ml) garlic-flavored vinegar

4 tablespoons (60 g) lightly salted butter

salt and pepper to taste

Preheat the oven to 375°F (190°C). Scatter half of the onion over the bottom of a heavy, 4-quart (4-liter) baking pot, preferably earthenware. Scatter one-third of the cabbage over this, then one-third of the chard. Sprinkle half of the lovage and dill over this, then cover the mixture with the mushrooms. Scatter the remaining onions over this, another one-third of the cabbage, and all the remaining chard, lovage, and dill. Cover with the rest of the cabbage, and add 1 cup (250 ml) of water and the vinegar. Cut the butter into thin pieces and dot the top of the cabbage with them. Cover the pot with a tight lid and bake in the oven for 45 minutes. Then stir the mixture and serve immediately.

Stew of Parsnips, Leeks, and Alexanders (Duszony Por z Pasternak i Gier)

This fasting dish, designed to take timely advantage of garden produce available during the early spring, would be a typical one-pot meal for a noble family living on a large rural manor in Little Poland. Cheese dumplings (see recipe page 152) may have been served with this as a substitute for meat. The menu would also have included a pot of mush made with millet kasha, perhaps boiled in milk rather than water.

Alexanders, one of the ingredients in this dish, looks very much like angelica, but the taste of the leaves resembles cubeb, a popular spice in the Middle Ages. Since alexanders is slightly bitter, it was often played against the sweetness of honey or used to counter the strong taste of "black" recipes—that is, recipes containing blood. In this stew, which is both sweet and aromatic, the alexanders provides a somewhat Oriental accent consistent with the old Polish fascination for things Asian.

Serves 4 to 6

4 pounds (2 kg) leek greens (use the leafy part that is normally discarded)

3 pounds (1.5 kg) small parsnips, trimmed, pared, and sliced on a slant to resemble thick potato chips

2 cups (175 g) sliced leek, white part only

2 cups (175 g) white cabbage shredded as for sauerkraut

1 cup (200 g) coarsely chopped onion

4 cloves rocombole garlic sliced in half lengthwise

6 tablespoons (90 ml) honey

1/8 teaspoon ground saffron

1/2 teaspoon ground cinnamon

1/2 teaspoon ground cumin

1 tablespoon salt

2 tablespoons (30 ml) Hungarian white wine vinegar

1 cup (100 g) coarsely chopped alexanders (leaves and small stems only)

Boil the leek greens in 1 gallon (4 liters) of water until soft and until the stock is reduced by one-fourth (about 1 hour). Strain and reserve the liquid, discarding the leek greens. Put the stock in a stewing pot with the parsnips, sliced leeks, cabbage, onion, and garlic. Cover and stew 45 minutes, or until the parsnips are tender, then add the honey, saffron, cinnamon, cumin, salt, and vinegar. Stew 15 minutes, then add the alexanders. Let the alexanders cook for about 5 minutes, then serve immediately over pieces of stale manchet bread or cheese dumplings (see following recipe).

Cheese Dumplings (Kluski z Bryndzą) *

These dumplings have been suggested as an accompaniment to the manor dish above. The cheese dumplings absorb flavors, neutralize the sharpness of the herbs, and help to soften the overall flavor of this dish. This interplay of tastes was considered an important feature in Polish medieval cookery, particularly in households with sophisticated kitchens. Not that everyday cooking was fancy, even for the well-off. In both cases, the manor fare emphasizes frugality. This aspect should be contrasted against the more elaborate dishes served to important guests, as in the conceit of cucumber and pears (page 153) or the spit-roasted marinated venison (page 197).

Yield: 32 to 36 dumplings (serves 8 to 10)

---

1 cup (125 g) bread crumbs

1 cup (125 g) barley flour

1 teaspoon ground mace

4 tablespoons (60 g) lightly salted butter

2 pounds (1 kg) bryndzą *farmer's cheese or any feta-type cheese*

8 chicken egg yolks or 4 goose egg yolks

Mix the bread crumbs, flour, and mace in a large work bowl. Melt the butter and combine with the crumbs, mixing thoroughly until the mixture is loose. Grate the cheese on the small holes of a vegetable grater and add this to the crumbs. Beat the yolks until frothy, then combine with the mixture. Work this with the hands into a soft paste. Mold the dumplings so that each weighs about 2 ounces (60 g) and resembles a long potato or gefilte fish. Set the dumplings on a baking sheet or large plate to dry for about 20 minutes.

While the dumplings are drying, bring 1 gallon (4 liters) of salted water to a rolling boil in a large stewpan or soup kettle. Turn back the heat to medium-low so that the water is barely quivering. Add the dumplings. When they rise to the surface (in about 15 minutes), they are done. For each individual, place 2 or 3 dumplings in a bowl and serve the parsnip stew over them. These dumplings should be served immediately; once they are cold, they become tough and heavy.

Pears Stewed with Cucumbers and Figs (Gruszki Duszone z Ogórkami i Figami) *

This court dish, which was mentioned in the records of the royal garrison at Korczyn in 1389, is not just a compote. It is a conceit meant to imitate poached melon, doubtless something similar to a casaba, and therefore draws its inspiration from Byzantium or the eastern Mediterranean. After the opening of trade with Constantinople in the 960s, Byzantine goods and culinary ideas reached the Polish royal court through overland trade routes from the Black Sea.

Serves 4 to 6

4 cups (500 g) cucumbers, pared, seeded, and diced

1 cup (175 g) dried figs, chopped

1 cup (250 ml) honey

⅛ teaspoon ground cloves

½ teaspoon ground cinnamon

4 cups (750 g) under-ripe pears, pared, cored, and diced

1 tablespoon (15 ml) rosewater

fresh cream (optional)

Put the cucumbers, figs, honey, cloves, cinnamon and 1 cup (250 ml) of water in a stewpan. Cover and cook gently over medium-low heat until the cucumbers are tender (about 20 minutes). Add the pears and cover. Continue to cook the mixture for 5 minutes, or until the pears are hot, then remove from heat. The cucumbers and pears should have a similar texture. Let the compote cool to room temperature, then add the rosewater. Serve at room temperature either as a side dish for a banquet or as a dessert with fresh cream. At the medieval Polish table the cream would have been served from a small ewer.

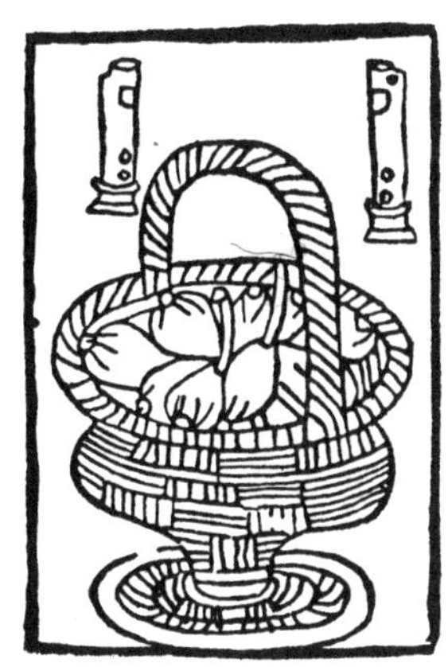

Basket of figs.

Chicken Baked with Prunes (Kurczak Pieczony z Suszonymi Śliwkami) *

This dish, first mentioned in a fourteenth-century menu from Weissenfels in Saxony, was just one of many dishes prepared for a two-day reception in honor of the Bishop of Zeitz.[5] *According to subsequent ethnographic evidence, as well as archaeological finds in the form of covered earthenware baking pans, similar dishes were also prepared farther east in Poland. This would have been true for the types of menus served to the prince-bishops in their castles at Kwydzyn (Marienwerder, begun 1322) and Lidzbark Warmiński (Heilsberg, built 1350) in former Prussia. The ingredients for this recipe also appear together in some of the Polish royal registers, so there is ample evidence to suggest that this was once a standard dish, at least in noble establishments. A red Hungarian wine and other imported ingredients give the recipe a courtly character with Polish nuances.*

The chicken was prepared in one of two ways. The hen was split down the middle. Then it was either cut in half and the two parts wrapped separately in dough and baked so that they came from the oven like giant turnovers, or, the split chicken was laid in a shallow earthenware pan, covered with a lid, and baked. Doubtless the method using dough was reserved for festive occasions, since the crust could be ornamented with intricate patterns and thus add to the grand visual effect of the meal. I have chosen the second method to reflect a more intimate, family-style dinner rather than a state occasion. But either way, it is a fine dish for a bishop, a high nobleman and his family, or a starosta in his tent.

Serves 6 to 8

1 medium onion, cut in half lengthwise and sliced thin

3 cups (260 g) white cabbage, shredded as for sauerkraut

1 pound (500 g) large prunes with pits (pits add flavor)

1½ cups (150 g) chopped parsley

30 juniper berries

5 pound (2.5 kg) roasting chicken, gutted and cleaned (the head and feet were not removed in the Middle Ages)

8 bay leaves, bruised

4 ounces (125 g) streaky slab bacon thinly sliced

¾ teaspoon ground ginger

½ teaspoon ground cinnamon

2 cups (500 ml) red Hungarian wine

½ teaspoon dill seed

Preheat the oven to 375°F (190°C). Spread the onion over the bottom of a large earthenware baking pan, then cover this with the cabbage, prunes, 1 cup (100 g) of parsley, and the juniper berries, taking care to distribute the ingredients evenly. Cut the chicken in half and spread the two halves butterfly fashion and cavity side down on top of vegetables and prunes. Tuck the bay leaves into spaces around the chicken. Place strips of bacon on top of the chicken. Mix the ginger and cinnamon with the wine and pour this over the bird. Scatter the remaining parsley over the top and then scatter the dill seed over this. Cover with a tight-fitting lid and bake 1 hour.

Serve hot with the chicken on a platter and the vegetables and fruit in a shallow basin. Boiled millet refried in oil or butter may be served as a side dish to be eaten like rice. The chicken may be accompanied by a green mustard sauce (see following recipe).

Green Mustard Sauce (Zielony Sos z Musztardą) *

This sauce is actually a type of pesto originally made in a mortar. It was normally eaten with fowl, pork, or veal. The luxury of olive oil defines this as a condiment limited strictly to royal and princely kitchens, although Syrennius specifically mentioned olive oil in connection with Polish mustard preparations in general and even provided a recipe. Until the disruption of trade by the Turks in the 1450s, olive oil came to medieval Poland from Cyprus and Greece as well as from Spain. It was purchased for the king exclusively by trading salt from the royal mines, one of Poland's leading export products at that time.

Serves 4 to 6

½ cup (125 ml) prepared Dijon-style mustard (grainy type)

¼ cup (60 ml) honey

¼ cup (60 ml) red Hungarian wine

2 tablespoons Cypriot olive oil

½ teaspoon anise seed, ground to a powder

½ teaspoon salt

2 cups (200 g) chopped parsley

1 teaspoon coarsely grated pepper

Combine the mustard, honey, wine and olive oil in a mixing bowl. Add the anise and salt, then the parsley. Pour this into a blender and puree until it attains the thickness of a pesto. (The old method was to pulp the parsley in a mortar, then combine it with the rest of the ingredients.) Pour this into a bowl, add the pepper, and serve at room temperature. This sauce should be eaten the same day it is made.

Lentils and Skirrets with Bacon
(Soczewica i Kruczmorka z Boczkiem)

*Syrennius's remark that skirret (*Sium siarum*) was introduced into Poland from Mainz, Germany, suggests a possible contact or exchange between the bishop of Mainz and someone of similar importance in Poland. If such were the case, then the skirret surely began its career in Poland as a foreign curiosity on noble tables. But it quickly found favor on all levels of society, perhaps because the climate and soil of Poland are so well suited to its culture.*

The skirret is a root vegetable that can be eaten only while it is dormant during the winter. In the spring, the roots become woody and covered with small hairs, since the plant is readying itself to shoot up to a height of as much as six feet. The best skirrets come from sandy ground, which encourages root growth. For culinary purposes, only the longest and thickest roots were harvested, that is, roots about 8 to 9 inches (20 to 23 cm) long and about half an inch (1 cm) thick. Parts of the root rejected for cooking can be stuck back in the ground to regrow the next year.

Since skirrets are not pared like parsnips, the roots must be washed thoroughly with a brush. For cooking, they are normally sliced very thin at an angle like French cut string beans, that is, as héricot. *This makes them easier to eat medieval-style because the whole dish can be scooped up with a piece of bread. This is probably the best way to prepare skirrets, even today.*

Although this recipe has been reconstructed to fit a fall menu, it could also serve as a meal in the spring following Easter. In this case, it might also be served with a fried egg or two on top. This is true Polish medieval middle-class fare, and as such this recipe is merely an outline, with all sorts of possible variations implied.

Serves 4 to 6 (as a side dish)

4-ounce (125g) piece of streaky slab bacon

heart and giblets of a chicken (or discarded bones and carcass from a previous meal)

8 leaves of rocombole garlic, or small leek leaves

1 pound (500 g) green or brown lentils

3 teaspoons salt

½ teaspoon ground ginger

1 cup (100 g) skirrets, cut on a slant into thin slices

¼ cup (25 g) chopped parsley

½ cup (50 g) chopped spring onion (green part only)

¼ cup (25 g) chopped dill

Put the bacon, chicken giblets, and garlic leaves in a stewing pan with 1 quart (1 liter of water and cook 30 minutes, skimming often. Strain and reserve the bacon and giblets. Put the stock in a clean stewing pan with 3 cups (750 ml) of water. Add the lentils, salt, and ginger. Chop the giblets and add this to the pot. Chop part of the bacon, enough to yield half a cup (50 g), and add this to the lentil mixture.

Cook 20 minutes over medium heat, then add the skirrets. Continue cooking until the skirrets are tender (about 15 minutes), then add the parsley, spring onion, and dill. Serve immediately in a bowl with the remaining piece of boiled bacon on top.

Beer Soup with Cheese and Eggs (Zupa Piwna z Bryndzą, lub Caseata) *

Even today most Poles are familiar with gramatka *or* farmuszka, *beer soups thickened with rye bread. This beer soup, however, is somewhat more refined in its use of egg yolks and fried spelt flour as thickeners. The soup was first mentioned under the name* caseata *as part of a royal fasting menu at Korczyn in 1394. As such, the soup contains no meat products but does take advantage of spring vegetables and herbs. The cheese used was similar to* bryndzą *farmer's cheese, but any feta-type cheese can be substituted. And last, the beer must be a wheat beer; any good, light German Weissbier will work. Spaten Premium Weissbier, from a Franciscan brewery founded at Munich in 1397, was used for testing this recipe.*

Serves 4 to 6

½ pound (250 g) leek greens

3 cups (260 g) white cabbage, shredded as for sauerkraut

1 cup (100 g) chopped chervil

4 tablespoons (60 g) lightly salted butter

4 tablespoons (30 g) spelt flour

2 cups (500 ml) Weissbier (wheat beer)

4 egg yolks

2 cups (500 ml) cold whole milk

½ tablespoon caraway seed

½ teaspoon ground ginger

¼ teaspoon ground mace

¼ teaspoon ground saffron

1 tablespoon salt

½ pound (250 g) bryndza *farmer's cheese or any feta-type cheese, cut into ½-inch dice*

Put the leek greens in a stewing pan with 1 quart (1 liter) of water, cover, and stew over medium-low heat for 30 minutes. Strain the broth and discard the leek greens. Return the broth to the stewing pan and add the cabbage. Cover and stew over medium-low heat for 30 minutes, then add the chervil and puree the hot mixture in a blender until it is smooth. Set aside.

In a large stewpan or stock pot, melt the butter and brown the flour in it over medium-high heat until the roux turns a golden brown. Then add the reserved puree, 2 cups (500 ml) water, and the beer. Whisk the egg yolks into the milk, then add this to the soup mixture. Add the caraway seed, ginger, mace, saffron, and salt. Continue to cook the soup for 10 minutes, then add the cheese. Let the cheese heat in the soup for about 5 minutes, then serve immediately.

Millet Flour Soup (Zacierki) *

There are both meat and fasting versions of this old Polish dish, which was once popular among the nobility, especially because it could be prepared very quickly (in less than 30 minutes). Both types of zacierki *were rich and filling, and this recipe is no exception. Ham or beef stock can be used instead of water and chicken stock, and saffron was always thought appropriate in recipes containing eggs. The soup may be served alone, over bread rolls, or with cheese curds, as suggested here.*

Serves 4 to 6

---

6 tablespoons (90 g) lightly salted butter

¾ cup (90 g) millet flour

⅛ teaspoon ground saffron or to taste

2 cups (500 ml) cold chicken stock

4 egg yolks

2 cups (500 ml) cold whole milk

3 tablespoons (45 ml) honey, or to taste

2 teaspoons salt or to taste

freshly grated pepper

large curd cottage cheese

*dried pot marigold (*Calendula officinalis*) petals (optional)*

Melt the butter in a deep stewing pan or soup kettle. Add the millet flour and brown lightly over medium heat for 5 minutes. Stir the paste with a wooden spoon from time to time to prevent it from sticking. Dissolve the saffron in the chicken stock and combine with 2 cups (500 ml) of cold water. Pour this into the millet and whisk vigorously to remove any lumps. Cook over medium heat for about 10 minutes, letting the mixture come to a gentle boil to thicken. Beat the egg yolks until frothy, then combine with the milk. Reduce the heat under the soup and add the egg mixture, whisking gently to keep it from curdling. Once the eggs have cooked and thickened the soup, add the honey, adjust seasonings, and serve immediately over bread torn into small pieces or with a spoonful or two of fresh curds. If served alone as a first course soup, garnish with dried marigold petals (use fresh when in season), pink radish flowers, or a mix of both.

Oat Flour Soup (Kucza)

The range of preparations characterized as pulmentum avenaticum *(oat gruel) in Polish medieval texts was evidently quite broad. Like* zacierki, *the recipe here represents the most refined end of the spectrum. Polish taste preferences ran against oats to begin with, thus the dish had to display a certain artifice to get beyond that. This is a dish likely to have appeared on the table of a petty noble or a well-off burgher. A peasant version would certainly have had a coarser texture, more bran and fat, for example, and a noticeable lack of ingredients like saffron and ginger.*

The old popularity of preparations like this is evident in its texture, for when properly made the soup is highly versatile. It can be served alone as a first course soup or ladled over bread, cooked hulled millet, or boiled dry peas. It can also serve as a sauce over boiled vegetables (such as parsnips, cow parsnips, or turnips), and if ground mustard is added, it can become a sauce for chicken or fish. For fasting days, the bacon drippings would have been eliminated in favor of butter or poppy seed oil.

Serves 4 to 6

---

8 leek greens or 2 medium onions, chopped

4 cloves garlic, cut in half lengthwise

6 cups (1½ liters) capon stock or water

⅛ teaspoon ground saffron

3 tablespoons (45 ml) bacon drippings or lard

4 tablespoons (30 g) fine oat bran

4 tablespoons (30 g) oat flour

4 egg yolks

¾ teaspoon ground ginger

3 tablespoons (45 ml) Hungarian white wine vinegar

salt and pepper to taste

Put the leek greens, garlic, and capon stock in a heavy saucepan and cook over medium heat for 30 minutes. Strain the stock and discard the vegetables (medieval cooks would have tossed them into a slop pot for the chickens). Reserve 1 cup (250 ml) of the stock in a small bowl and dissolve the saffron in it.

Heat the bacon drippings in a heavy saucepan. Mix the oat bran and flour together and add this to the drippings. Stir to form a paste, then brown it lightly over medium high heat for about 3 minutes, or until it begins to smell nutty. Add 5 cups (1¼ liters) of stock and whisk until smooth. Cook over medium-high heat for about 20 minutes, or until the liquid thickens, whisking it from time to time to keep it smooth.

Beat the egg yolks into the saffron infusion and add the ginger. Pour this slowly into the soup, whisking vigorously. Let the soup cook until thick (about 10 minutes), then gradually add the vinegar, a little at a time, whisking it so that it does not curdle the eggs. Adjust seasonings and serve.

Polish Hydromel (Czemiga) *

Extremely easy to make, and quite refreshing during the hot days of summer, this hydromel can be kept up to a week in the refrigerator. The Polish use of fennel seed, as suggested by Syrennius, gives it a distinctive flavor, and the cassia, which was also used to flavor honey-based drinks, provides an interesting pepperlike bite. When hydromel was served at court or in noble houses, the jug was brought into the dining room and placed in a tub of cool water along with the wine and other beverages being served.

Serves 4

3 cups (750 ml) spring water

3 tablespoons fennel seed

½ teaspoon ground cassia or 1 tablespoon bruised cassia buds

1 cup (250 ml) honey

Bring the water to a boil and pour it over the fennel and cassia in a large jar. Cover and infuse until the liquid is room temperature. Strain through a filter or fine sieve. Dissolve the honey in the clear liquid. Store in a stoneware jug or wine bottle in the refrigerator until needed.

Fermented Barley Flour Soup (Kisiel)

This ancestor of the Polish soup now known as żur *was first documented in Polish texts in* A.D. *997. It is by far the oldest Polish dish in this book, and surprisingly, one of the easiest to make. In its medieval context, however, this was a food eaten on fast days. According to the reference to* kisiel *from 997, the king of Poland consumed this dish during Lent. And because it is so intertwined with the formation of Polish culture, kisiel is one of those dishes that is also closely connected with Polish identity and culinary roots.*

Slavic food historians have suggested that this dish is a substitute for koumiss, *fermented mare's milk, a food forbidden by the early Christian church due to its association with pagan religion. While this line of argument may be difficult to prove or disprove, it offers an insight into the controversial dynamics of food as cultural identity. Just as interesting is the Russian cognate* kiseli *(plural), referred to as kissels in English. These are thick puddings similar to blancmange and normally served with fruit or berries. Polish kisiel was likewise eaten with such additions as blackberries, blueberries, or wild currants.*

The ferment was usually strained and allowed to jell. This "white" version of the dish was traditionally served at Christmas in Poland, and even today, instant mixtures can be bought and cooked like blancmange. The modern descendant of the medieval preparation is more like its Russian counterpart and may have acquired this character during Russian occupation of the country. The recipe that follows is much more archaic, following the general outline of kisiel as mentioned in Cracow codexes from 1394. Water would be substituted for the milk if the dish were served during Lent, and flavor would be added with a little rocombole garlic or leek.

Serves 4 to 6

1 cup (250 ml) beer barm or 1 tablespoon dry active yeast in 1 cup (250 ml) lukewarm water

12 tablespoons (90 g) barley flour

2 cups water

1 cup (250 ml) thick beer (page 183)

3 cups (750 ml) milk, or 2 cups (500 ml) milk plus 1 cup (250 ml) buttermilk, or 3 cups (750 ml) sheep's milk whey

1 teaspoon salt

honey to taste

Proof the beer barm or dry yeast. Put the barley flour in a deep work bowl and pour 2 cups (500 ml) of boiling water over it. Stir well with a whisk to remove lumps. When lukewarm, add the proofed yeast and the thick beer. Cover and let stand overnight in a warm place to ferment or until desired sourness is achieved (2 to 5 days for a very sour soup). The flavor of this soup should be pleasantly tart, similar to yogurt. Fermentation time will vary greatly: during cool, dry weather more time is required.

Once the ferment settles, strain off the water and pour the mixture into a large saucepan and bring to a gentle boil over medium heat. Add the milk and salt. When the mixture is scalded, it is ready to serve. Honey may be added to the soup before serving or individuals may sweeten it to taste at the table. This dish was eaten with a wooden spoon or with sops in medieval times.

Fish Aspic (Galareta z Ryby)

Simple yet difficult would be an honest assessment of this dish, for the cooking is easy but the jelling is not. Medieval recipes are often quite particular about the various ways to achieve a good jell, but the most direct one is to start with the right sort of fish. Fish with oily skins jell better, but this alone will not guarantee success because a good quantity of bones, fins, heads, and tails are necessary to stiffen the stock. Thus before even attempting this recipe, have on hand a quart (liter) or two of fish stock prepared by boiling a large quantity of fish parts and reducing this by one-third. You can also cheat and use packaged gelatin. Modern packaged gelatin is generally made from pigs' feet, so it would never have been allowed in meatless dishes, but it will definitely take the guesswork out of aspic.

Last, a few words about ingredients. Medieval Polish cooks did not use much wine in aspic-making; rather, they relied on vinegar. Polish cooks could choose from a great number of flavored vinegars to take the place of the variety of wines then available elsewhere in Europe. One of the favored vinegars for fish aspic was lavender vinegar, and in French texts from the same period lavender also appears in a number of aspic recipes. Lavender vinegar is best made with fresh blossoms (see recipe on page 168), and it will keep for several years. To carry the lavender theme through the course of the meal, serve lavender comfits at the beginning, and at the end and use the flowers, either fresh or dried, as ornamental "plumes" on some of the display dishes. This of course is court cookery, fare for only the wealthiest of nobles and merchants.

This aspic was probably served as an ornamental component of a larger display dish. It can be treated in much the same manner as quince or medlar paste, with which it was sometimes served. If the aspic is cast in shallow pans, it can be cut into shapes to create the sort of inlay work that characterized truly elaborate presentation pieces at court. Aspics of various colors, hard cooked eggs, mushrooms or truffles, all of these ingredients could be assembled to create a coat of arms or some other appropriate figure. The most common method, however, was to fill halves of hard cooked egg whites (after removing the yolks) with the fish aspic and letting this set. This was done at manor houses and in homes of lesser nobility, a conceit worthy of the trouble since the yellowish aspic looks like egg to begin with.

Serves 6 to 8

2 buck shad, 4 small trout, or other freshwater fish equal to 2 pounds (1 kg) after gutting and scaling (heads and tails are not removed)

1 medium onion, sliced

6 cloves rocombole garlic, gently crushed

8 fresh bay leaves, bruised

2 cinnamon sticks about 4 inches (10 cm) in length

1 tablespoon cubebs

1 tablespoon shredded mace

1 cup (250 ml) lavender vinegar (see page 168)

1 cup (250 ml) spring water

1 quart (1 liter) prepared fish stock (see following recipe)

4 envelopes unflavored gelatin (optional)

1 teaspoon ground ginger

1 teaspoon salt

1/8 teaspoon ground saffron

4 tablespoons (60 ml) honey or to taste

Place the cleaned fish in a shallow pan with the onion, garlic, bay leaves, cinnamon, cubebs, and mace. Combine the vinegar and spring water and pour this over the fish. Poach for about 20 minutes, or until the fish falls away from the bones. Remove the fish and separate the flesh from the bones. Reserve the flesh. Put the bones, skins, heads, tails, and fins in a small stock pot with the prepared fish stock. Strain the poaching liquid and add this to the pot. Cook the fish stock until reduced by one-third, then strain. Add the ginger, salt and saffron, and mix this with the reserved fish. Beat with a whisk so that the fish breaks down into very small pieces. Sweeten with honey and add more lavender vinegar if a sour flavor is preferred (about 3 tablespoons per 45 ml). Pour the mixture into a loaf-shaped pan for a standing aspic, onto tin sheets with raised edges for inlay work or ornamental figures, or fill halves of hard-cooked eggs as suggested above. Refrigerate to jell (at least 3 hours). Four envelopes of commercial unflavored gelatin can be dissolved into the strained stock to ensure a proper jell.

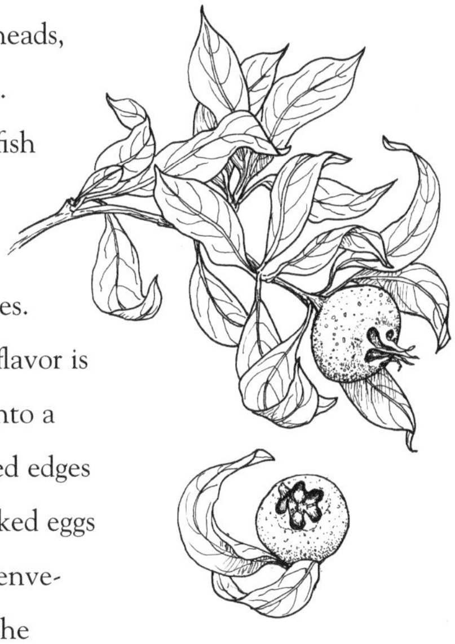

Medlars.

To serve as a standing aspic, turn out the aspic and send to the table on a fine dish well ornamented with flower petals, buckler leaf sorrel, parsley, cooked crayfish, truffles, and other garnishes of this sort.

Prepared Fish Stock (Rosół z Ryby)

6 cups (1½ liters) unflavored strained fish stock

4 bruised bay leaves

4 cloves rocombole garlic, gently crushed

1 cinnamon stick, about 4 inches (10 cm) long

2 tablespoons celery seed

All sorts of fish trimmings, bones, skins, heads, and the like should be boiled in a large stock pot with 1 gallon (4 liters) of water for about 1 hour, then strained and reserved. Stock that has been made ahead and frozen will work perfectly. This stock recipe is designed to fit the requirements of the aspic above.

Put the stock, bay leaves, garlic, cinnamon, and celery seed in a stock pot and boil over medium heat until reduced to 4 cups (1 liter), about 40 minutes. Strain and use as directed above for making the aspic.

Lavender Vinegar (Ocet Lawendowy)

15 sprigs of fresh lavender flowers

1 sterilized wine bottle (750 ml)

3 cups (750 ml) Hungarian white wine vinegar

Yield: 3 cups (750 ml)

Put the flowers in the wine bottle and add the vinegar. Cork tight and set in a dark, cool closet. Allow to infuse at least 3 weeks before using.

Game Stewed with Sauerkraut (Miszkulancja, lub Bigos) *

Bigos is one of those Polish dishes that has been romanticized in poetry, discussed in its most minute details in all sorts of literary contexts, and never made in small quantities. Historically, it was served at royal banquets or to guests at meals following a hunt. It was made invariably from several types of game and served during the winter. Bigos has gradually assumed the character of a Christmas and Easter dish in Poland, and today the recipes are as varied and as complex as any Italian recipe for tomato sauce. In fact, some Poles even add tomato sauce to the mixture. (It does not need it.)

In the manor house where my grandfather was born, the bigos was kept warm in a compartment in the great tile stove that heated the parlor where guests were received. It was handed out as a welcoming snack served on poppy seed toast, along with a glass of iced vodka or champagne. While Polish villagers often make a plain version of bigos in huge cauldrons over an open fire for wedding feasts, real bigos is best when it is baked very slowly at a low temperature in a ceramic pot. The evaporation alone should be enough to thicken it. Furthermore, it should not be served until at least one day old, preferably three; it needs time for the flavors to fuse into a highly complex and concentrated taste.

The old-style recipe that follows has been written so that the bigos can be made according to modern cooking techniques. However, one key feature that cannot be altered is the flavor of the various meats; if they are not spit-roasted, they should be grilled over a barbecue so that there is a pronounced browned meat taste. The precise choice of game is entirely personal, but by implication the meat is first marinated before it is roasted, so this adds a further dimension to the complex flavors.

Serves 16 to 18 as hors d'oeuvres

2 pounds (1 kg) sauerkraut

1 pound (500 g) white cabbage, shredded as for sauerkraut

8 ounces (250 g) streaky country bacon cut into 4 pieces

3 cups (750 ml) well-flavored ham stock or game stock

3 ounces (90 g) dried mushrooms

1 cup (200 g) coarsely chopped onion

6 ounces (185 g) pitted prunes or a mix of prunes, dried cherries, and dried pears, coarsely chopped

8 ounces (250 g) spit-roasted elk (łoś) or bison (żubr), cut into ½-inch (1 cm) dice

4 ounces (125 g) spit-roasted rump of wild boar (dzik), cut into ½-inch (1 cm) dice

4 ounces (125 g) spit-roasted pheasant or peahen, cut into ½-inch (1 cm) dice

4 ounces (125 g) spit-roasted ham, cut into ½-inch (1 cm) dice

4 ounces (125 g) veal sausage, cut in half lengthwise and sliced

4 ounces (125 g) smoked sausage, cut in half lengthwise and sliced

2 cups (500 ml) red wine

1 teaspoon ground cubebs

½ teaspoon ground cinnamon

1 teaspoon ground cumin

1 tablespoon (15 ml) honey (optional)

Combine the sauerkraut and cabbage in a deep baking dish or heavy stewpan. Add the bacon and stock. Cover and braise 40 minutes or stew over medium heat so that most of the liquid cooks out. While braising, pour 3 cups (750 ml) boiling water over the mushrooms and infuse until soft. Remove the mushrooms and cut into shreds, reserving 2 cups (500 ml) of the strained liquid.

Remove the bacon from the cabbage mixture and coarsely

chop it into small bits. Put the bacon in a skillet and brown lightly over medium-high heat. Add the chopped onion and brown lightly for 3 minutes, then cover and sweat over low heat for 10 minutes, or until the onion becomes yellow. If too dry, add excess mushroom stock to moisten.

After the onions are cooked, add the bacon and onion mixture to the cabbage, along with the mushroom infusion and the mushrooms. Stir well so that the cabbage turns light brown, then add the meats, wine, and spices. Stew over medium heat for 15 minutes, stirring often so that most of the liquid is cooked out. Remove from the heat, cover, and set aside to cool. Store in a cold place at least one day before reheating to serve. Best if made several days in advance.

Hashmeat in the Cypriot Style (Zrazy po Cyprjsku) *

This dish is the central component of several preparations that were considered foreign or exotic by the Polish court. It was served baked in the form of "meatloaf" patties or zrazy *used as filling in standing pies and turnovers, and wrapped in chard leaves in the manner of dolmates. After being braised in wine, the stuffed leaves were brushed with honey (or with aspic reduced until sticky), then rolled in a mixture of sesame seeds and gith (*Nigella sativa*). This is probably one way in which the hashmeat was served for the banquet held at Cracow in honor of King Peter of Cyprus in 1364, since variations of this basic idea appear in a number of later court cookbooks in France, England, and Germany, often under the designation* heidenisch *("heathen"—perhaps in reference to King Peter's victory over the Arabs at Alexandria). Indeed, some food historians have speculated that many of the so-called Cypriot recipes appearing in late medieval cookbooks relate in some way to the legendary banquet held for King Peter and the international character of the Cypriot court.*

The hashmeat was also mixed with various ingredients like cooked rice, cooked kasha manna, or cooked green rye or green spelt grits. In Cyprus, cooked cracked wheat and sun-dried chondro *were used the same way. In any event, if a grain is used, the proportion of bread crumbs should be reduced accordingly or omitted altogether. The bread crumbs must be made from the white part of manchets (wheat-flour dinner rolls), not the crust.*

Serves 16

1¼ cups (175 g) ground cooked ham

1¼ cups (175 g) ground cooked beef

2½ cups (315 g) white bread crumbs

1 teaspoon freshly grated pepper

1 teaspoon salt

½ teaspoon ground cinnamon

½ teaspoon ground cumin

½ teaspoon ground ginger

½ cup (75 g) chopped raisins

1 tablespoon minced garlic

¼ cup (25 g) minced parsley

3 tablespoons (45 ml) Cypriot olive oil

1½ cups (375 g) pureed onion

¼ cup (60 ml) cubeb vinegar (page 199)

2 eggs

2½ cups (625 ml) ham stock (see note)

Preheat the oven to 400°F (200°C). Combine the meat, bread crumbs, pepper, salt, cinnamon, cumin, ginger, raisins, garlic, and parsley in a deep work bowl. Heat the olive oil in a sauté pan or skillet and add the onion. Cover and sweat over medium heat for 5 minutes, then add the vinegar and combine this with the meat mixture. Beat the eggs until frothy, then combine with the ham stock. Pour this into the meat mixture and stir thoroughly to form a thick batter. Pour the batter into greased, shallow 4-inch (10 cm) earthenware tart dishes and bake 20 minutes or until set.

Note: When using this as a stuffing or pie filling, reduce the ham stock by one-fourth to one-half, depending on how moist a filling is wanted. Red Cypriot wines are perfect with this and may be used as the basis of a sauce to serve over the patties or for dipping if the patties are served medieval-style as finger food.

Saffron Wafers (Opłatki Szafranowe) *

Saffron was more expensive in Gdansk than in Cracow or Lvov during the Middle Ages, which suggests that distance from market source played a key role in determining the cost of such imported goods. A large portion of Polish saffron appears to have come from regions bordering the Black Sea where saffron originated, via Genoese middlemen. Its use in Polish cookery was a mark of high status, so it may seem contradictory that it also was commonly used in foods associated with fasting. Yet saffron wafers were served at the Polish court during meatless days or at the end of the meal with various confections and Malvasia wine.

Because they also contained sugar, the wafers were generally made by specialized confectioners and were therefore not only sweet but also expensive. Part of the expense (aside from the saffron and sugar) was high-quality flour, which had to be farina alba cribrata*—the finest sort. Another reason for the cost was manufacture, for the art of wafer making is a distinct craft unto itself, and rather tedious. In spite of this, a good wafer baker was said to produce about one thousand wafers a day. Indeed, it was sometimes a specialty of nunneries or monasteries, which derived income from the sale of such goods.*

Wafers were made with irons ornamented with various patterns that were impressed into the surface of the wafer as it baked. Polish irons were normally round, although rectangular North German and Dutch types were also used in Gdansk and Pomerania.[6] *Metal wafer irons are mentioned in several medieval sources and on occasion they are depicted, but none have survived intact. The images were generally religious, and an especially good wafer maker would have several sets of irons on hand to meet the demand of funerals, weddings, and special religious feasts, such as Easter or Christmas. For everyday use, the royal court probably served wafers impressed with the royal coat of arms, or the coat of arms of a special guest if the intention was to flatter or impress.*

Since sugar absorbs and amplifies flavors, wafers must be made over a smokeless heat source, the most common being a charcoal stove. This technique requires considerable practice because the iron must be turned constantly to keep both halves evenly heated. The iron must be also kept hot while it is being refilled with wafer batter. Last, the wafers must be trimmed while they are hot and soft and still in the iron; once cool, they become brittle and break easily. All of this implies speed and a steady hand with a very sharp knife. Having tested this recipe with a wafer iron from the 1500s, I can report that total baking time per wafer should be about 6 minutes, or 3 minutes per side, depending on the type of metal from which the iron

1 cup (250 g) double sifted pastry flour

1 cup (250 g) superfine sugar (white sugar ground to a fine powder, called bar sugar in the United States)

1/4 teaspoon finely ground saffron

4 egg whites

2 to 3 tablespoons (30 to 45 ml) rosewater

poppy seed oil

is made (there are several alloys) and its thickness. Accomplished wafer bakers could probably do this in half the time; I was somewhat restrained by the cautious use of antique equipment.

Yield: About 30 wafers, depending on the size of the iron

Before assembling the ingredients, which should be at room temperature, light a charcoal grill or old-style charcoal stove so that the coals have a good 30 minutes to heat and reduce to embers. Do not use self-lighting charcoal, since this will give the wafers a burned petroleum flavor.

Sift together the flour, sugar and saffron three times. Whisk the egg whites until they are stiff and form peaks, then fold them into the dry ingredients. Moisten with rose water so that it forms a thick batter.

Heat both sides of the wafer iron (or a pizzelle iron) over the charcoal stove or grill. When evenly hot on both sides, open the iron and grease it liberally. Put some of the batter on one side and let it spread. Slowly close up the iron but do not press hard, just enough to force the batter out to the edges. Turn the iron over the coals often until the batter begins to bubble around the edges, then press tightly and hold it firmly together, turning the iron several times (this will caramelize the sugar and cause the wafer to stiffen). Batter that has run out of the edges can now be trimmed off neatly with a very sharp knife. Once the wafer tests done, the iron can be opened and the wafer removed with the help of a knife. Repeat until all the batter is used. Perfectly made wafers will bake paper-thin and turn out a golden fawn color. Once cool, they can be stored several months in airtight containers.

Pike in Polish Sauce (Szczupak w Polskim Sosie)

Because many medieval recipes were mere outlines, it was up to the cook to fill in the missing elements with local ingredients or to prepare them in a regional manner.[7] *Fortunately, while this recipe was written down in 1553 by Augsburg patrician Sabina Welser, it represented a much older, traditional Polish mode of saucing fish.*[8] *It appears to come from a collection of Polish recipes now lost.*

Welser's exact words were "Welt ihr ain bollischen brei jber ain hecht machen" (how to make Polish sauce for pike). Most interesting, the Welser version explicitly called for finely minced onions in a puree of peas, the peas (we assume) to make the sauce green. Much was left unsaid, except that spices were used and that the pieces of fish were cooked in the sauce until done. Here we have the classic vagueness of a recipe meant only to jog the memory, with crucial elements left out because they were givens.

Understood in this case is the pea puree, which is not made from fresh peas but from dried peas ground to flour and enhanced with various potherbs and beer—the key elements that make it Polish. In fact, Queen Jadwiga dined on perch-pikes in July 1393, and the purchase order listed quite a few of the common ingredients found in Polish sauce: peas, millet flour, onions, and vinegar. Other fish on her menu may have been stewed this way, for the perch-pikes were specifically designated ad galeretam*—that is, for galantines.*[9]

Welser also included a recipe in the Hungarian style, again, a dish of a much older type. Instead of pureed peas or pea flour, the fish was stewed in finely minced apples cooked with wine, lemon, pepper vinegar (or vinegar flavored with csombor*), and saffron. One of the meals prepared for King Władysław Jagiełło in October 1393 was based on a purchase order for raw apples and whole herrings. It is quite possible that these ingredients were prepared in a similar Hungarian manner. The use of saffron, sweet wines, and lemons, in any case, was perceived as Hungarian by Polish cooks of this period, so perhaps it was this in the apples that suggested the name of the Hungarian preparation recorded by Welser. It is also possible that the Polish style imitated this sweet-and-sour yellowness by using yellow peas rather than green ones. Both the old seventeenth-century Gdansk pea and Wrocław pea are yellow (both cultivars are extant) and were used exclusively for stewing and for purees. They may descend from medieval Polish strains that were also yellow.*

In any event, the pike was prepared in one of two ways in the kitchens of the Polish nobility. As a display piece, the fish was cooked whole and stuffed with a

¼ cup (60 ml) poppy seed oil

2 cups (200 g) coarsely chopped onion

1 cup (100 g) chopped parsley

1 cup (100 g) chopped dill

1 cup (125 g) pea flour

½ cup (65 g) millet flour

1½ cups (375 ml) fish stock

1½ cups (375 ml) Weissbier (wheat beer)

½ teaspoon ground mace

½ teaspoon ground ginger

1 tablespoon (15 ml) lavender vinegar, or to taste

1 tablespoon (15 ml) honey, or to taste

4 pounds (2 kg) pike cut into steaks at least 1 inch (2½ cm) thick

red peppercorns for garnish

minced dill for garnish

mixture of diced cucumber, minced onion, chopped hard-cooked egg yolks, parsley, and precooked kasha manna. The stuffing was inserted through the top of the fish, not the bottom. A slit was made in the back, along the dorsal fin, and the entrails were removed. The cavity was then filled with stuffing and closed up. The fish was tied into a bent shape so that it looked as though it were swimming. After cooking, it was untied and served "swimming" through its sauce.

The other method of preparation is the one referred to by Welser. The fish is cleaned and cut up into thick "steaks" that are then laid in the sauce and baked or braised. This is the easiest mode of preparation for home cookery and probably the most common one outside the royal court.

Serves 4 to 6

Heat the oil in a broad, shallow stewing pan and add the onion. Cover and sweat over medium heat for 5 minutes, then add the parsley and chopped dill. Combine the pea and millet flour with the fish stock and add this to the herb mixture. Add the beer, mace, and ginger. Stew for about 20 minutes, or until thick. Then add the vinegar and honey. Lay the fish in the sauce and continue stewing until the fish is cooked (about 20 minutes). Serve immediately garnished with red peppercorns and minced dill. Salt is added to taste after each portion is served.

Fast Day Pancakes (Naleśniki Postne) *

This type of crepe was popular at the Polish court. The pancakes are fairly rich but easy to make. While they would be treated as a dessert food today, they were probably served during dinner, along with the beer soup with cheese (page 159), fish aspic (page 166), or another meatless dish. On a technical note, these pancakes were not made in the kitchen, but prepared in or near the dining area over a charcoal stove.

Good Friday pancakes were also served at the Polish court. These were made with the fermenting batter from kisiel (page 164) and fried in poppy seed oil. They were served with poppy seeds, chopped nuts, and honey, a far cry from the rich recipe that passed for fasting.

Makes about 30 small pancakes or 15 large ones

Filling

The texture of the filling should be fine and loose, thus the cheese should be grated on the small holes of a vegetable grater. More cardamom may be added if desired.

1 cup (125 g) finely chopped hazelnuts

3 tablespoons poppy seeds

½ teaspoon ground cardamom, or to taste

6 ounces (185 g) grated* bryndza *farmer's cheese, or any feta-type cheese drained of whey

---

Combine the nuts, poppy seeds, and cardamom in a deep work bowl then gently stir in the cheese with a fork, taking care that it does not form lumps. Set aside and prepare the pancake batter.

Pancake Batter

4 whole eggs

3 egg yolks

1 cup (250 ml) cream

1 cup (250 ml) sour cream (*śmietaną*)

½ teaspoon salt

7 tablespoons (50 g) barley flour

5 tablespoons (30 g) spelt or club wheat flour

poppy seed oil or hazelnut oil

honey

poppy seeds

Beat the eggs and yolks until lemon color, add the cream, then add the sour cream. Sift together the salt and flours, then fold into the egg mixture to form a thick, ropy batter. Heat a little oil in an omelet pan, and pour in about ½ cup (125 ml) of the batter for a large-sized pancake. Let this brown on one side, then flip it over to brown on the other side. When it is done, spread some of the nut mixture (about 2 tablespoons) over the middle and fold the pancake over or roll it up into a tube. Let the filling heat only enough to melt the cheese slightly, then move the pancake to a hot dish. Brush the pancake with honey and scatter poppy seeds over it. Serve immediately while hot. Repeat until all the batter and filling is used.

Ham Stewed with Cucumbers
(Szynka Duszona z Ogorkami) *

Although this dish first appeared on a fourteenth-century menu from Weissenfels, the stew presents a strange familiarity because it is a predecessor of dishes later characterized in French cookery as salpicons. The finely diced ingredients are probably the connecting factor, yet the antecedent to this concept traces to the Eastern Mediterranean so it is part of an ongoing culinary continuum.

The meat may be prepared in a number of ways without changing the rest of the recipe. I decided that the meat must have been cut into bite-sized cubes (like meat for bigos), into diamond-shaped lozenges, or into thick strips. Any of these forms of presentation would be correct but the cubes stand up better to prolonged cooking.

Last, when the dish was brought to table for initial inspection, it was garnished with rose petals. This was a treatment at the court, not in home cookery among the nobles, unless they were entertaining. The old English term for this form of presentation was floreye, *that is, "flowered."*

Serves 6 to 8

4 tablespoons (60 g) lightly salted butter

1 cup (100 g) chopped leek or onion

1 cup (125 g) finely diced white carrot or the root of Hamburg parsley

4 pounds (2 kg) country ham cut into 1-inch (2.5 cm) cubes

1 tablespoon minced rocombole garlic

1 cup (45 g) chopped parsley

1 quart (1 liter) Weissbier (wheat beer)

1 quart (1 liter) ham stock (ham trimmings cooked with leek tops and bay leaves)

½ cup (75 g) dried** żurawina **(European cranberries), substitute American dried cranberries

½ cup (75 g) raisins

4 cups (500 g) diced cucumber (seeds removed)

4 tablespoons (60 ml) honey

2 tablespoons (30 ml) cubeb vinegar (page 199)

Sour cream (**śmietaną**) to taste

Freshly grated pepper

Rose petals

Heat the butter in a large, heavy stewing pan and add the leek and carrot. Cover and sweat over low heat for 10 minutes. Add the ham, garlic, and parsley. Stir to coat the ham with all the ingredients, then cover and cook over medium heat for 10 minutes. Add the beer, ham stock, dried cranberries, and raisins. Stew uncovered for 35 minutes or until the liquid is reduced by one third. Add the cucumber, honey, and vinegar. Cook an additional 15 minutes, then serve with sour cream. The sour cream may be added directly to the stew to thicken it, or each person may add it to individual taste. Season with pepper. Garnish with rose petals and serve over pieces of manchet rolls or bread.

Note: It was also customary to thicken stews of this sort with flour. If a very thick gravy is preferred, dust the ham with spelt or whole wheat flour before adding it to the vegetables. Polish sour cream (*śmietaną*) is thinner than American sour cream and therefore more of it is required for thickening.

Wrocław Trencher Bread (Worcławski Chleb Żytni)

8 cups (1 kg) stone ground rye flour

7 cups (875 g) stone ground spelt or whole club wheat flour

2 cups (500 ml) thick beer (see page 183)

1 cup (250 ml) active beer barm or ½ ounce (14 g) active dry yeast proofed in 1 cup (250 ml) lukewarm water

4 cups (1 liter) water at room temperature

2 tablespoons salt

In many parts of Europe, trenchers were made from old bread, which was often sold in the marketplace specifically for this purpose. However, the Polish court appears to have used one type of bread for trenchers and another for general consumption. This practice is confirmed in medieval bread regulations and seems to have been imitated by the lesser nobility and wealthy townspeople. Since the Wrocław bread laws have been analyzed the most fastidiously, they are now the most reliable for reconstructing the sort of bread favored for trenchers, at least for the region now encompassing Silesia and southern Poland. The medieval Polish word for trenchers is tallari, *a cognate of the German word* Teller *for plate. Both terms appear to derive from vulgar Latin* taliare, *to cut or split.*

This bread requires a sourdough starter, which will be key to the success of other recipes in this section, so it would be advisable to make a batch three to five days in advance of baking. Directions for making the starter (called "thick beer" in Polish) are provided below.

*The precise composition of Wrocław trencher bread is at best an educated guess, but we do know that it was a blend of wheat and rye flours because of its texture. Therefore it was a type of middling bread. Furthermore, this bread was meant to be eaten upon, thus its texture was far more important than its flavor, at least to the nobles who disposed of their trenchers like wet paper plates. At the Polish court, the crusts and trimmings of the trencher loaves were reserved for the servants' table or for a table with guests of low status. Used trenchers were not thrown away but often distributed to the poor or fed to the royal hounds. These were placed in a "voider" by the pantler (*panetier *in French), the person in charge of the pantry who carved the bread. It was not unusual to use such leftovers as thickeners in middle class cookery, especially in gruels and porridges.*

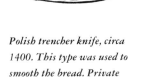

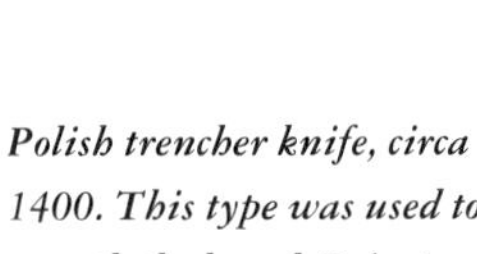

Polish trencher knife, circa 1400. This type was used to smooth the bread. Private collection.

As a rule the pantler cut the bread into trenchers away from the dining table—medieval dinner scenes rarely show trencher bread except as finished trenchers in front of diners, sometimes neatly stacked in anticipation of several courses. The pantler accomplished his carving with three knives: one to cut the loaf, one to trim it, and one to smooth the trenchers (above).

The loaf was molded into a boule *(round, inverted bowl-like shape) about 6 inches (15 cm) in diameter at the base and weighing roughly 11½ ounces (350 g) after baking. Each loaf yielded two trenchers measuring 4 inches (10 cm) square and ½ inch (1 cm) thick. The dough itself is dense, similar to the dough used in modern American bagels. Not surprisingly, trencher bread dough was also molded into rings, boiled in lye, then baked and sold as a type of poor man's dinner roll.*

For the bread to conform to these fixed specifications, which appeared in the bread assize in 1362, gluten-rich spelt or club wheat flour must have been added to the mix, the proportions of which varied according to the quality of the harvest. Both of these wheat crops were often raised specifically for the baking trade, just as spelt is still raised in Germany today expressly for the pretzel bakers. Because flour is milled differently today, some experimentation may be required to achieve the correct size loaves. If they do not rise enough during baking, more wheat flour is needed. Reduce the rye and increase the spelt flour accordingly. If nice trenchers are more important than loaf size, bake six loaves of equal size instead of ten. Then trim as directed below.

Last, the baking directions below are designed to reproduce the effect of a brick oven. After they were heated, the old ovens were swept out and then swabbed with rye straw brooms dipped in water. The steam trapped in the oven gave the crust of the bread a rich golden color. In the countryside, this same effect was achieved by baking the bread wrapped in cabbage leaves or the leaves of Tartar bread plant brushed with poppy seed oil. The crust is very hard when it comes from the oven, but softens after the loaves cool. Like most bread of this type, it is much better when a day old.

Yield: 9 to 10 loaves, depending on grade of flour

Combine the flours in a mixing bowl. Measure out 7½ cups (950 g) and put this in a large work bowl or bread trough. Combine the thick beer, yeast, and water. Add this to the flour and stir to create a slurry. Cover and let stand overnight until foamy. Combine the salt with the remaining flour, and stir down the slurry. Add the salted flour to the slurry and knead this into a ball of dough on a well-floured work surface. Knead for at least 20 minutes, vigorously striking the dough from time to time with a bat or long rolling pin to break down the gluten. Set aside, cover, and let the dough rise until doubled in bulk. When it is fully risen, knock down and knead again, breaking it with a bat or rolling pin as before. When the dough is soft and spongy, mold it out into 9 or 10 round loaves (each about 12 ounces or 375 g to allow for water loss during baking). Cover and let the loaves rise in a warm place until they are roughly 6 inches (15 cm) in diameter.

While the loaves are rising, preheat the oven to 400°F (205°C). When the loaves are fully risen, set them on greased pizza sheets and cut a small sign of the cross or some other preferred pattern into the top of each loaf (see note). Set the loaves in the oven and bake for 15 minutes. Then reduce the temperature to 375°F (190°C) and continue baking for another 15 minutes. Last, reduce the temperature to 350°F (175°C) and finish baking the bread for 10 to 20 minutes or until it sounds hollow when tapped on the bottom. Cool on a rack. Do not cut the bread until it is room temperature.

Note: Some bakeries impressed pictorial images into the bread, including cyphers or initials of the baker, the arms of the bakers' guild, the arms of the city of Wrocław, or in the case of the royal bakery, the coat of arms of the king. These bread stamps were generally lozenge-shaped and carved of wood in a design similar to the signet ring on page 117.

Thick Beer or Sourdough Starter (*Gęstwina z drożdzy*)

*Thick beer was made one of two ways. Hulled spelt and barley were sprouted then fermented in spring water with hops and Labrador tea (*Ledum palustre*) or, for home use, a beery batter was made with flour. I have chosen the latter method.*

Yield: Roughly 1 quart (1 liter) of starter

20 dry hops blossoms

2 cups (250 ml) Weissbier (wheat beer)

1 cup (125 g) barley flour

1 cup (125 g) spelt or whole wheat flour

Pour 2 cups (250 ml) of boiling water over the hops and infuse 20 minutes. When the tea is lukewarm, combine it with the beer and pour this over the barley and spelt flours in a large, wide-mouthed jar. Stir to form a slurry. Let this stand uncovered for 3 to 5 days or until foamy (this will depend on the weather and room temperature). It should smell like sour milk. Once active, use as needed. The starter can be revived and continued by adding more flour and liquid as the old is used up.

Turnip Kugel (Kugiel z Rzepki) *

The German Jews who settled in Poland in the 1300s brought with them a variety of early medieval dishes that were borrowed from non-Jewish sources and adapted to fit their own dietary needs. Several of these dishes undoubtedly date to late classical antiquity and were familiar to the Diaspora Jews living in many parts of Roman Europe. The early Jewish utilization of this dish-concept is evidenced by the use of the word Kugel *(also* Küchl, Kaichl, Koichl*), the archaic German name under which it was transferred to medieval Poland. The root meaning is simple: cake or flat breadlike cake.*

In the Rhineland, the area of Germany from which many Polish Jews emigrated, turnip Kugel *is called* Schales, *in reference to the shallow gratin dish in which it is prepared and served. Multifunctional ceramic baking dishes called* patinae, *with or without lids, have been found in many archaeological sites from Roman Europe. They provide an archaeological antecedent for this genre of medieval recipe, for not all foods cooked in a patina were egg mixtures, as one might incorrectly surmise from reading the Roman cookery book of Apicius.*

The manufacture of patina-shaped ceramic vessels continued during the Middle Ages, although not in all parts of Europe and not among all classes of people. Its modern counterparts may be found in the traditional Greek baking dish known as a tigani *or the Italian* pignate.

In medieval Poland, kugel covered a range of preparations baked in shallow or deep (usually round) pans without reference to type of ingredients or elaborateness of preparation. The fancier deep-dish versions of kugel resembled bread puddings and were made almost exclusively for Chanukah. However, kugel also provided the practical advantage of being made in advance and then kept warm overnight for serving on Shabbos, when cooking was forbidden. Kugel made with shredded turnips is one of those old Sabbath dishes. It predates later preparations made with potatoes and represents the sort of recipe that might have been served in the home of a middle-class merchant in Kazimierz, the Jewish Quarter across the Vistula River from Cracow. It is designed to use leftover kasza grutan *(buckwheat kasha) and was served as a side dish with boiled chicken feet or chicken aspic. Preparation of the kasha has been included here for convenience.*

Serves 6 to 8 (as a side dish)

½ cup (125 ml) poppy seed oil or ½ cup (125 g) chicken or goose fat

1½ cups (225 g) buckwheat grits (see note)

3 cups (460 g) turnip pared and shredded on the large holes of a vegetable grater

1 cup (150 g) cooked lentils

*1 cup (100 g) chopped orache (*Atriplex hortensis*)*

½ cup (50 g) minced parsley

1 cup (100 g) chopped leek or onion

6 tablespoons (90 g) poppy seeds

1½ teaspoons ground anise seed

1 teaspoon ground ginger

1 cup (250 ml) chicken stock

4 eggs, separated

matzo crumbs (about 1 tablespoon)

Kazimierz, old Jewish ghetto at Cracow.

Heat 4 tablespoons (60 ml) of oil or fat in a skillet. Add the buckwheat grits and stir over high heat for 3 minutes so that the grits acquire a toasted, nutty flavor. Add 3 cups (750 ml) water, then cover, and reduce the heat to low. Simmer gently for 5 minutes or until the grits are tender and all the liquid is absorbed. Pour this into a large work bowl and allow to cool.

While the grits are cooling, preheat the oven to 375°F (190°C). When the grits are room temperature, stir with a fork to loosen, or rub the grits through the large holes of a vegetable grater so that the mixture is loose. Add the turnip, lentils, orache, parsley, leek,

4 tablespoons (60 g) of poppy seeds, anise, ginger, and remaining oil or fat. Beat the egg yolks until frothy, then combine with the stock. Add this to the turnip mixture. Beat the egg whites until stiff peaks form and fold this into the turnip mixture. Pour into a greased round 2-quart (2-liter) casserole or gratin dish dusted with matzo crumbs. Bake for 40 minutes or until set. Remove from the oven and scatter the remaining poppy seeds over the top.

Note: Buckwheat grits are not the same as American kasha. The whole seeds or groats are called kasha in the United States, but these must be broken down in a mortar or hand mill to resemble coarse oatmeal. This is not sifted. All of the particles, including the flour, are used. In addition to cooking more quickly, it creates a thick, pudding-like consistency.

Tripe in Sauerkraut (Flaczki w Kiszonej Kapuście)

While in Hungary in 1983, Maria Dembińska and I went over a list of old foods that we wanted to learn more about, one of them being tripe. At that time, tripe was almost impossible to obtain in Poland unless one bought it directly from a farmer who had just butchered a cow. This modern scarcity was all the more peculiar given the abundance of tripe according to medieval Polish records. It was often served at the royal court, but elaborate recipes from the period do not exist. Even passing comments on methods of preparation are difficult to find because, like most traditional dishes, there was no fixed recipe, just multitudes of variations passed along orally. This recipe is based in part on ethnographic research and in part on royal purchase orders.[10]

It seems that the basic dish consisted of cooked tripe laid down in sauerkraut and horseradish. It was a cold-weather emergency food consumed by all classes of people, for it could be made ahead, stored, and then cooked and elaborated as required. Corned beef and pork were also preserved in sauerkraut in a similar manner. The meat traveled well in casks during cold weather, and in this form, appears to have served as nourishing food to boatmen on the Vistula and Oder rivers.

Many versions of this dish have been preserved among ethnic Germans in Poland, especially in northern sections of the country, but the basic idea was shared by both Poles and Germans during the Middle Ages. Furthermore, in its plainest version, the sauerkraut and tripe mixture was used among country people as a home remedy for the common hangover, and therefore a reprieve after heavy feasting.

*Like sauerkraut, this dish was made only in large quantities, thus the recipe that follows is just a sample on a very small scale presenting the dish in an upper-class form. Rather than starting with a keg full of sauerkraut, tripe, and horseradish, the recipe has been adapted to start from scratch. This recipe is intended to represent what happened to the stored tripe and sauerkraut once it was unkegged, cooked in a more elaborate manner, and served as a side dish with roasts. As a one-pot meal, it was common to add meat to the dish, especially bacon or pork. Smoked sausage, game, or almost any combination of meats was deemed appropriate, but meatballs roasted on small wooden skewers (*brochettes *in French) were always considered the most elegant addition. However, as a delicate side dish for a large menu, rich texture and the flavor of expensive spices predominated, especially cassia or cinnamon, which seem to be the most favored spices in northern Polish*

1 pound (500 g) cleaned tripe (see note)

3 pounds (1½ kg) sauerkraut

2 cups (500 ml) veal reduction stock or 2 envelopes unflavored gelatin dissolved in boiling water

2 cups (500 ml) Weissbier (wheat beer)

1 cup (200 g) chopped onion

1 tablespoon minced fresh horseradish

2 teaspoons ground mustard

2 cinnamon sticks measuring 4 inches (10 cm) each

1 tablespoon dill seed, or more to taste

2 tablespoons (30 ml) dill-flavored vinegar or a mixture of chopped dill and 2 tablespoons (30 ml) vinegar

2 tablespoons (30 ml) honey

cookery of this period. There should be enough tripe in the dish to make it jell when cold. This stiff texture is implied by the fact that the mixture was often cut into slices before reheating. In addition to the tripe, or to ensure the jelling, veal or pork knuckles were sometimes cooked and reduced to aspic consistency, with the liquid added to the mixture to further enhance its jelling qualities. (Fish glue, a common thickener in this period, was never used in meat preparations by Polish cooks, only in fish dishes on meatless days.)

A horseradish sauce consisting of finely grated horseradish and minced dill pureed with bread soaked in beer or vinegar can be prepared to accompany the dish. Historically, this sauce would have been cooked in a pipkin. As it contained no animal products, it was also used as a fasting day sauce on fish dishes, especially on fish dumplings. A recipe is provided below. The green mustard sauce (see page 156) can also be served with this.

Serves 4 to 6

Soak the tripe overnight in salted water, then drain and rinse. Cut the tripe into ½-inch (1 cm) squares. Bring 2 quarts (2 liters) of salted water to a rolling boil, then reduce the heat so that the water is barely quivering. Add the tripe and poach gently for 2 hours or until tender. Drain and combine with the sauerkraut.

Put the sauerkraut-tripe mixture in a deep stewing pan with the stock, beer, onion, horseradish, mustard, cinnamon sticks, and dill seed. Cover and cook slowly over medium-low heat for 2 hours, then add the vinegar and honey. Pour this into a scalded stoneware crock or glass container and let cool. In medieval times, the top was sealed with fat and the crock then stored in a cool cellar until needed.

The souse could be served cold with blood sausage or reheated and served with additional ingredients as the situation demanded. It was commonly eaten hot over *binavice* (rusks) or over bread broken into coarse pieces. If meatballs were part of the meal, they would be made separately, browned on a skewer, then added to the hot sauerkraut mixture shortly before serving.

Note: Pre-cooked tripe is sometimes sold in butcher shops, normally in 1-pound (500 g) blocks. This will eliminate the preparation step.

Polish Sauce for Fast Days and Tripe
(Polski Sos na Dni Postne i Do Flaków)

*4 ounces (125 g) white bread or rolls (*bulki*), crusts removed*

1½ cups (375 ml) Weissbier (wheat beer)

1 cup (100 g) chopped dill

1 cup (100 g) chopped parsley

4 tablespoons (75 g) freshly grated horseradish

½ cup (125 ml) poppy seed oil

½ teaspoon salt or to taste

1 tablespoon (15 ml) honey

pepper to taste

This sauce is very easy to prepare and does not take long to cook. Poppy seeds may be added if desired.

Serves 4

Soak the bread in the beer until completely soft (at least 4 hours). Combine with the dill, parsley, horseradish, poppy seed oil, salt, and honey in a food processor and work to a thick, smooth puree. (This was done in a mortar in the Middle Ages, then pressed through a hair sieve.) Heat the mixture in a small saucepan and cook over medium heat until thick (about 5 minutes). Add beer if a more liquid consistency is desired. Season to taste with pepper.

Court Dish of Baked Fruit (Pieczone Owoce po Królewsku) *

Much discussion has been given to gruels and porridges but little has been said about their transformation into baked dishes that serve as a meatless course at a court dinner. This is one of those dishes, and it may have come to Poland from Germany or more likely from Hungary. Indeed, it resembles the so-called Schmarren *of the Danube basin, although the Polish dish is heavier and would seem to fall into that category of sweet dish called a* conkauelit *by medieval court cooks. The ingredients like almonds, lemons, and sugar are clearly luxury items and would have stood out for their unusual taste even at the Jagiellon court.*

Serves 10 to 12

½ pound (250 g) apples, pared, cored, and chopped

½ pound (250 g) pears, pared, cored, and chopped

½ cup (75 g) chopped raisins, dried cherries, or figs (or a mix of all three)

½ cup (60 g) slivered almonds

juice and grated zest of 1 lemon

¾ cup (185 g) sugar

1½ teaspoon ground cinnamon

8 ounces (250 g) lightly salted butter

2 cups (250 g) fine white bread crumbs

1 quart (1 liter) boiling milk

4 eggs, separated

Dried or candied fruit for ornamentation

Combine the fruit, almonds, lemon, sugar, and cinnamon in a deep work bowl. Cover and let stand 2 hours.

Preheat the oven to 425°F (220°C). Cream the butter until fluffy, then add the crumbs. Put this in a deep stewing pan over medium heat and stir until the crumbs are hot. Add the boiling milk and beat vigorously to form a thick porridge. Cook the mixture for about 5 minutes or until thick, then set aside to cool.

Beat the egg yolks until frothy and combine with the porridge. Whisk the egg whites until stiff and forming peaks. Grease an earthenware baking dish measuring 9 by 14 inches (23 cm by 35 cm) and dust it with bread crumbs. Fold the egg whites into the batter and pour half of this into the baking dish. Spread the fruit mixture over this and then add the rest of the batter to form a top layer.

Bake in the preheated oven for 15 minutes, then turn back the heat to 350°F (175°C) and continue baking for 35 to 40 minutes or until the mixture sets in the center and forms a nice crust. Remove from the oven and serve hot or at room temperature, ornamented with dried fruit cut and arranged into patterns. This dish was probably eaten in a bowl with milk or cream, or perhaps even a sweet wine poured over it.

Skirrets Stewed with Fish (Kruczmorka Duszona z Ryby) *

1 cup (85 g) white cabbage, finely shredded as for sauerkraut

1 cup (45 g) finely chopped rocket

1 cup (45 g) finely chopped sorrel (preferably the buckler-leaf type)

1 cup (100 g) chopped leek (white part only)

½ cup (50 g) finely chopped chervil

3 fresh bay leaves, bruised

2 quarts (2 liters) strained fish stock (see page 168)

6 tablespoons (90 g) lightly salted butter

6 tablespoons (45 g) pea flour

3 cups (300 g) skirrets, cut into thin, diagonal slices

2 pounds (1 kg) filleted wels (European catfish) cut into bite-sized chunks

4 egg yolks

1 cup (250 ml) milk or cream

⅛ teaspoon ground cinnamon

⅛ teaspoon ground cumin

3 tablespoons (45 ml) cubeb vinegar (page 199)

salt and ground pepper to taste

chopped hard-cooked egg whites (optional)

*This recipe was selected not only because it is specifically mentioned in the royal accounts; it also reveals the complex nature of what passed for "fasting" among the upper nobility. Furthermore, the dish uses pea flour, an ingredient not often discussed in medieval records, but once widely used as bread flour and as a thickener in "green" dishes and sauces. A starchy thickener was also made from the dried tubers of asphodel (*Asphodelus aestivus*) for use in sauces in the royal kitchen much the way cornstarch is used today. But since this was generally imported (mostly from Mediterranean sources), it was also expensive.*

Pea flour, however, was made by grinding field peas or dry split peas to a very fine powder. When raw, the flour has the same bitter taste found in mature pea pods, but when cooked it becomes rich, mellow, and creamy. It provided an easy way to make instant pea soup. In stews such as this, it added body and texture.

In this recipe, the amount of fish may be doubled, therefore increasing the portion count, or the fish stock may be cut in half to produce a thick, filling one-course meal. In either case, the fish stock must be rich enough to jell when cold. To make it, use heads, tails, and fish bones. The stew, without the fish, may be used as a sauce over whole poached trout, mackerel, or herring. If the stew is served as one course in a succession of dishes, as it would have been served at court, it was customary to follow it with something sweet, like a strudel stuffed with honey and cheese or an apple kolacz.

Serves 6 to 8

Put the cabbage, rocket, sorrel, leek, chervil, and bay leaves in a large saucepan with the fish stock. Cover and boil gently over medium heat for 30 minutes. Remove the bay leaves and puree the vegetables and liquid so that all the ingredients are broken down into tiny flecks of green.

In a clean stock pot, heat the butter and pea flour. Cook the flour until it begins to bubble, then add the vegetable-fish stock and skirret. Cook the skirret until tender (15 to 20 minutes), then add the fish. Heat the fish for 10 minutes in the stock. While the fish is cooking, beat the egg yolks together with the milk and add the cinnamon and cumin. Whisk this into the stew and cook for about 10 minutes, or until thick. Add the vinegar, a little at a time to keep the eggs from curdling. Serve immediately with salt and pepper to taste. Finely chopped hard-cooked egg white can also be sprinkled over the top.

Stewed Pig Tails with Buckwheat Gruel (Wieprzowe Ogony Duszone z Kaszą Gryczaną)

This is based in part on ethnographic research and has many parallels in other central European cultures. In terms of technical logistics, it is a two-part recipe that was prepared concurrently on the same hearth. By virtue of the ingredients, it is clear that this is a dish attuned to the economics of rich farmers or the poorer rural nobility. Buckwheat did not become fashionable at the Polish court until the reign of Queen Anna Jagiełłonka (1523–1596), wife of Stephen Bathory—the Duke of Transylvania who was crowned king in 1576. At that time the grain was received into stylish circles, mostly due to the queen's passion for buckwheat kasha. Furthermore, the grade of buckwheat that Poles now value most—the finely ground "Cracow-style" kasha—is not mentioned in early Jagiellonian records. Therefore, buckwheat groats must be the most appropriate choice, even though they are ground up after cooking to make a thick gruel. The dish was served in a wooden trough or bowl set in the middle of the table.

Serves 4 to 6

---

2 pounds (1 kg) pig tails (about 4), singed and cleaned

2 ounces (60 g) salt pork, diced

2 ounces (60 g) slab bacon, diced

3 cups (750 ml) beer (optional)

1 tablespoon peppercorns or juniper berries

3 tablespoons (45 g) lard

4 medium onions (about 14 ounces/445 g), cut in half and sliced very thin

1 tablespoon (15 ml) honey

1 tablespoon ground mustard

salt to taste

Stewed Pig Tails

Cut the tails into 2-inch (5-cm) segments, or smaller toward the thick end. Heat the salt pork and bacon in a deep stewing pan, add the tail pieces, and brown over medium-high heat for 5 minutes. Add 3 cups (750 ml) water or beer (optional) and the peppercorns. Cover and simmer over medium-low heat for 1 hour or until the tails are tender but not falling apart. Remove the tails with a slotted spoon and set aside, but keep warm. Strain and reduce the broth to 1 cup (250 ml).

In a separate pan, heat the lard and add the onion. Cook over medium heat for 3 minutes or until wilted. Add the honey and mustard and continue cooking for another 3 minutes, but do not scorch the mixture. Add the strained tail stock and boil up so that it thickens. Pour this into the "valley" in the buckwheat gruel and serve the reserved pig tails as directed below.

Buckwheat Gruel

This can be prepared while the pig tails are cooking so that everything is ready at once. Start the gruel halfway through the cooking time of the tails. Buckwheat was either parched in a hot oven, to give it a toasted flavor, or quickly browned in a hot skillet without fat, to give it a rich, nutty flavor.

2 ounces (60 g) salt pork, coarsely chopped

8 ounces (500 g) parched or toasted buckwheat groats

½ cup (100 g) coarsely chopped onion

5 cups (1¼ liter) ham or pork stock

2 teaspoons dried savory or thyme rubbed to a powder

1 to 2 teaspoons salt or to taste

freshly grated pepper

chopped parsley

caraway seeds

Put the salt pork in a skillet and brown lightly over medium-high heat. As soon as the pork begins to dissolve, add the buckwheat and onions. Stir to coat the ingredients with the drippings, then add the stock. Cover and simmer 30 minutes over medium-low heat or until the buckwheat is completely soft. Puree the mixture to the consistency of smooth mashed potatoes, then add the herbs, salt, and pepper.

Put the gruel in a large serving dish, shaping it into a low circular "ridge" with the center area open like a valley. Fill this with the stewed onions from the pig tails, then lay the cooked tails on top of the onions. Scatter parsley and caraway seed over the top and serve.

Pomeranian Trójniak (Trójniak Pomorski) *

Herbord's Vita *Ottonis (Life of Bishop Otto of Bamberg) noted that honey and beer mixtures had been drunk in Pomerania since the twelfth century. In this case,* trójniak *means a beverage consisting of beer and spring water sweetened with honey. The addition of spices was variable; ginger and cardamom have been chosen as flavorings because they are known ingredients in flavored beers from this period. Grains of paradise (*Aframomum melegueta*) were also popular, although they are somewhat difficult to locate today. In addition to these spices, dried raspberries may be added instead of the juniper berries to give the infusion a fruity character.*

Serves 4 to 6

2 tablespoons bruised juniper berries

1 tablespoon ground ginger

2 teaspoons ground cardamom

1 cup (250 ml) honey

3 cups (750 ml) Weissbier (wheat beer) or to taste

Pour 2 cups (500 ml) boiling spring water over the juniper berries and spices in a large jar or jug. Cover and infuse until the mixture is room temperature. Strain through a jelly bag, then dissolve the honey in it. Pour the beer into a large stoneware pitcher and add the sweetened infusion. Serve immediately.

Hungarian-Style Spit-Roasted Shoulder of Venison (Mostek Jeleni z Roźna po Węgiersku) *

This recipe represents an alternative method for preparing meat flavored with csombor *in the "Hungarian" style (see page 92). It should be fairly close to one of the ways in which venison was prepared at the Polish court, with special reference to Queen Jadwiga's fastidious passion for things Hungarian. Furthermore, the special nature of the recipe is implied by the size of the roast, a shoulder taken from a stag (* jeleń*) rather than from a roe deer (*sarna*), the latter being quite small.*

Aside from the ingredients listed, the following equipment is required: two fire dogs with spit hooks, a long spit with a turning handle on one end, a fan-operated turn-spit (the medieval ones operated on hot air rising from the fire), two to three skewers and four to six small onions, a rectangular trivet with four feet, a dripping pan to fit on top of the trivet, a flesh fork, and a basting spoon. In the absence of these, the meat may be treated as a pot roast and cooked in some of the marinade at 375°F (190°C), allowing 25 minutes per pound. After 2 hours, reduce the heat to 350°F (175°C).

Serves 8 to 12

1 shoulder of venison weighing 8 to 10 pounds (4 to 5 kg)

4 cups (1 liter) cubeb vinegar or balsamic vinegar

8 cups (2 liters) spring water

1 tablespoon coarsely ground caraway seed

1 tablespoon coarsely ground dill seed

¼ cup (25 g) chopped fresh savory

¼ cup (25 g) chopped fresh tarragon

*2 tablespoons long pepper (*Piper longum*), or to taste*

8 to 10 cloves rocombole garlic, gently crushed

4 ounces (125 g) lightly salted butter, melted

*sliced crustless manchet rolls (*bulki*), optional*

Score the meat with an extremely sharp knife and set it in a deep, non-reactive vessel, ideally 1 gallon (4 liter) in size. Cover the meat with the vinegar and water, then add the herbs, pepper, and garlic. Cover with a lid and marinate overnight in a cool place. The next day, remove the meat from the liquid and reserve half the marinade for basting. (The rest of the marinade would have been reused for other recipes in medieval times.)

After building the fire and creating sufficient hot coals, run the spit through the meat, following the bone. Cut a delicate hatch pattern in the surface of the meat, then insert the skewers, using half an onion on each skewer handle and tip to keep the skewer from baking into the meat and pulling off a piece of the roast when removed. The skewers pass through the meat entirely as well as through the holes in the spit made for this purpose. Otherwise, if the spit lacks holes, the skewers must pass tightly against the spit to lock the meat in place. In this case, string may be tied from one skewer to the next in a criss-cross fashion (handle to tip) so that everything is held firmly in place, a precaution that is recommended in any case when a roast is heavy.

Set the spit on the spit hooks. The firedogs should be about 18 inches (45 cm) from the heat source, a little farther away if there is a fireback (firebacks reflect a more intense heat). Set the trivet and dripping pan beneath the roast. Put bread in the bottom of the pan if a thick sauce is wanted.

Put the reserved marinade and the melted butter in separate pans (or pots) and set near the roast. Turn the meat often and baste alternately with the marinade and butter. Stick the roast from time to time with a flesh fork so that juice drips from the meat. The accumulated drippings in the pan are skimmed of grease and cooked in a pipkin with additional marinade, then bound with drawn butter as a liaison (vinaigrette style), or thickened with the bread worked to a smooth puree. Indeed, three sauces can be made: a clear one, one with butter and fresh herbs (the same used in the marinade), and a very thick one made with bread.

When the roast is finished cooking (after about 4 hours), remove it from the skewers and spit and set it on a hot serving platter. The sauces would be sent up to the banquet separately in covered bowls. The meat would be carried into the great hall with considerable fanfare and then carved.

Cubeb Vinegar (Ocet Kubebowy) *

Various types of pepper vinegars were used at the Polish royal court for marinades, and numerous vendors sold such vinegars in Cracow during the 1300s.[11] *Guinea pepper (*Piper guineense*) was used when a mild pepper taste was preferred; Indian long pepper (*Piper longum*) supplied a heat similar to the New World capsicums that eventually replaced it. Cubeb, however, is uniquely pungent, with overtones of allspice. It is excellent with venison. However, the vinegar was not, like venison, restricted to royalty, and in fact it was probably made by merchants specializing in imported food products. Therefore, the vinegar also found a place in the larders of wealthy merchant families and doubtless a rather wide range of high nobles and clergy. It is also quite likely that less expensive versions of sherry vinegar were made in Cyprus or Hungary for export so that something of similar taste and acidity was also available to those of lesser economic means. Rich peasants, for example, might have chosen juniper berries instead of cubebs, or an infusion made with the leaves of alexanders, and used the marinade on a shoulder of pork.*

Yield: 2 cups (500 ml)

1 tablespoon cumin seed

1 tablespoon cubebs

1 clove of garlic

2 cups (500 ml) sherry vinegar or vino cotto vinegar

Put the cumin, cubebs, and garlic in a sterilized wine bottle. Add the vinegar and cork it tight. Shake well, then let the spices infuse for 3 months before using. When this vinegar ages (over 5 years), it tastes similar to balsamic vinegar.

Turnip Gruel (Kleik z Rzepy) *

While the name may imply a certain rooty heaviness, this dish is in fact quite delicate. It represents the sort of sweet vegetable preparation that was considered elegant by medieval Polish standards and was eaten with sops. It is almost a soup, but not quite, and can be served as a sauce over meat dumplings. It marries well with the saltiness of smoked tongue, salt pork, and corned beef and should be treated as a recipe for meat days in the context of the medieval menu.

Serves 4 to 6

2 ounces (60 g) bread

1½ cups (375 ml) Weissbier (wheat beer)

2 pounds (1 kg) turnips, pared and cubed

2 medium onions (400 g), chopped

1 quart (1 liter) beef stock

2 cups (200 g) chopped parsley

2 ounces (60 g) lightly salted butter

1 tablespoon (15 ml) honey

3 tablespoons (45 ml) cider vinegar

¾ teaspoon ground anise

salt to taste

Soak the bread in the beer for at least 2 hours or until soft. Put the turnips, onion, and beef stock in a deep saucepan with the beer and bread and cook over medium heat for 20 minutes. Add the parsley and cook an additional 10 minutes. Puree the mixture in a food processor until thick and batterlike (the medieval method was to pound it in a mortar). Return this to the pan and add the butter, honey, cider, and anise. Cook over medium heat until thoroughly heated, then season and serve immediately.

Notes

Citations to the Polish edition of this work (Dembińska, 1963) have been added as markers for sources or more detailed discussion.

Editor's Preface

1. Polish food historian Maria Lemnis wove many of Maria Dembińska's findings into the fabric of her book, which is both a series of essays and a collection of recipes. It was published in 1979 in Polish, German, and English.

2. It has been suggested recently that the recipes are French in origin, although the late Rudolph Grewe assigned them a German provenance. If French, then whose French? A Norman court in Sicily? A Picard handbook? It was also Maria Dembińska who first led Rudolph Grewe to this recipe collection (I was present during that exchange). He later published an article about the Danish recipes, but did not mention Maria's earlier work. In all fairness, she does deserve some sort of acknowledgment.

Chapter 1. Toward a Definition of Polish National Cookery

1. M. Kubasiewicz, "Z badań nad resztkami wczesnośredniowiecznych zwierząt łownych Pomorza zachodniego" (Concerning Research on Remnants of Early Game in Western Pomerania), *Z Otchłani Wieków* (Poznan), 24, no. 2 (1958), 101–107. Since the appearance of this article and others at the time, there is now a huge collection of literature on the subject.

2. Dembińska's colleagues at the Institute of Material Culture often joked that she learned the ethnographic approach firsthand from her experience managing the various fisheries, orchards, hops plantations, and mills on the huge Dembiński estate, not to mention her active participation in the life of the adjoining town and village. She understood the value of ethnographic evidence and appreciated the fact that it is not often easy to use.

3. That ethnography can be used to successfully analyze the past has been confirmed even further by the recent work of Polish ethnographer Zofia Szromba-Rysowa of Cracow, a scholar much influenced by Maria Dembińska's research. Szromba-Rysowa's book *Przy wspólnym stole* (At the Common Table) explored the daily eating habits and festive meals of the mountain villages of southern

Poland and linked them to old traditions and lost symbolic meanings tracing to the Middle Ages.

4. Zdzislaw Rajewski, "Piło się własny miodek," *Z Otchlani Wiekow* (Poznan), 15, nos. 3–6 (1946), 45.

5. Andrzej Wyczański, "Uwagi o konsumpcji żywności w Polsce XVI w," *Kwartalnik Historii Kultury Materialnej*, 8, no. 1 (1960), 15–42. Hereafter cited as Wyczański (1960).

6. Evidence for Montigny's identity is discussed by Nicole Crossley-Holland in *Living and Dining in Medieval Paris* (Cardiff, 1996), 185–211.

7. Kitowicz's work was republished with editorial comments by Roman Pollak in *Biblioteka Narodowa*, series I, no. 88 (Wrocław, 1950).

8. Mikołaj Rej, "Zywot człowieka poczciwego," ed. J. Krżyzanowski in *Biblioteka Narodowa*, series I, no. 152 (Wrocław, 1956), 206.

9. Zygmunt Gloger, "Kuchnia polska," in *Encyklopedia staropolska* (Warsaw, 1900–1903).

10. The basis for this false etymology appears to trace to Aleksander Brückner's *Slownik etymologiczny języka polskiego* (Warsaw, 1957). Maria Dembińska did not cite it specifically because she was not convinced that it was correct. Elsewhere in her book she pointed to instances where he had not used his ethnographic materials carefully.

11. See Albert Hauser, *Vom Essen und Trinken im alten Zürich* (Zurich, 1961), 42.

12. Joyce Toomre, ed. and trans., *Classic Russian Cooking* (Bloomington, Ind., 1992), 217–218.

13. Maria Dembińska, *Konsumpcja Żywnościowa w Polsce Średniowiecznej* (Wrocław, 1963), figure 23, page 255. Hereafter cited as Dembińska (1963). Dembińska referred to this as a "skillet," based on the archaeological report, but it is a type of braising pan on legs. Those made of iron could be used as bake kettles.

Chapter 2: Poland in the Middle Ages

1. Paul W. Knoll's outline of Polish history in the *Dictionary of the Middle Ages* (New York, 1987) is recommended to the general reader; it is accessible in most libraries. His *Rise of the Polish Monarchy* (Chicago, 1972) is an excellent study of the late 1300s.

2. Dembińska consulted two versions of the chronicles. The first, in the original Latin, was edited by Karol Maleczyński as *Galli Anonymi Cronica* in the series *Monumenta Polonia historica*, 2 (Cracow, 1952); the other was a Polish translation which appeared in *Kronika polska* (Cracow, 1932), edited by Roman Grodecki.

3. The original text of the St. Hedwig *Vita* was edited by A. Semkowicz and

published in the old series of *Monumenta Polonia historica*, 4 (Lvov, 1884), later reprinted at Warsaw in 1961. Dembińska also used the Semkowicz edition of the *Vitae Annae ducissae Silesiae* in the same volume. Anna, Duchess of Silesia (d. 1265), was evidently quite well known as an accomplished cook. She was the daughter-in-law of St. Hedwig and helped to establish a cloister at Krzeszów in 1242.

4. See Ewald Walter, *Studien zum Leben der hl. Hedwig, Herzogin von Schlesien* (Stuttgart, 1972).

5. The texts of these works can be found in such collections as the *Monumenta Polonia historica* (1864–1893) and the *Monumenta mediiaevi historica res gestas Poloniae illustrantia* (1874–1927).

6. For recent studies of the szlachta, see Maria Koczerska's *Rodzina szlachecka w Polsce* (Warsaw, 1975) and Antoni Gasiorowski's *Polish Nobility in the Middle Ages* (Wrocław, 1984). The latter work is a collection of papers.

7. Anton Boczek, *Codex Diplomaticus et Epistolaris Moraviae*, I (Olomouc, 1836), 309.

8. See *Monumenta mediiaevi historica res gestas poloniae illustrantia*, 3 (Cracow, 1876), 138.

9. Harleian MS 279 as published in Thomas Austin, ed., *Two Fifteenth-Century Cookery Books* (London, 1996), 21.

10. Majer Bałaban's 1931 history of the Cracow Jewish community is still one of the most detailed studies of the period.

11. The two works mentioned are only a few of the vast quantity of materials Dembińska consulted. See Walther Ziesemer, *Das grosse Ämterbuch des deutschen Ordens* (Danzig, 1921); and Jadwiga Karwasińska, "Rachunki żupne bocheńskie z l. 1394–1421," in *Archiwum Komisji Prawa Polskiej Akademii Umiejętnosci*, volume 15.

Chapter 3: The Dramatis Personae of the Old Polish Table

1. This house still stands although much renovated in later styles and is presently a well-known restaurant called U Wierzynka (Chez Wierzynek). It was also commemorated in a famous nineteenth-century Polish painting called *The Banquet at Wierzynek's* by the Polish artist Jan Matejko (1838–1893).

2. Jerzy Sadomski, *Gotyckie Malarstwo Tablicowe Malopolski: 1420–1470* (Warsaw, 1981).

3. Juraj Spiritza and Ladislav Borodáč, *Podoby Starého Spiša* (Bratislava, 1975), 119.

4. Dembińska (1963), 200.

5. This weight was calculated by Roman Grodecki in "Dawne miary zboża w Polsce: Przyczyński do dziejów rolnictwa w Polsce średniowiecznej," *Tygodnik Rolniczy* (Cracow, 1919), 2–8.

6. Edward Kuntze, ed., "Expens dworu królowej Katarzyny, zony Zygmunta Augusta," in: *Archiwum Komisji Historycznej Polskiej Akademii Umięjetnosci*, 9 (Cracow, 1913), 116–132.

7. Dembińska (1963), 189.

8. Wyczański (1960), 15–42.

9. Stefan Falimirz, *O ziołach i o moczy gich* (Cracow, 1534).

10. Dembińska (1963), 150–152 and note 238.

11. The list is based on the research of Jerzy Kruppé and A. Gardowski, "Poznosredniowieczne naczynia kuchenne i stolowe" (Late Medieval Kitchen Utensils and Tableware), in *Szkice Staromiejskie* (Warsaw, 1955), 123–139.

Chapter 4: Food and Drink in Medieval Poland

1. See Louis-Claude Douët-d'Arcq, "Un petit traité de cuisine écrit en français au commencement du XIVième siècle," in *Bibliothèque de l'Ecole de Chartres*, 1, 5th series (Paris, 1860), 209–227; Taillevent, *Le Viandier*, Jérôme Pichon and Georges Vicaire, ed. (Paris, 1892).

2. Henrik Harpestraeng, *Incipit libellus de arte coquinaria*, ed. M. Kristensen (Copenhagen, 1908–1920).

3. For example, "Die Speiseordnung der Klosterbrüder von Werden vor 1063," ed. Hans Lichtenfelt in *Die Geschichte der Ernährung* (Berlin, 1913), 73. The diet of monks and nuns was so different from those who lived outside the cloister that it represents a specialized category of study far too broad a topic for the focus of Dembińska's original monograph. However, subsequent authors, particularly Johanna Maria Van Winter of the University of Utrecht, have dealt more thoroughly with this area of research.

4. Dembińska (1963), 94.

5. Dembińska (1963), 76–79; also footnotes 120–124.

6. Dembińska (1963), 95.

7. Dembińska (1963), 143. The original reference appeared in *Regestrum Dni Hynczconis Vicesthezaurarii*, which is part of Piekoskiński's edition of the royal accounts for 1388–1420 (Cracow, 1896), 156. The most money was spent on expensive imports during the period 1393–1395.

8. Maria Kwapien has explored this subject in some depth. See "Początki uprawy winorosli w Polsce," in: *Mat. Arch.* 1 (Cracow, 1959), 353–400. Also see Dembińska (1963), 70.

9. Dembińska (1963), 95–96.

10. Dembińska (1963), 135. Here she lists several references to beer. The original citation by Długosz appeared in *Opera Omnia*, II, Book 1.

11. Dembińska (1963), 123.

12. Rej, *Zywot człowieka poczciwego*, 210.

13. Dembińska (1963), 176.

14. Dembińska (1963), 139. She cited Matheus Silvaticus's *Pendecta Medicinae*

as it appeared in Maurizio, *Pozywienie roślinne i rolnicze w rozwoju* (Warsaw, 1926), 145.

15. Olaus Magnus, *Historia de gentibus septentrionalibus* (Basel, 1567), 341 and 342.

16. Syrennius, *Księgi pierwsze o ziołach rozmaitych* (circa 1616/1617), 379.

17. Dembińska (1963), 140. The original references appeared in "Księga skarbowa Janusza II, ks. mazowieckiego, z 1. 1477–1490," ed. J. Senkowski, *Kwartalnik Historii Kultury Materialnej*, 7, no. 3 (Warsaw, 1959), 549–718.

18. The queen's lamb consumption is discussed by Edward Kuntze, "Expens dworu królewej Katarzyny," in *Archiwum Komisji Historycznej Polskiej Akademii Umiejętnosci*, 9 (Cracow, 1913), 116–132. Also see Dembińska (1963), 82.

19. Dembińska (1963), 96, 146, and footnote 228.

20. Dembińska (1963), 50–51. Footnote 19. There are several varying accounts of this diplomatic gift, and only the Augsburg version actually stated that it was an aurochs. The quotation is translated (with emendations) from an edition of the Vienna codex prepared by M. Solokowski in *Spr. Komisji dla Badania Historii Sztuki*, 8 (Cracow, 1907), 77–78. Similarly, not all of the versions mention that the aurochs was rubbed down with gunpowder. Gunpowder contains saltpeter, a meat preservative. Dembińska also consulted another version of the story as cited under Kaulsche (1804) in the bibliography, extracting missing information from both.

21. Valerie Porter, *Cattle* (New York, 1991), 162–164.

22. Dembińska (1963), 97.

23. Dembińska (1963), 81–82; see also footnote 139.

24. Many still-life paintings depict this type of coarse bacon. The Italian artist Jacopo Chimenti (1554–1640) included it in a number of his works. See for example his pantry scene in Traudl Seifert and Ute Sametschek's *Die Kochkunst in zwei Jahrtausenden* (Munich, [1977]), 65.

25. Dembińska (1963), 97–98.

26. Alfred Gottshalk, *Histoire de l'alimentation et de la gastronomie depuis la préhistoire jusqu'à nos jours* (Paris, 1948), 415; Dembińska (1963), 100.

27. Szymon Syrennius, *Księgi pierwsze o ziołach rozmaitych*, 1006.

28. Adolf Pawiński, *Młode lata Zygmunta Starego* (Warsaw, 1893), 161. Dembińska also checked the original quotation in documents in the Polish National Archives at Warsaw.

29. Dembińska (1963), 98.

30. Dembińska (1963), 99 and 104, including footnote 49.

31. This is mentioned by Długosz in his *Opera Omnia*, III (under the year 1141), 3; and further discussed by Dembińska (1963), 105.

32. Stanisław Krzyżanowski, "Rachunki wielkorządowe krakowskie z. 1. 1461–1471," in: *Archiwum Komisji Historycznej Polskiej Akademii Umiejętnosci*, 11 (Cracow, 1909–1913), 466–526. Refer to document 456.

33. Dembińska (1963), 100 and 117.

34. Gottschalk, *Histoire de l'alimentation et de la gastronomie*, 415.

35. Dembińska (1963), 47. Several pages are devoted to the controversies surrounding the interpretation of this archaeological material.

36. Gallus Anonymus, *Chronicon*, I, 409. Gallus was quite expansive about the generosity of this king and the sorts of foods he provided his most honored guests. Polish historians have pointed out that Gallus's motives were political, so his claims must be read with caution.

37. Jan Długosz, *Opera Omnia*, IV, 511; V, 1 and 317. Dembińska (1963), 49.

38. Dembińska (1963), 103.

39. Dembińska (1963), 201.

40. Dembińska (1963), 51. Jagiełło's original letter from circa 1411 was quoted in T. Lewicki, ed., *Codex epistolaris saeculi XV*, 3 (Cracow, 1891), 48.

41. Dembińska (1963), 51 and footnote 21.

42. Dembińska (1963), 108.

43. Dembińska (1963), 54–55 and footnote 31. The original citation may be found in the *Codex Pomeraniae Diplomaticus*, I (Greifswald, 1843), 99.

44. Dembińska (1963), 103. Zdzislaw Rajewski, "Settlements of the Primitive and Early Feudal Epochs in Biskupin and its Surroundings," in: *Archeologia Polona*, 2 (Warsaw, 1959), 119.

45. Dembińska (1963), 57 and footnote 47.

46. Dembińska (1963), 110.

47. Dembińska (1963), 110.

48. *Chiquart's "On Cookery": A Fifteenth-Century Savoyard Culinary Treatise*, ed. Terence Scully (New York: Peter Lang, 1986).

49. Ryszard Kiersnowski, "Roślinny uprawnę i pozywienie roślinne w Polsce wczesnofeudalnej," in *Kwartalnik Historii Kultury Materialnej*, 2, no. 3 (1954), 346–387.

50. Dembińska (1963), 123.

51. Stephen Mitchell, *Anatolia* (Oxford, 1995), 169. Mitchell cited a passage from Galen which contained the recipe. It appears to have been a type of polenta made in connection with a festivity focused on goat's milk.

52. Szymon Syrennius, *Księgi pierwsze o ziołach rozmaitych*, 1005 and 1006.

53. Dembińska (1963), 112. The recipe she discussed appeared in Taillevent (Paris, 1892), 16.

54. Dembińska (1963), 112, but citing the research of Muszyński (1924), 31–32.

55. Szymon Syrennius, *Księgi pierwsze o ziołach rozmaitych*, 404.

56. Janina Kruszelnika, *Pierniki torunskie i inne* (Toruń, 1956), is a history of Toruń honey cakes.

57. There is considerable research on this subject, especially by such cultural geographers as Ernst Burgstaller and Anni Gamerith. Refer to the bibliography in Burgstaller's *Österreichisches Festtagsgebäck* (Linz, 1983) and the reference archive at the Deutsches Brotmuseum, Ulm.

58. Dembińska (1963), 116.

59. Dembińska (1963), 157 and 177.

60. Dembińska (1963), 98 and 114, and especially footnote 95 for literature.

61. As illustrated in Dembińska (1963), 245, figure 5.

62. Dembińska (1963), 135.

63. Maria Dembińska explored this theme in much greater depth in her *Przetwórstwo zbożowe w Polsce średniowiecznej* (Grain Processing in Medieval Poland) (Wrocław, 1973).

64. For the serious reader wishing to pursue specific Polish plant histories, the *Acta Societatis Botanicorum Poloniae* provide a wealth of information on past and continuing research.

65. Dembińska (1963), 66.

66. Udelgard Körber-Grohne, *Nutzpflanzen in Deutschland* (Stuttgart, 1988), plate 38. The remains came from a barn floor excavated in 1958 at Feddersen Wierde on the North Sea. Dembińska noted that similar finds had come to light in Poland.

67. Dembińska (1963), 117–118. Also Mikołaj Rej, *Zywot człowieka poczciwego*, 366.

68. Szymon Syrennius, *Księgi pierwsze o ziołach rozmaitych*, 1060.

69. Dembińska (1963), 127. Syrennius also mentioned the European cow parsnip on page 673 of his herbal, although he discussed it under its common Polish name. See illustration on page 128.

70. Martin Grosser, *Krótkie i bardzo proste wprowadzenie do gospodarstwa wiejskiego*, ed. Stefan Inglot (Wrocław, 1954), 264–265.

71. Dembińska (1963), 119.

72. Dembińska (1963), 119 and footnote 124.

73. Mikołaj Rej, *Zywot człowieka poczciwego*, 367. Also see Dembińska (1963), 119.

74. Dembińska (1963), 70. The references actually appeared in the "Rachunki królewicza Zygmunta I z l. 1501–1506," unpublished manuscript documents in the Polish National Archives, Warsaw.

75. Dembińska (1963), 121.

Medieval Recipes in the Polish Style

1. The original pages of the broken copy of the *Kuchmistrzostwo* found in the nineteenth century were edited by Zygmunt Wolski and published in *Biała Radziwiłłowska* in 1891.

2. A history of this remarkable pamphlet cookbook was published by Mary Ella Milham in the *Gutenbergjahrbuch* for 1972.

3. Edith Hörandner, *Model: Geschnitzte Formen für Lebkuchen, Spekulatius und Springerle* (Munich, 1982), is a comprehensive account of gingerbread molds.

4. For example, Friederike Löffler, *Oekonomisches Handbuch für Frauenzimmer*

(Stuttgart, 1795), 458–459. The recipe in question is for *Sand-Torte,* which is made with thin layers of cake interfilled with fruit preserves or apple butter. This is not to imply that Löffler was a source for the Polish idea, for there are numerous versions of this basic concept in other cookbooks.

5. A. Gottschalk, *Histoire de l'alimentation et de la gastronomie*, addenda p. 415.

6. The history of the wafer iron and its regionalization are covered rather thoroughly in Ernst Thiele's *Waffeleisen und Waffelgebäcke* (Cologne, 1959).

7. Dutch medieval food scholar Johanna Maria Van Winter has written about the difficulties in discerning regionalisms in medieval cookery. Johanna Maria Van Winter, "Interregional Influences in Medieval Cookery," in Melitta Weiss Adamson, ed., *Food in the Middle Ages* (New York, 1995), 45–59. Jean-Louis Flandrin has also written on this subject. Refer to his article in the bibliography.

8. Hugo Stopp, ed., *Das Kochbuch der Sabina Welserin* (Heidelberg, 1980), 158.

9. Dembińska (1963), 195.

10. Personal correspondence. Maria Dembińska to William Woys Weaver, August 29, 1984.

11. Dembińska (1963), 85.

Bibliography

For the large number of sources cited in Polish, a translation into English has been supplied in brackets following the title. This does not imply that the source appears in full or partial translation; most of the Polish works listed below are not available in English. The publications of Maria Dembińska were selected only for their relevance to this book. Over the course of her career, Professor Dembińska published several books and nearly two hundred articles, far too numerous to include here.

Adamson, Melitta Weiss, ed. *Food in the Middle Ages*. New York and London: Garland, 1995.

Ameisenowa, Zofia. *Kodeks Baltazara Behema* [The Codex of Balthazar Behem]. Wrocław: Ossolineum, 1961.

Bałaban, Majer. *Historię Żydów w Krakowie i na Kazimierzu, 1304–1868* [History of the Jews of Cracow and Kazimierz, 1304–1868]. 2 vols. Cracow: "Nadzieja," 1931, 1936. Reprinted 1991.

Banach, Jerzy. *Dawne Widoki Krakowa* [Views of Cracow Long Ago]. Cracow: Wydawnictwo Literackie, 1967.

———. *Ikonografia Wawelu* [The Iconography of Wawel Castle]. 2 vols. Cracow: Ministerstwo Kultury i Sztuki, 1977.

Bayer, Erich. *Wörterbuch zur Geschichte*. Stuttgart: Alfred Kröner Verlag, 1965.

Benker, Gertrud. *Kuchlgschirr und Essensbräuch*. Regensburg: Verlag Friedrich Pustet, 1977.

Billy, Pierre-Henri. *Thesaurus Linguae Gallicae*. Hildesheim: Olms-Weidmann, 1993.

Boczek, Anton. *Codex Diplomaticus et Epistolaris Moraviae*. Olomucii: Ex Typographia Aloysii Skarnitzl, 1836. Vol. 1 (396–1199).

Bois, Désiré. *Les Légumes*. Paris: Paul Lechevalier, Editeur, 1927.

Borst, Otto. *Alltagsleben im Mittelalter*. Frankfurt: Insel Verlag, 1983.

Brunner, Karl, and Gerhard Jaritz. *Landherr, Bauer, Ackerknecht: Der Bauer im Mittelalter: Klischee und Wirklichkeit*. Vienna: Hermann Böhlaus Nachf., 1985.

Burgstaller, Ernst. *Österreichisches Festtagsgebäck*. Linz: Rudolf Trauner, 1983.

Bystroń, Jan Stanislaw (1892–1964). *Etnografia Polski* [The Ethnography of Poland]. Warsaw: "Czytelnik," 1947.

Chiquart's "On Cookery": A Fifteenth-Century Savoyard Culinary Treatise. Ed. Terence Scully. New York: Peter Lang, 1986.

Chmielewski, S. "Gospodarka rolna i hodowlana w Polsce w XIV i XV w" [Agriculture and Husbandry in Poland in the Fourteenth and Fifteenth Centuries]. *Studia z Dziejów Gospodarstwa Wiejskiego*, 5, no. 2. Warsaw, 1962.

Ciołek, Gerard. *Gärten in Polen*. Warsaw: Verlag Budownictwo I Architektura, 1954.

Czerniecki, Stanislaw. *Compendium Ferculorum*. Cracow, 1682. Subsequent editions of this exceedingly rare cookbook were printed at Cracow in 1753, at Sandomirz in 1784, and at Wilno in 1788.

Czolowski, Aleksander, ed. "Księga przychodów i rozchodów miasta Lwowa (1404–1414)" [Income and Expense Book of the City of Lvov, 1404–1414]. In *Pomniki Dziejowe Lwowa*. 4 vols. Lvov: Nakł. Gminy Król. stot. miasta Lwowa, 1892–1924. Refer to vol. 3 (1896).

Dembińska, Maria. "W sprawie stosowania metody statystycznej w babaniach archeologicznych" [On the Applicability of the Statistical Method in Archeological Research]. *Kwartalnik Historii Kultury Materialnej*, 5, no. 1 (1957), 100–103.

——. "Kilka uwag o roli bartnictwa w gospodarce wiejskiej polskiego średniowiecza" [Several Remarks on the Role of Beekeeping in the Rural Economy of Medieval Poland]. *Kwartalnik Historii Kultury Materialnej*, 6, no. 3 (1958), 347–356.

——. "Méthodes des recherches sur l'alimentation en Pologne médiévale." *Archeologia Polona*, 2 (Warsaw, 1959), 142–154.

——. "Udzial zbieractwa w średniowiecznej konsumpcji zbozowej — La participation de la cueillette dans la consommation de blés à l'époque médiévale." *Studia z dziejów gospodarstwa wiejskiego*, 9, no. 3 (1967), 83–103.

——. *Konsumpcja Żywnościowa w Polsce Średniowiecznej* [Food Consumption in Medieval Poland]. Wrocław: Wydanictwo Polskiej Akademii Nauk, 1963.

——. *Przetwórstwo zbożowe w Polsce średniowiecznej (X–XIV wiek)* [Grain Processing in Medieval Poland: Tenth to Fourteenth Centuries]. Wrocław: Zakłład Narodowy im. Ossolinskich, 1973.

——. "Food Products, Consumption, and Dishes in the Light of Polish Historical Sources from the Tenth to Eighteenth Century." In Niilo Valonen and Juhani U. E. Lehtonen, ed., *Ethnologische Nahrungsforschung/Ethnological Food Research*. Helsinki, 1975, 54–63.

——. "Wild Corn Plants Gathered in the Ninth-Thirteenth Centuries in the Light of Paleobotanical Materials." *Folia Quarternaria*, 47 (Cracow, 1976), 97–103.

——. "Diet: A Comparison of Food Consumption Between Some Eastern and Western Monasteries in the Fourth-Twelfth Centuries." *Byzantion*, 55 (1985), 432–462.

Długosz, Jan. *Opera omnia. Historia Polonicae libri XII*, ed. Alexander Przeździecki. Cracow: F. Kluczyncki & Soc., 1863–1878.

———. *Roczniki czyli Kroniki sławnego Królestwa Polskiego*, ed. Jan Dabrowski, trans. Stanislaw Gaweda. Warsaw: Panstwowe Wydawnictwo Naukowe, 1961.

Dorson, Richard M., ed. *Folklore and Folklife: An Introduction*. Chicago: University of Chicago Press, 1972.

Douët-d'Arcq, Louis-Claude. "Un petit traité de cuisine écrit en français au commencement du XIVème siècle." In *Bibliothèque de l'Ecole de Chartres*, vol. I, 5th series (Paris, 1860), 209–227.

Duft, Johannes. *Notker der Arzt: Klostermedizin und Mönchsarzt im frühmittelalterlichen St. Gallen*. St. Gallen: Verlag der Buchdruckerei Ostschweiz, 1975.

Dutkiewicz, Józef. *Małopolska rzeźba średniowieczna, 1300–1450* [The Medieval Sculpture of Southern Poland, 1300–1450]. Cracow: Nakladem Polskiej Akademii Umiejetnosci, 1949.

Falimirz, Stefan Hieronim. *O ziołach i o moczy gich* [On Herbs and Their Properties]. Cracow: Florian Ungler, 1534.

Flandrin, Jean-Louis. "Internationalisme, nationalisme et régionalisme dans la cuisine des XIVe et XVe siècles: Le témoignage des livres de cuisine." *Manger et boire au Moyen Âge: Actes du colloque de Nice (15–17 octobre 1982)*. Paris, Les Belles Lettres, 1984, vol. 2, 75–91.

Fuchs, Leonhard. *De historia stirpium comentarii insignes*. Basel: In Officina Isingriniana, 1542.

Gallus Anonymus. *Cronicae et gesta ducum sive principum Polonorum*. Dembińska used two editions: Karol Maleczyński, ed., in "Galli Anonymi Cronica.," *Monumenta Poloniae Historica*, series 2, vol. 2 (Cracow, 1952); and a translation into Polish, Roman Grodecki, ed., "Anonym, tzw. Gall," in *Kronika Polska* (Cracow, 1932).

Gasiorowski, Antoni, ed. *The Polish Nobility in the Middle Ages: Anthologies*. Aleksandra Rodzinska-Chojnowska, trans. Wrocław: Zaklad Naradowny im. Ossolinskich, 1984.

Genealogisches Handbuch des Adels. Glücksburg and Ostsee: Verlag von C. A. Starke, 1953.

Gessner, Adolf. *Abtei Rauden in Oberschlesien*. Kitzingen-Main: Holzner-Verlag, 1952.

Gloger, Zygmunt. *Encyklopedia Staropolska* [Old Polish Encyclopedia]. 4 vols. Warsaw: Gebethner & Wolff, 1900–1903.

Gołębiowski, Łukasz. *Domy i Dwory* [Town Houses and Country Houses]. Warsaw: A. Galezowski, 1830.

Górnicki, Łukasz. *Dworzanin polski* [The Polish Courtier]. The most recent edition is edited by Roman Pollack in: *Biblioteka Narodowa*, series I, no. 9 (1954). The work was originally published at Cracow in 1566.

Górski, Karol. *Dzieje Malborka* [The History of Malbork]. Gdansk: Wydawnictwo Morskie, 1973.

Gottschalk, Alfred. *Histoire de l'alimentation et de la gastronomie depuis la préhistoire jusqu'à nos jours*. 2 vols. Paris: Editions Hippocrate, 1948.

Grewe, Rudolf, ed. *Libri de Sent Soví*. Barcelona: Editorial Barcino, 1979.

Grodecki, Roman. "Dawne miary zboża w Polsce. Przyczynki do dziejów rolnictwa w Polsce średniowiecznej" [Old Weights and Measures of Grain. Contributions to the History of Agriculture in Medieval Poland] in *Tygodnik Rolniczy* (Cracow, 1919), 2–8.

———. *Kongres Krakowski w roku 1364* [The Congress of Cracow in the Year 1364]. Cracow: Universitas, [1995]. This is a reprint of the first edition (Warsaw, 1939).

Grosser, Martin. *Krótkie I bardzo proste wprowadzenie do gospodarstwa wiejskiego* [A Short and Very Simple Introduction to Farm Economy], ed. Stefan Inglot. Wrocław: Zakład Ossolineum, 1954. This is a Polish edition of Grosser's *Kurtze und gar einfeltige Anleytung zu der Landwirschafft*, originally published in 1590. See also Schröder-Lembke below, which includes considerable scholarly apparatus.

Guerquin, Bohdan. *Zamki w Polsce* [The Castles of Poland]. Warsaw: Arkady, 1974.

Hammond, P. W. *Food and Feast in Medieval England*. Phoenix Mill and Stroud: Alan Sutton Publishing, 1995.

Harleian MS 279. As published in Thomas Austin, ed. *Two Fifteenth-Century Cookery Books*. London: Oxford University Press, for the Early English Text Society, 1996. Reprint of the original edition of 1888.

Harpestraeng, Henrik. *Incipit Libellus de Arte Coquinaria. Gample Danske Urtevøgner, Stenbøger, og Kogebøger*, M. Kristensen, ed. Copenhagen: H. H. Thielse, 1908–1920.

Hauser, Albert. *Vom Essen und Trinken im alten Zürich*. Zurich: Verlag Berichthaus, 1961.

Hegi, Gustav. *Illustrierte Flora von Mittel-Europa*. Munich: J. F. Lehmann, 1907–1931.

Heitz, Paul, ed. *Primitive Holzschnitte: Einzelbilder des XV. Jahrhunderts*. Strasbourg: J. H. Ed. Heitz, 1913.

Henel von Hennefeld, Nicolaus. *Silesiographia; hoc est, Silesiae delineatis brevis et succincta*. Frankfurt: Typis I. Bringeri, 1613.

Henisch, Bridget Ann. *Fast and Feast*. State College: Pennsylvania State University Press, 1976.

Hieatt, Constance. *An Ordinance of Pottage*. London: Prospect Books, 1988.

Hieatt, Constance, and Sharon Butler, ed. *Curye on Inglysch: English Culinary Manuscripts of the Fourteenth Century*. London and New York: Oxford University Press, 1985.

Hörandner, Edith. *Model: Geschnitzte Formen für Lebkuchen, Spekulatius, und Springerle*. Munich: Verlag Callwey, 1982.

Hoyt, Robert S., ed. *Life and Thought in the Early Middle Ages*. Minneapolis: University of Minnesota Press, 1967.

Jacob, Heinrich Eduard. *Sechstausend Jahre Brot*. Hamburg: Rowohlt Verlag, 1954.

Jasienica, Pawel. *Polska Pisatów* [Piast Poland]. Wrocław: Zakład Ossolineum, 1960.

Jeffery, George E. *Cyprus Under an English King*. London: Zeno, 1973. Reprint of the 1926 London edition.

Jelicz, Antonina. *Das Alte Krakau*. Leipzig: Koehler & Amelang, 1981.

Kaeuper, Richard W., and Elspeth Kennedy. *The Book of Chivalry of Geoffroi de Charny*. Philadelphia: University of Pennsylvania Press, 1996.

Kajzer, Leszek. *Uzbrojenie i Ubiór Rycerski w Średniowiecznej Małopolsce* [The Arms and Armor of Medieval Knighthood in Southern Poland]. Wrocław: Wydawnictwo Polskiej Akademii Nauk, 1976.

Kalesný, František. *Das Weinbaumuseum in Bratislava*. Bratislava: Pallas, 1977.

Karbowiak, Antoni, ed. "Obiady profesorów Uniwersytetu Jagiellońskiego w XVI i XVII w" [Dinners of the Jagiellonian University Professors in the Sixteenth and Seventeenth Centuries.] *Biblioteka Krakowska*, no. 13 (Cracow, 1900).

Karwasińska, Jadwiga, ed. "Rachunki żup solnych z XIV i XV w" [Salt-Mine Accounts from the Fourteenth and Fifteenth Centuries]. *Archeon*, 3 (1928).

———. "Rachunki żupne bocheńskie z l. 1394–1421" [The Accounts of the Bochnia Salt-Mine from 1394 to 1421]. *Archiwum Komisji Historycznej Polskiej Akademii Umiejętnosci*, 15 (Cracow), 123–232.

Kaulsche, R. "Die Handschriften Ulrich von Richentals Chronik des Contanze Concils." *Zeitschrift für die Geschichte des Oberrheins*, 9 (1804), 19.

Kiersnowski, Ryszard. "Roślinny uprawne, pozywienie roślinne w Polsce wieczenofeudalnej" [Plant-Based Nutrition and Plants Cultivated in Early Feudal Poland]. *Kwartalnik Historii Kultury Materialnej*, 2, no. 3 (1954), 346–387.

Kitowicz, Jędrzej. *Opis obyczajów i zwyczajów za panowania Augusta III* [Customs During the Reign of August III]. Ed. Roman Pollack, in *Biblioteka Narodowa*, series I, no. 88 (1950).

Klichowska, M. "Najstarsze zboża z wykopalisk polskich" [The Oldest Types of Grain from Polish Archeological Sites]. *Archeologia Polski*, 20 (1975), 83–143.

Kluge, Friedrich. *Etymologisches Wörterbuch der deutschen Sprache*. Strasbourg: Verlag von Karl J. Trübner, 1910.

Knoll, Paul W. "Poland." *Dictionary of the Middle Ages*, ed. Joseph R. Strayer. New York: Charles Scribner's Sons, 1987. 9:716–731.

———. *The Rise of the Polish Monarchy: Piast Poland in East Central Europe, 1320–1370*. Chicago: University of Chicago Press, 1972.

Koczerska, Maria. *Rodzina szlachecka w Polsce póznego średniowiecza*. Warsaw: Pantwowe Wydawn. Naukowe, 1975.

Konarski, Szymon. *Armorial de la noblesse polonaise titrée*. Paris: Chez l'auteur, 1958.

Körber-Grohne, Udelgard. *Nutzpflanzen in Deutschland*. Stuttgart: Konrad Theiss Verlag, 1988.

Kramer, Karl-S. *Fränkisches Alltagsleben um 1500*. Würzburg: Echter Verlag, 1985.

Kruppé, Jerzy. *Studia ceramika XIV- i XV-wieczna* [Studies of Fourteenth- and Fifteenth-Century Ceramics]. Warsaw, 1962.

Kruppé, Jerzy, and A. Gardowski. "Późnośredniowieczne naczynia kuchenne i stołowe" [Late Medieval Kitchen Utensils and Tableware]. In *Szkice Staromiejskie*. Warsaw, 1955, 123–139.

Kruszelnicka, Janina. *Pierniki toruń skie i inne* [Toruń and Other Gingerbreads]. Toruń: Ministerstwo Kultury i szłuky, 1956.

Krzyżanowski, Stanisław, ed. "Rachunki wielkorządowe krakowskie z l. 1461–1471," [Accounts of the Voivode of Cracow, 1461–1471]. In *Archiwum Komisji Historycznej Polskiej Akademii Umiejętnosci*, 9 (Cracow, 1909–1913), 466–526.

Kubasiewicz, M. "Z badań nad resztkami wczesnośredniowiecznych zwierząt łownych Pomorza Zachnodniego" [Concerning Research on Remnants of Early Game in Western Pomerania], in *Z Otchłani Wieków* (Poznan), 24, no. 2 (1958), 101–107.

Kuchowicz, Zbigniew. *Obyczaje staropolski XVII–XVIII wieku* [Old Polish Customs of the Seventeenth and Eighteenth Centuries]. Łodz: Wydawnictwo Lozkie, 1975.

Kuntze, Edward, ed. "Expens dworu królowej Katarzyny, żony Zygmunta Augusta" [Expenses of the Court of Queen Katarzyna, Wife of King Sigismund August]. *Archiwum Komisji Historycznej Polskiej Akademii Umiejętnosci*, 9 (Cracow, 1913), 116–132.

Kwapien, Maria. "Początki uprawy winorośli w Polsce" [The Beginnings of Grapevine Cultivation in Poland]. *Mat. Arch.*, 1 (Cracow, 1959), 353–400.

Labahn, Patricia. "Feasting in the Fourteenth and Fifteenth Centuries: A Comparison of Manuscript Illuminations to Contemporary Written Sources." Ph.D. diss., St. Louis University, 1975.

Lambert, Carole, editor. *Du manuscrit à la table*. Montreal: Presses de l'Université de Montréal, 1992.

Laurioux, Bruno. *Le règne de Taillevent*. Paris: Publications de la Sorbonne, 1997.

Le Goff, Jacques. *Time, Work, and Culture in the Middle Ages*. Chicago: University of Chicago Press, 1980.

Lemnis, Maria, and Henryk Vitry. *Old Polish Traditions in the Kitchen and at the Table*. Warsaw: Interpress Publishers, 1979.

Lichtenfelt, Hans. *Die Geschichte der Ernährung*. Berlin: G. Reimer, 1913.

Löffler, Friederike. *Oeconomisches Handbuch für Frauenzimmer*. Stuttgart: Johann Friedrich Steinkopf, 1795.

Maczyński, Jan. *Lexicon Latino-Polonicum*. Regiomonti: Daubmann, 1564.

Magnus, Olaus. *Historia de gentibus septentrionalibus*. Basel: Exofficina Henric-Petria, 1567.

Manteuffel, Tedeusz. *The Formation of the Polish State: The Period of Ducal Rule, 963–1194*. Trans. Andrew Gorski. Detroit: Wayne State University Press, 1982.

Maurizio, Adam. *Pozywienie roslinne i rolnicze w rozwoju dziejowym* [Plant and Agricultural Nutrition in Human Development]. Warsaw, 1926. It originally appeared in German, *Die Getreidenahrung im Wandel der Zeiten*. Zurich, 1916.

Milosz, Czeslaw. *The History of Polish Literature*. New York: Macmillan, 1969.

Mitchell, Stephen. *Anatolia: Land, Men, and Gods in Asia Minor. Part I: The Celts in Anatolia and the Impact of Roman Rule*. Oxford: Clarendon Press, 1995.

Mohs, Karl. *Die Entwicklung des Backofens vom Backstein zum selbsttätigen Backofen*. Stuttgart: Verlag von Werner and Pfleiderer, 1922.

Muszyński, Jan. *Warzywa, owoce i przypawy korzenne w Polsce w XIV x* [Vegetables, Fruit, and Condiments in Poland During the Fourteenth Century]. Warsaw: 1924.

Niesiecki, Kaspra. *Herbarz Polski* [Armorial of the Polish Nobility]. Leipzig: Breitkopf und Härtel, 1842.

Ochorowicz-Monatowa, Maria. *Uniwersalna książka kucharska* [The Universal Cookbook]. Lvov: Nakládem B. Polonieckiego, 1910. Adapted versions are available in English, none of which convey the full extent of the author's voluptuous use of ingredients or, for that matter, her creative persona.

Okolski, Szymon. *Orbis Polonus*. 3 vols. Cracow: In officina typographica F. Caesarii, 1641–1645.

Padulosi, Stefano, Joachim Heller, and Karl Hammer, ed. *Hulled Wheats: Proceedings of First International Workshop on Hulled Wheats, 21–22 July 1995*. Rome: International Plant Genetic Resources Institute, 1996.

Pawiński, Adolf Stanisław. *Mlode lata Zygmunta Starego* [The Young Days of Sigismund the Old]. Warsaw: Gebethner and Wolff, 1898.

Piekosiński, Franciszek. *Heraldyka Polska, Wieków Średnich* [Polish Heraldry of the Middle Ages]. Cracow: Nakladem Akademii Umiejetnosci, 1899.

Piekosinski, Franciszek, ed. *Kodeks Dyplomatyczny Małopolski. 1178–1386. Monumenta mediiaevi historia res gestas poloniae illustrantia*. Cracow: Sumptibus Academiae Literum Cracoviensis, 1876–1905.

———. "Rachunki dworu króla Władysława Jagiełły i królowej Jadwigi za lata 1388–1420" [Accounts of the Royal Court of King Władysław Jagiełło and Queen Jadwiga from the Years 1388–1420]. In *Pomniki dziejowe wiekow średnich (Polska Akademia Umiejętnosci)*, 15 (Cracow, 1896).

Piekosiński, Franciszek, and F. Szujski, ed. *Najstarsze księgi i rachunki m. Krakowa od 1300–1400 r* [Oldest Books and Bills of the City of Cracow from 1300 to 1400]. Cracow: 1877–1878.

Platina Cremonensis (Bartolomeo Sacchi di Piadena). *Von der Eerlichen zimlichen auch erlaubten Wolust des Leibs*. Augsburg: Heinrich Stayner, 1542. First German edition.

Pohl-Weber, Rosemarie, ed. *Aus dem Alltag der Mittelalterlichen Stadt*. Bremen: Bremer Landesmuseum für Kunst-und Kulturgeschichte (Focke-Museum), 1982.

Porter, Valerie. *Cattle: A Handbook to the Breeds of the World*. New York: Facts on File, 1991.

Rajewski, Zdzislaw. "Pije sie własny miodek" [One Used to Drink Home Made Mead]. *Z Otchłani Wieków* (Poznan), 15, nos. 3–6 (1946), 45.

———. "Settlements of the Primitive and Early Feudal Epochs in Biskupin and Its Surroundings." *Archeologia Polona*, 2 (Warsaw, 1959).

———. *Biskupin: Polish Excavations*, trans. Leopold Widymski. Warsaw: Polonia Publishing House, 1959.

Redon, Odile, Françoise Sabban, and Silvano Serventi. *The Medieval Kitchen: Recipes from France and Italy*. Chicago: University of Chicago Press, 1998.

Rej, Mikołaj. "Żywot człowieka poczciwego" [Life of An Honest Man], ed. J. Krzyżanowski. *Biblioteka Narodowa*, series 1, no. 152 (Wrocław, 1956).

Rose, P. Ambrosius, O.S.B. *Kloster Grüssau*. Stuttgart: Konrad Theiss Verlag, 1974.

Rumpolt, Marcus. *Ein new Kochbuch*. Frankfurt: Sigmund Feyerabend, 1581. Facsimile reprint of the first edition, Hildesheim: Olms Press, 1977. The original work reproduced by Olms is not paginated, although there is an index.

Sadomski, Jerzy. *Gotyckie Malarstwo Tablicowe Małopolski: 1420–1470* [Gothic Panel Art in Southern Poland, 1420–1470]. Warsaw: Panstowowe Wyawnictwo Naukowe, 1981.

Schröder-Lembke, Gertrud, ed. *Anleitung zu der Landwirschaft [von] Martin Grosser. Oeconomia [von] Abraham von Thumbshirn. Zwei frühe deutsche Landwirschaftsschriften*. Stuttgart: G. Fischer Verlag, 1965.

Scully, Terence. *The Viandier of Taillevent*. Ottawa: University of Ottawa Press, 1988.

Seifert, Traudl, and Ute Sametschek. *Die Kochkunst in Zwei Jahrtausenden*. Munich: Gräfe and Unzer, 1977.

Senkowski, J., ed. "Księga skarbowa Janusza II, ks. mazowieckiego, z l. 1477–1490" [Treasurer's Accounts of Duke Janusz II of Mazovia, 1477–1490]. *Kwartalnik Historii Kultury Materialnej*, 7, no. 3 (Warsaw, 1959), 549–718.

Skirgiełło, Alma. *Polska bibliografia mikologiczna*. [Bibliography of Polish Mycology]. Warsaw: Państowowe Wydawn. Nauk, 1988.

Spiritza, Juraj, and Ladislav Borodáč. *Podoby Starého Spiša* [Images of Old Spis]. Bratislava: Pallas, 1975.

Starykón-Kasprzycki, Stefan, and Michata Dmowski. *Polska Encyklopedja Szlachecka*. [Encyclopedia of the Polish Gentry]. 12 vols. Warsaw: Wydawnictwo Instytutu Kultury Historycznej, 1935–1938.

Steinhausen, Georg. *Kaufleute und Handelsherren in alten Zeiten*. Leipzig, 1899; reprint, Düsseldorf: Eugen Diederichs Verlag, 1976.

Stoffler, Hans-Dieter. *Der Hortulus des Walahfrid Strabo*. Sigmaringen: Jan Thorbecke, 1978.

Stopp, Hugo, ed. *Aus Kochbüchern des 14. bis 19. Jahrhunderts*. Heidelberg: Carl Winter/Universitätsverlag, 1980.

———. *Das Kochbuch der Sabina Welserin*. Heidelberg: Carl Winter/Universitätsverlag, 1980.

Syrennius, Szymon. *Zielnik, Herbarzem z jezyka lackinskiego zowia* [Herbs. Herbarium in Latin]. Cracow, 1613.

———. *Księgi pierwsze o ziołach rozmaitych* [First Books on Various Herbs]. Undated imprint from about 1616 to 1617 (or earlier) in the manuscript collection of Warsaw University Library. Call number: 5.1.2.29. An edition of the herbal containing extensive annotations.

Szafer, Władysław. *The Vegetation of Poland*. Oxford: Pergamon Press; Warsaw: Polish Scientific Publishers, 1966.

Szromba-Rysowa, Zofia. *Przy wspólnym stole* [At the Common Table]. Wrocław: Ossolineum, 1988.

Thiele, Ernst. *Waffeleisen und Waffelgebäcke*. Cologne: Odra-Verlag, 1959.

Tirel dit Taillevent, G. *Le Viandier*, Jérôme Pichon and Georges Vicaire, ed. Paris: Leclert and Cormuau, 1892.

Toomre, Joyce. *Classic Russian Cooking: Elena Molokhovet's A Gift to Young Housewives*. Bloomington: Indiana University Press, 1992.

Ulewicz, Tadeusz. *Wśród impresorów krakowskich doby renesansu* [Studies on Cracow Printers of the Renaissance]. Cracow: Wydawnictwo Literackie, 1977.

Valonen, Niilo, and Juhani U. E. Lehtonen, ed. *Ethnologische Nahrungsforschung/Ethnological Food Research*. Helsinki: Kansatieteellinen Arkisto 26, 1975. Proceedings of the Second International Symposium on Ethnological Food Research held at Helsinki, Finland, in 1973.

Van Winter, Johanna Maria. *Van Soeter Cokene: Recepten uit de Oudheid en Middeleeuwen*. Haarlem: Fibula-Van Dishoeck, 1976.

———. "Interregional Influences in Medieval Cooking." In Melitta White Adamson, ed., *Food in the Middle Ages*. New York: Garland, 1995, 45–59.

Walter, Ewald. *Studien zum Leben der hl. Hedwig, Herzogin von Schlesien*. Stuttgart: Konrad Theiss Verlag, 1972.

Wasylikowa, K. "Makroskopowe szczatki roslin znalezione w warstwie średniowiecznej na Rynku Głównym w Krakowie" [Microscopic Plant Remains Found in the Medieval Layer at the Main Market Place in Cracow]. *Mat. Arch.*, 6 (1965), 191–196.

———. "Fossil Evidence for Ancient Food Plants in Poland." *Proceedings of the Sixth Symposium of the International Work Group for Palaeoethnobotany* (Rotterdam, 1984), 257–266.

Weczerka, Hugo, ed. *Handbuch der Historischen Stätten: Schlesien*. Stuttgart: Alfred Kröner Verlag, 1977.

Weiss, Hans U. *Gastronomia. Eine Bibliographie der deutschsprachigen Gastronomie: 1485–1914*. Zurich: Bibliotheca Gastronomica, 1996.

Wirkowski, Eugeniusz. *Kuchnia Żydów Polskich* [Cooking the Polish-Jewish Way]. Warsaw: Wydawnictwo Interpress, 1988.

Wiswe, Hans. *Kulturgeschichte der Kochkunst*. Munich: Heinz Moos Verlag, 1970.

Wolski, Zygmunt. "Kartki z nieznanych ksiazek znalezione wraz z brosczura," in: *Biała Radziwiłłowska* (1891).

Wurzbach, Constantin. *Die Kirchen der Stadt Krakau*. Vienna: Verlag der Mechitharisten-Congregations-Buchhandlung, 1853.

Wyczański, Andrzej. "Uwagi o konsumpcji żywności w Polsce XVI w" [Remarks on Food Consumption in Poland during the Sixteenth Century], *Kwartalnik Historii Kultury Materialnej*, 8, no. 1 (1960), 15–42.

Ziesemer, Walther, ed. *Das Grosse Ämterbuch des Deutschen Ordens*. Danzig: A. W. Kafemann, 1921. Reprint, Wiesbaden: M. Sändig, 1968.

Acknowledgments

The contributions of a number of people are deeply appreciated and were essential to the completion of this book. Roman Plaskota, a botanist from Pabianice, Poland, must be thanked for providing me with seeds for several species of *manna*, for European cow parsnips, and for various other old Polish food plants. His help with taxonomy and with sorting out some very confusing Polish plant names was invaluable. Likewise, Alzbeta Kovacova-Decarova of Kosice, Slovakia, generously supplied seeds for rare medieval vegetables and rocombole garlics from the Carpathian region.

Lidia Bartkowiak-Rachny (formerly of Toruń) deserves a very special mention for acting as translator and ethnographer at Nowy Sącz in 1985 during my conversations with the farm women who prepared some of the trial recipes for the recipe section of this book. One of those women presented me with handmade wooden implements copied from medieval prototypes by her talented husband. It was warm generosity like this that often reminded me of the keen pleasure Poles take in sharing their cultural riches; that reminder later served as inspiration to keep going during difficult periods when I thought that the parts of this book would never fall into place.

Another individual of very special importance was Anita Gorzkowska, one of Maria Dembińska's daughters. Anita helped me many times to get through to her mother, supplied me with missing information about the family, and provided me with an eloquent translation of the tribute to her mother that was published by the Institute of Material Culture in Warsaw. Like the other children, Anita experienced all the tragedies that fell on the Dembiński family during and after World War II. But she also had the very special pleasure of watching her mother's extraordinary career unfold. This book is as much a thank-you to her as it is a tribute to her mother.

Chef Fritz Blank of Deux Cheminées in Philadelphia must be thanked for sharing with me his material on Hungarian *csombor*. This research originally came from the late Louis Szathmary, who before his death had taken an interest in my foray into the Polish Middle Ages. Louis knew full well that there were Hungarians lurking in the culinary shadows, and had he not taken ill so suddenly, I am sure he would have gotten involved more directly in the recipe section of this book. I only regret that he and Maria Dembińska never had the opportunity to meet, for they were two of a kind.

On the linguistic front, I must thank the eagle eyes of Joseph Czudak, as well as André Baranowski and his wife, Anna, for helping me check the Polish throughout the book. I came to know André through work for *Kitchen Garden* magazine and our mutual love of things culinary, but his artistic career began in Poland where he exhibited widely before emigrating to the United States. I now consider him a very special friend.

While on the subject of art, I should also mention my friend and colleague Signe Sundberg-Hall, who graciously provided the supplementary line drawings for this book. Realizing that many readers would not know some of the old plants mentioned in the text, I called upon Signe's excellent abilities to render botanical drawings from life.

All the plants she drew came from my garden, the same ingredients used in the various recipes.

Signe also created the drawing of the rare Byzantine fork on page 42. That fork belongs to Mr. and Mrs. William H. Brown of Beckenham (Kent), England, who possess one of the largest and finest cutlery collections in the world. They graciously supplied me with a transparency of the fork so that I could include it in this book.

The Byzantine connection leads me directly to Nicholas Andilios of Nicosia, Cyprus, for his help with the Cypriot materials. I must thank him heartily.

The IACP Foundation, operated by the International Association of Culinary Professionals, provided a grant to help underwrite the translation of Maria Dembińska's book into English. Without that money, this edition would never have been possible. For this reason I am especially indebted to Dr. Joyce Toomre of Harvard University for her written recommendations that proved so useful in the application process.

The grant money enabled me to hire Magdalena Thomas in 1993 to translate the text. Magdalena worked steadily and with utmost patience. Because of her knowledge of Polish literature, she was able to help define words that might confound non-Polish speakers. Those bits of parenthetical information dropped into the text and marked MT made my task as editor much, much easier. Magdalena's working translation provided me with the basis for this book, and I salute her contribution with deep gratitude.

The most extraordinary patience of all was that of Jerome E. Singerman of the University of Pennsylvania Press. He watched and waited for almost fifteen years for this project to take shape. In fact, he was not the original editor who took on the book. The university press moved twice, faces changed, yet the book inched forward. One day, I received a message by email from Jerry that said simply: Persevere. I did. I thank him for helping me keep my promise to Maria.

And finally I would like to acknowledge the extraordinary copyediting of Noreen O'Connor, who suggested ways to make the manuscript a better book.

Index

Page numbers in **boldface type** refer to recipes.

INDEX

Index

Index of Recipes by Polish Name